MW00612386

CHOOSE to Engage

leveraging personal stories to empower dialogue about race and ethnicity

The Classroom Index

foreword by Ruha Benjamin, Ph.D.

produced by
Winona Guo, Priya Vulchi
and the CHOOSE team

The creation of this book was partially funded by the Princeton University
Department of African American Studies and the Princeton Education Foundation.

❝ A wealth of **important, essential** and **potentially healing** information presented in **clear, thoughtful and compassionate** ways to touch individual hearts and minds. I believe that if teachers really want to make a difference... this will be an **invaluable tool** for inspiring themselves and each other. This format is **engaging and user-friendly**, with so many touching real life stories. People's stories have been healing lights since the beginning of time. Telling the real history is the way out of the darkness."

—Roberto Schiraldi
Counselor

Books may be purchased in quantity and/or special sales by contacting Princeton CHOOSE at princetonchoose@gmail.com.

ISBN: 978-0-692-77772-5
Second Edition
Produced by Winona Guo, Priya Vulchi, and the CHOOSE team
Printed by Princeton University

*dedicated to all the courageous people
who shared their stories for this book*

Contents

Foreword

" It is time to CHOOSE. "

Will we make our classrooms laboratories of democratic participation—experimenting with new ways of knowing and relating to the world and one another—*or* will we allow our schools to reproduce racial and class equalities that exist in the broader society?

To choose the former, we must abandon the notion that the passage of time necessarily leads to progress. Social change has always required enormous effort, struggle, and sacrifice, and students too often have to push the adults in their communities to live up to ideals to which we give lip service. "Liberty and justice... *for all*?" It is youth, after all, that stand to inherit a world in crisis.

Watch any evening news program or read through any online comments section, and what we see is a world at war with itself, where racial divisions and hatred are alive and well, and where the very idea of a cohesive society is undermined by inequality and indifference. Even without extensive study of the social science literature, discerning young people have a sense that our institutions are not meeting their basic functions, and that many people cannot turn to hospitals for health,[1] police for safety,[2] legislators for principled administration,[3] or schools for true education.[4] This is the world they stand to inherit. In this context, it is not just *jobs* they want, but *purpose*, as well as the *tools* to more accurately read their reality so they can begin to change it. That is where "racial literacy" and CHOOSE come in.

Remember the etymology of *crisis*: a decisive moment. The word has its root in the process of medical diagnosis, referring to the 'turning point' of a disease. Therefore, when it comes to the cancer of racism, what will we decide to do?

Will we get angry with the doctors who make the diagnosis? If only they would be more cheerful in describing the tumor, we would listen. Perhaps we will pop an aspirin and hope racism will magically heal on its own? Maybe we should seek a second opinion—one that misdiagnoses the disorder as a "problem for a few ignorant individuals"?

Or, will we act on the knowledge that racism is *endemic* to all of our institutions, including our educational system, and CHOOSE to work together to regenerate our ailing body politic? If and when we begin to seriously grapple with this difficult diagnosis, the next step is to think carefully about how we can each contribute to racial justice and healing.

Administrators, teachers, parents, and community members *all* have a part to play, including students of all ages! Before most us can even read, we learn the value society assigns to different kinds of people: "...children show evidence of stereotyping and prejudice by age 3 or 4."[5] From books to cartoons, video games to religious iconography, they read between the lines. And without the adults in their lives explicitly countering these narratives, they quickly learn that lighter means good and darker means bad.[6] But the solution is not to skirt the issues with the mantra "I don't see color."[7] Colorblindness is like applying a Band-Aid on a tumor, when what is urgently needed is a thorough and *honest* diagnosis of the social ills that impact us all.

As educators, our role is to incubate a better world in the minds and hearts of our students. And let's face it: the potential to shape the next generation is powerful and even dangerous. This is one of the reasons why, I believe, the teaching profession is under such consistent and virulent attack, undermined at every turn in terms of autonomy, respect, and resources.

Teachers, if actually unified, empowered, and equipped, can change the direction of history.

Schools are places where the next generation either comes alive with possibility, or gets crushed by the weight of the odds stacked against them.[8] And in many locales, these two processes occur simultaneously, where some children are nurtured and others disparaged,[9] some given room to make mistakes[10] while others face harsh penalties as they try to find their way.[11]

When it comes down to it, racism is a form of theft—robbing some people of the material and symbolic resources to realize their full potential while others monopolize these goods under the banner of meritocracy. In this context, working for a just and equitable society in our schools and communities is not a form of charity... something the privileged do "for the underserved."

Rather, we must come to see how the fortunes of each of us, is bound up with all others.

To understand and act on this reality—of the oneness of humanity—we must develop racial literacy as a 21st century life skill. Learning to carefully *read the reality* of racism that encompasses our everyday lives, especially for those who are the beneficiaries of an unjust system, is a daunting and humbling process that requires a commitment to deep learning and courageous action. It is a necessary process for anyone who wants to effectively contribute to the community in which they live. And it is lifelong work not for the faint of heart. But, *oh*, is it worth it! A poignant reminder of why we must all put in the work comes from the Bahá'í Writings:

Children are the most precious treasure a community can possess, for in them are the promise and guarantee of the future. They bear the seeds of the character of future society which is largely shaped by what the adults constituting the community do or fail to do with respect to children. They are a trust no community can neglect with impunity. An all-embracing love of children, the manner of treating them, the quality of attention shown them, the spirit of adult behavior toward them -- these are all among the vital aspects of the requisite attitude. Love demands discipline, the courage to accustom children to hardship, not to indulge their whims or leave them entirely to their own devices. An atmosphere needs to be maintained in which children feel that they belong to the community and share in its purpose.[12]

Professor Ruha Benjamin
Department of African American Studies
Princeton University

[1]See *Reproducing Race: An Ethnography of Pregnancy as a Site of Racialization* (University of California Press 2011), by Khiara M. Bridges.;
[2]See *Down, Out, and Under Arrest: Policing and Everyday Life in Skid Row* (University of Chicago Press 2016), by Forrest Stuart.;
[3]See *Democracy in Black: How Race Still Enslaves the American Soul* (Crown 2016), by Eddie S. Glaude.;
[4]See *Inequality in the Promised Land: Race, Resources, and Suburban Schooling* (Stanford University Press 2014) by R. L'Heureux Lewis-McCoy.;
[5]See "Reading, Writing, Arithmetic, and Racism? Risks and Benefits to Teaching Children About Intergroup Biases" (*Child Development Perspectives* 2014), by Rebecca S. Bigler and Yamanda R. Wright: http://onlinelibrary.wiley.com/doi/10.1111/cdep.12057/full;
[6]Study: White and black children biased toward lighter skin: http://www.cnn.com/2010/US/05/13/doll.study/;
[7]See "I Don't See Color": Challenging Assumptions about Discussing Race with Young Children *Journal of Early Childhood Education* 2012), by Terry Husband Jr.: http://link.springer.com/article/10.1007/s10643-011-0458-9;
[8]See *Kids Don't Want To Fail: Oppositional Culture and the Black-White Achievement Gap* (Harvard University Press 2011), by Angel L. Harris.;
[9]See *Despite the Best Intentions: How Racial Inequality Thrives in Good Schools* (Oxford University Press 2015), by Amanda E. Lewis and John B. Diamond.;
[10]US Department of Education Office for Civil Rights, "Data Snapshot: School Discipline," March 2014: http://ocrdata.ed.gov/Downloads/CRDC-School-Discipline-Snapshot.pdf;
[11]See *Punished: Policing the Lives of Black and Latino Boys* (New York University Press 2011), by Victor M. Rios; see also: "Black Girls Matter: Pushed Out, Overpoliced, and Underprotected" by Kimberle Williams Crenshaw: http://www.law.columbia.edu/null/download?&exclusive=filemgr.download&file_id=613546;
[12] The Universal House of Justice (2000) Ridvan Message: http://www.bahai.org

CHOOS

Why talk about race in K-12?

In August of 2014, Michael Brown, an unarmed black teenager, was shot by a white police officer in Ferguson, Missouri. Protests erupted around the country. Nevertheless, when our nation's schools started a few weeks later, most of our classrooms were largely silent about the event.

I often imagine a world without racism. A world in which all people move freely and without fear. A world in which levels of education and income are accessible to all. A world in which the ideas, contributions and culture of each individual are celebrated.

But we don't live in such a world. We live in a post-Ferguson, post-Chicago, post-Dallas world. The news is filled with incidents and commentary regarding racial differences and the tension and violence associated with them. The conversation and the conflict are all around us.

Our students want and need to be a part of that conversation and to make sense of that conflict. I believe schools have a responsibility to give them a safe space to do that. More importantly, I believe schools have a responsibility to lead the conversations—and the actions—to propel our world to a place beyond racism. Indeed, one could argue that the stability and enhancement of society is our most important function.

But how? How can we possibly help our students and our society move beyond racism? The answer I cling to: Courage. Humility. Hope.

We have to have the courage as educators to wade into conversations about race with one another even when we are afraid we might misstep and offend someone else or embarrass ourselves. We have to have the courage to look honestly at our curricula and in some cases radically revise it to reflect cultural balance. We have to have the courage to pose the questions to our students that challenge their world view—and ours: Is history the story of the "winners"? Is the Civil War still being fought today?

Humility. As individuals and as institutions, we have to be humble enough to recognize that we all have internalized beliefs about race, we all harbor unconscious prejudices, we all have made mistakes, and that none of us hold all the answers. All of our perspectives are necessarily incomplete without those of others.

Hope. I still get chills when I hear the words, "I have a dream that someday my children will be judged not be the color of their skin but by the content of their character." That dream gives me hope. Our own students give me hope. All of you who have picked up this book to increase your own understanding and those of others give me hope.

Racism is not something we are born with. It is something we learn. It invades our psyche, sometimes violently, sometimes slowly and subtly.

But if it can be learned, it can be unlearned. There is no more important work we can do, no more important lessons we can teach than empathy for others and respect for our world's diversity of races, religions, and cultures.

I believe this book is fundamental to that work. It contains the stories of individuals both locally and internationally that help to personalize our appreciation of diversity. Some of the stories are tragic. Others are celebratory. All are deeply moving.

The two remarkable young women who compiled and catalogued these stories envision them as entry points into class discussions about race and culture. They have consulted and collaborated with teachers and administrators in the Princeton Public Schools, and we intend to integrate their work into our approved curriculum.

The students in this community—and in communities throughout our country—are amazing. It is their voices and their vision that should give us all hope and inspire us to persevere in teaching our way to a world without racism.

Thank you for choosing to engage.

Stephen C. Cochrane
Superintendent
Princeton Public Schools

How to Use
the **Classroom Index**

What is in this book?

It is often difficult or uncomfortable to talk about race. For the educator, Engage's Classroom Index provides an easily-accessible, successfully-tested solution. A reference guide, story index, and racial literacy toolbox, the Classroom Index enables educators to supplement their lesson plans with personal stories to spark meaningful and effective conversations about race.

Each story consists of an interview, a visual, thematic tags, and discussion points that support, refute, or qualify the story with historical or contemporary events and research. The list of tags and corresponding stories on page 16 makes it simple to choose content relevant to the themes of an existing lesson or unit. Stories are color-coded to **indicate appropriate age & grade levels**—including elementary, middle, and high school. Short interviews, longer interviews, written reflections, current event features, and Teacher Talks (interviews with educators discussing racial literacy and/or reviewing the Engage program) **provide**

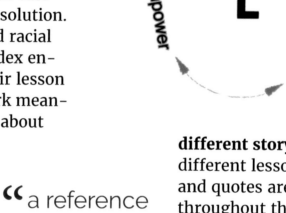

> **"**a reference guide, **story index,** and **racial literacy toolbox."**

different story formats to fit different lesson plans. Cartoons and quotes are also reprinted throughout the book. To ensure our stories can **accomodate all class subjects**, page 197 contains content, activities, and ideas for dialogue for eight core subjects taught in schools globally. Opinion pieces covering essential questions that often confuse students are also answered on page 208, along with a racial literacy test for pre- and/or post-assessment on page 214.

The Engage program also includes Virtual Packages (page 13) as a solution for teachers who cannot find relevant stories in the Classroom Index, or who would like a tool tailored to their specific lesson plan.

Step 1: How Do I Connect My Lesson Plan to a Story?

Refer to the tags list on page 16 to choose an appropriate story based on your lesson or subject, theme, time constraints, and age level. Stories can be used as both stand-alone lessons, or inserted as a single activity into a larger lesson plan.

Step 2: What Does a Story Look Like?

This book contains 5 story formats: 100 short interviews (see below), 8 long interviews (**black background**), 17 written reflections (**purple headings**), 20 current event features (**yellow boxes**), and 8 Teacher Talks (**orange Teacher Talk text**).

tag based on interview & discussion point content themes; index starting on page 16
color of theme/tag text represents recommended age level (red=elementary school and up; green=middle school and up; purple=high school and up)

photograph of interviewee

THEME/TAG

" STORY. "

Key phrase from the story.
Discussion point analysis, with data and statistics that support, refute, or qualify the story.[1]

Key phrase from the story
Discussion point analysis, with data and statistics that support, refute, or qualify the story.[2]

1 citation, source 1
2 citation, source 2

stories, collected around the globe by the CHOOSE team, are always in blue boxes and enclosed by quotation marks

discussion points place story in a larger historical or contemporary framework

Step 3: How Do I Use a Story to Initiate Dialogue?

Each story exposes teacher and student to knowledge and experience outside the walls of a classroom. As a result, the teacher does not necessarily **need** to speak from or to a personal perspective, and can rely solely on the story to spark conversation about race. (Keep in mind, often, the conversation will prompt students to share their own stories and opinions.)

Before
Your Lesson

1. Read and complete steps 1 and 2: choose appropriate stories and familiarize yourself with format and content.
2. Read the **"How to Talk about Race"** guide on page 16, which has more information regarding why and how to initiate dialogue about race in your class.
3. Recommended: Administer pre-test (page 214).

During

For class access to chosen stories, provide each student with a copy of the *Classroom Index*, photocopy appropriate pages, or enlarge the pages on a projector.

Ideas for sparking conversation:
1. Read the story and ask students a series of guided questions to expand dialogue:
—*What is the person in this story trying to say?*
—*How does this story relate to our recent discussions?*
—*Refer to the pullout quotes in discussion points: What does the speaker mean? Why have these been pulled out as key phrases?*

—Read the discussion points. *How does the story fit into a larger historical or contemporary context?*
—Refer to the tag(s): *How does this story fit the larger assigned theme or category?*
—*Can anyone relate to this story or form any personal connections?*

2. Read an excerpt from the lesson or unit, read the story, and ask students to compare/contrast

3. If your lesson/unit covers a historical topic, and the story serves to connect it to a contemporary context by theme, compare and/or constrast race relations over time

Recommended:
After using it in class, provide the Classroom Index to students as an optional independent reading at home, or photocopy more stories for them to read.

After

1. Ask students for feedback: What worked and what did not? What did they learn from the discussion? Assign written self-reflections or essays for students to process. (Along with other feedback, share student work with us at princetonchoose@gmail.com for consideration in the Classrooom Index's Third Edition!)
2. Administer post-test (page 214).
3. Considering feedback, choose other stories or revise lesson plan to meet students' needs.

Step 4: What Else Can I Include in My Lesson?

Ideas for Dialogue & Activities by Class Subject

Are you a world language, math, performing or visual arts, history, science, English, business, computers, or economics teacher? Tips and action steps for all disciplines and subjects are listed on page 197. Recommended reading for elementary, middle, and high schoolers, race-related vocabulary, and U.S. history curriculum are also included.

Thematic Tag Descriptions

To clarify the definitions and meanings of each tag we've chosen, refer to page 16. These primarily systemic racial themes can serve as a foundation for your discussion.

Racial Literacy Tests

For pre- and/or post- assessment, our racial literacy tests on page 214 can be used to measure progress and/or hold students accountable for learning. Questions cover essential content from this book.

Opinion Pieces

Seemingly simple questions—such as "Are you racist?", "Are racial jokes and slurs okay?", "Should we be colorblind?", and "What is white privilege?"—nevertheless stump students. Find opinions to seven crucial questions on page 208.

Quotes & Cartoons

Throughout the book, we have included famous quotes, as well as cartoons created by Barry Deutsch and reprinted with his permission.

Some of Our Favorites:
—page 104: original poetry
—page 108: police brutality feature
—page 198: U.S. History curriculum
—page 40, 54: interviews in Spanish
—page 77: interview in Urdu
—page 207: plan for racial reconciliation

Virtual Packages

Cannot find what you are looking for here? Customized to a specific lesson plan, CHOOSE's Virtual Packages provide a direct (and free-of-cost) opportunity for initiating conversations about race.

Steps:
1. Visit www.princetonchoose.org to sign up for a Virtual Package; you will need to describe your existing lesson objectives.
2. Upon receiving your request, the CHOOSE team will collect personal stories, write discussion points, and create a list of key terms—tailored to your lesson.
3. The finalized Virtual Package will be emailed to you within five business days.

How to Talk About *Race*

3. Understand the Issue

Students are constantly feeling pressured to act a certain way, pursue certain hobbies, believe certain things, just because they are Black, White, Asian, Hispanic, or any other race/ethnicity. We might not always hear obvious racial slurs or see racial conflicts, but it's subconscious discrimination that still creates a weight on our shoulders and stays with us our whole lives. If we don't deal with it now, in the classroom, racism can grow and develop and amplify. We've seen this phenomenon in communities like Ferguson, in which racial conflicts didn't happen overnight—they were the result of years and years of growing prejudice.

When we refuse to talk about and understand racial terms, we miss the opportunity to address uncomfortable racial inequalities. People don't understand the danger of refusing to talk about racism, and refusing to face it. Systematic racism will never be eliminated if this culture of denial and silence persists.

1. Understand Why You are Needed

Classrooms are perfect environments for student transformation into activists and allies. If students don't want to speak about race right now, in the comfort of a welcoming classroom, how can they be expected to do it as adults? A lack of dialogue has become habitual from generation to generation, and is one of the root causes of the festering large-scale incidents seen all around the country. We teach students how to understand Newtonian math, write 12-page-long analytical essays, and learn about the complexities of the human anatomy, so why not take the time to go through the basics of talking about equality? Shouldn't this be one of the first things we teach in school? Regardless of what it should be, you have the power to define what it is. Aim to set a precedent for future generations, a precedent that exemplifies a teacher's ability to mold a student's perspective on an age-long conflict: race.

2. Move Past Personal Inertia

Human psychology seems to follow a trend nicknamed the "Starting Problem." When we have to try something new—be it a new food, school, or general routine—we drag our heels and cross our arms in protest. We don't like risking our comfort, but teachers must understand that it is their responsibility to. Teachers don't have a written law requiring them to step out of their comfort zones, but rather a moral one. There is no escape where fulfillment is not required. If race is ignored, teachers risk perpetuating the same behavior of a bystander. Don't allow fear of the conversation going wrong cut off your activism; rather, allow it to serve as a cautionary tool that monitors instead of prohibits your courage to speak up.

How NOT to Talk about Race:

Credit: Barry Deutsch,
leftycartoons.com

4. Be Aware of Your Surroundings

Whether it be with interpersonal relationships, local and national news, or historical information, make sure you are actively engaging in informed activism through self-education. Awareness of the role race is playing in our world will ensure that you don't come off as indifferent or ignorant.

5. Don't Leave Anything Lying on the Table

If the book you're teaching deals with race, talk about it. If the historical figure who you're asking your students to research faced or perpetuated discrimination, talk about it. If the scientific theory you are introducing was invented by people who had to fight their way into a laboratory because of their skin color, talk about it. If the artwork you are displaying contains race-related symbolism, talk about it. It doesn't have to be an hour-long conversation, just mention it before you move on, and you will be on your way to a more inclusive classroom.

7. Stress Themes and Values

Attempting to equate races with one another can cause devaluation, disinterest, and embarrassment. For example, if a teacher attempts to initiate a dialogue focused on the specific experience of an Asian American's encounter with racism, anyone who isn't an Asian-American student might become disconnected from the main purpose of the conversation. However, by stressing themes and values, a connection can be formed between all students, regardless of race, creating an overall more productive experience.

6. Avoid the "Expectation of the Minority Student"

Too often, minority students are expected to speak for their entire race, stripping them of their individuality and forcing them into the constraints of an identity solely based on race. While White students have the luxury of living outside their racial identity, it is important for teachers to understand that minorities must, unfortunately, navigate around it daily. Therefore, when speaking about race-related topics, avoid the temptation to point a finger at a student and ask him or her, "What do you think? Do you have something to share?"

So, if you can't individually prompt students to speak up, what are you expected to do? Instead, wait for students to participate themselves. Organize them into small groups to experience that transformative moment when they realize the value of participating in a dialogue from which so many are absent—that's when their participation will be meaningful, and not forced. Elicit this response through the sharing of personal anecdotes, which shatter the misconception that race-related issues are miles away from being a problem worth worrying about.

CHOOSE Your Story:
The *Tags* List

Short Interviews

Aesthetic

In the United States, beauty is measured by whiteness. Lighter skin and straighter hair not only attract admiration, but also power and privilege, while non-White features are fetishized, denigrated, or appropriated in popular culture.

A few examples: *Light-skinned Black women are incarcerated 12% less than dark-skinned Black women.[1] In 2016, a prestigious high school in South Africa asked Black girls to "fix" their hair by using chemical straighteners and put limitations on cornrows, dreadlocks, and braids.[2]*

Economic

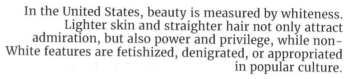

The historical and contemporary intersections between race and class are inseparable with systemic and intergenerational oppression. White supremacy and centuries of economic benefit from colonialism, slavery, Jim Crow Laws, and the urban apartheid fuel racial inequality.

A few examples: *In 1983, the median household net worth for Whites was eight times greater than Blacks; by 2013, it had grown to thirteen times greater. People with "Black-sounding names" have to send out approximately 50% more job applications just to get a call back.[3] White women earn 78%, Black women 64%, and Hispanic women 54% of every dollar a White man earns.[4]*

Educational

In 1964, the Civil Rights Act guaranteed equal access to education regardless of race, color, or national origin. However, the inequities in our educational institutions are still widely prevalent.

A few examples: *5% of White students are suspended, compared to 16% of Black students. 17% of Whites drop out of high school, compared to 29% of Hispanics and 24% of Blacks.[5]*

Identity & Familial

Racial and ethnic backgrounds—including family history, experiences, and relationships—are key to the framework of an individual's identity. Amidst a White social standard, finding and retaining this identity prove difficult for many minorities.[6]

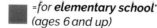

Key: ■ =*for elementary school*
(ages 6 and up)   □ =*for middle school*
(ages 10 and up)   ■ =*for high school*
(ages 14 and up)

CHOOS

Interpersonal

Interpersonal racism involves unconscious or conscious prejudice between individuals. Manifesting itself in beliefs and behaviors, this racism is reinforced by larger systemic structures.[7]

International

Israel

Nigeria

China

Phillipines

Hong Kong

South Africa

China

Additional countries are featured throughout the book in different formats.

Nigeria

South Africa

Guatemala

While this book focuses primarily on race in the United States, race is not an issue in this nation alone. Whether it be the Apartheid Laws in South Africa, the Syrian Refugee Crisis, increasing hostilities in the Middle East, Western European racist attacks against Arabs and Jews, or the anti-Semitic influences in Austria, many forms of racial and ethnic discrimination still exist around the globe.[8]

Brazil

South Africa

Mexico

Political & Legal

Since the beginning of our nation's history, the government and its laws have played a significant role in the creation and preservation of racial inequality. Even today, the narrative of a "colorblind" society veils the issue and the necessity of top-down change toward justice.

A few examples: *Black children constitute only 16% of our nation's children, yet make up 60% of all children in prisons.[9] Blacks are five times—and Hispanics are two times—more likely to be incarcerated than Whites.[10]*

Residential

In many towns and cities, the racial segregation of neighborhoods and public schools is perhaps one of the most obvious lasting manifestations of historical inequality. Racist housing policies such as the 1934–1968 Federal Housing Administration, which did not allow Blacks to take out loans, existed to keep minorities out of White neighborhoods; today, many racial, social, and economic barriers prevent relocation.

A few examples: *Blacks and Hispanics are 1.6 times more likely to be rejected when applying for a bank loan.[11] 73% of homeowners are White; 43% are Black.[12] Gentrification of urban areas continues to push minorities out.*

*A. The colored tags refer to the **minimum recommended age level**; for example, interviews with a green "middle school" tag can and should be used in high school classrooms; B. While the CHOOSE team is based in Princeton, the majority of interviews are not limited to local experiences and are of **national relevance***

Long Interviews

Sumaiyya Stephens, Princeton High School Class of 2016, discusses racial discrimination within the predominantly White public school system she grew up in and how her parents shaped her understanding of identity.

48

Yuki Moore Laurenti, Trenton (NJ) resident and Harvard University alumna, reflects on growing up with an African-American father and a second-generation Japanese-American mother who survived the World War II Japanese Internment Camps.

135

Born in Ethiopia to Indian parents and raised in 7 nations, **Kalpana Peck** shares her views on her international upbringing, her interracial marriage, and the impact she had on her children.

64

Youth Services Librarian **Jocelyn Jimenez** talks about the role of race in her career and in the publishing industry, as well as her family background, culture, colorism, and her interracial relationship.

156

Amir Latif, Rawalpindi renowned Dermatologist, shares his father's experiences migrating from Kashmir to Pakistan in a time of death and discrimination. Interview conducted in Urdu.

77

Robert Karp shares his stories of growing up Jewish in Philadelphia and how his experience as an activist in the Civil Rights Movement shaped his medical career.

168

Treniya Bronaugh, Cornell High School Class of 2017, discusses her search for family history, as well as the intersectionality between race, religion, gender, and class.

100

Christian Joachim, Wheaton College Class of 2019, shares four personal stories from private school, a trip to the Dollar Tree, and construction jobs.

176

<u>Sources for Tag Introductions:</u> Educational: 5 http://blogs.edweek.org/edweek/rulesforengagement/CRDC%20School%20Discipline%20Snapshot.pdf; Political/Legal: 9, 10 http://www.prisonpolicy.org/reports/rates.html; Economic: 4 http://www.infoplease.com/ipa/A0882775.html. 3 http://www.usnews.com/news/blogs/at-the-edge/2015/05/06/institutional-racism-is-our-way-of-life; International: 8 http://www.globalissues.org/article/165/racism; Aesthetic: 1 http://newsone.com/2000618/light-skin-vs-dark-skin/; 2 https://www.washingtonpost.com/world/africa/protests-over-black-girls-hair-rekindle-debate-about-racism-in-south-africa/2016/09/02/27f445da-6ef4-11e6-993f-73c693a89820_story.html; Interpersonal: 7 http://www.health-psych.org/InterpRacism.cfml; Identity & Familial: 6 http://isites.harvard.edu/fs/docs/icb.topic551690.files/Chavez%20and%20Guido%20Debrito.pdf, 12 http://blackyouthproject.com/report-more-than-73-of-homeowners-are-White-compared-to-43-of-blacks/

Stories

CHOOS

" We're Sikh, and we're originally from India. I've been living here for over 25 years now. When we were young and going to school in Texas, they hadn't seen very many Sikhs. Most Americans actually confuse us with Muslims. So it's indirect racism. It's in a way trying to be racist against the Muslims. And what we see the most is not so much walking in the street, but in the media. Online, you see a story, you see a picture, you read people's comments—it's more media-bullying racism rather than on the street."

"That and the TSA."

"We both do analytics for a living, and it's amazing how frequently you get randomly selected. We have both been randomly selected many times."

"We both have TSA-pre cards, and even then we get randomly selected. The people who work at the airport have absolute power. You can't be logical with them at all; any logic is considered an argument."

"It's fascinating actually, there are many parts of the world that are much more ahead of the U.S. in terms of awareness, but other parts have no clue. So the U.S. is actually more ahead of most parts, but not Canada, Australia, the United Kingdom, the Netherlands, some of the more progressive, globally-aware, integrated countries."

"The whole world is going through the [War on Terrorism]; the U.S. is not alone. We are not necessarily just the victims, and I think we seem to have created a lot of these problems ourselves, in terms of the wars that we have created, the people that we have supported through money and arms. In some ways, it's what goes around, comes around. If you look at the current so-called terrorism and war against it, there's a lot more domestic—we don't call it terrorism—[deaths], still more Americans getting killed by guns than by 9/11, for example. But we don't consider that to be terrorism, that's gun violence. If someone takes a gun and shoots someone, if he or she is a person of color, that's terrorism, but if he or she is White, that's someone who is mentally unstable. So there are many different shades of the War on Terrorism. "

When we were young and going to school in Texas, they hadn't seen very many Sikhs. Most of Americans actually confuse us with Muslims. Physical markers like a turban, a beard, and brown skin are commonly associated with Islamic radicalism ever since the September 11, 2001 terrorist attacks. Sikhism, a religion founded in India (Islam was founded in the Arabian peninsula), also requires men to wear turbans as an important article of faith. Sikhism is a distinct religion from Islam and the world's fifth largest organized religion, yet many Americans know little about it. In fact, 60% of Americans claim to know nothing at all about Sikh Americans, and only one in ten Americans (11%) personally knows someone who is Sikh.[1]

Online, you see a story, you see a picture, you read people's comments—it's more media-bullying racism rather than on the street.
Digital platforms, such as Facebook, Instagram, and Twitter, are prone to online racial harassment. A common misconception is that racial cyberbullying is inconsequential; however, in law, racism in online public spaces is still referred to as racial hatred and/or vilification and such racial hatred laws apply.[2] Furthermore, the Internet has enabled everyone to self-publish, which permits the existence of many factually incorrect sites with racist material.

continued on page 22

We both have TSA-pre cards, and even then we get randomly selected.
Sikhs, Muslims, and people of Middle-Eastern descent are often racially profiled at airports because of anti-Islam sentiment and discrimination, stemming from the 9/11 terrorist attacks. Although proven largely ineffective at catching terrorists, Transportation Administration Security officials commonly stop people for "looking" Muslim, which includes non-Muslim religious devotees like Sikhs and Arab Christians.[3] After the Paris and San Bernardino attacks, those affected by Islamophobia are complaining of profiling not only by the TSA, but also by airline companies and fellow passengers. In November 2016, for example, two Palestinian Americans were not allowed to board a plane in Philadelphia when a passenger claimed she felt uncomfortable because they were conversing in Arabic.[4]

If someone takes a gun and shoots someone, if he or she is a person of color, that's terrorism, but if he or she is White, that's someone who is mentally unstable.
The word "terrorism" will not be used to describe a White shooter in the media. However, when discussing a Muslim or African-American shooter, U.S. media outlets quickly characterize the individual as a terrorist or thug. According to mainstream media, White suspects are lone wolves, whose actions are characterized as single incidents of mental instability. A shooting by a Muslim, however, is systematic and considered on behalf of his entire religion or race. See the Current Events feature on page 155.

1 https://d3n8a8pro7vhmx.cloudfront.net/sikhcampaign/pages/40/attachments/original/1422251794/sikh-ES-final.pdf?1422251794
2 http://www.racismnoway.com.au/about-racism/cyber-racism/index.html
3 http://www.washingtontimes.com/news/2013/nov/14/tsa-profiling-at-airports-has-yet-to-nab-a-terrori/
4 https://thinkprogress.org/iraqi-man-removed-from-southwest-flight-for-speaking-arabic-786ff04fb344#.8rsnxd2zn

"At the Bus Stop"

Graphic Credit: Barry Deutsch, leftycartoons.com

CHOOS

" Everyone from Israel is coming from somewhere. There are very few people who are born in Israel. Immigration is 'aliyah' ... it's like coming to the holy land. So, everybody's different. [In the United States], everyone has been living here for more than 200 years. In Israel, everybody is new. It actually seems like there is an effort [to be open to different types of people]. For example, in kids' TV shows. But I think that in the United States, the Hispanics are doing the work that is very low. And with Black people, we see that also. They do the lowest jobs in America. Initially, you don't see it. You don't see that these kind of people do that, and these kind of people do that... but it seems that the [White people in] America have a better education. So maybe, if the public schools were much better, it would help. **"**

But it seems that the [White people in] America have a better education.
In a study of four-year-old children, researchers found that between 18.8% and 28.3% of Black, Latinx, and Native American children were proficient in recognizing letters, compared to between 36.8% and 49.4% of Whites and Asian-Americans. In a study of fourth graders, 29% to 36% of Black, Latinx, and Native American children scored below the basic proficiency level of mathematics, compared to 8%–9% of Whites and Asian-Americans. At the high school level, 26% of Black Advanced Placement test takers scored the passing 3 or above, compared to 43% of Latinx and Native American students and 62-64% of White and Asian-American students. From early to higher education, extensive research has shown racial disparities in educational achievement that reflect structural inequities in U.S. society.[1]

1 http://www.apa.org/ed/resources/racial-disparities.pdf

**CURRENT
EVENT**

originally a CHOOSE Facebook post
graphic credit: Ayesha Qureshi

November 14th, 2015

Terror attacks have taken the lives of hundreds of innocent civilians in places such as Paris, Baghdad, and Lebanon. In these tragic times, it is essential that instead of associating terror with a race or religion, we focus on giving our condolences and love to all victims and their families.

#terrorhasnoreligion

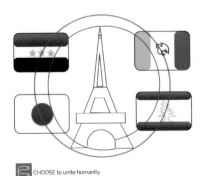

CHOOSE to unite humanity

The community that I live in is full of Western expatriates, so it seems like a very diverse place. But when you look at the rest of Hong Kong, 94% is Chinese.

Expatriates are individuals living outside the country of their citizenship. In Hong Kong, the number of expatriates have increased from 19,155 individuals in 2004 to 31,676 in 2014.[1]

And as a result, some of the more traditional Chinese ways of bringing up children, such as using strict discipline, were not enforced.

Numerous studies comparing traditional and modern Chinese and American cultural values have found that "Chinese parents set higher standards and work more often with their children on homework than their American counterparts, and Chinese cultural values help to ensure that children work diligently." While this may have contributed to China's higher average national test scores in mathematics, it has also contributed to the common, inaccurate stereotype that all Asian-Americans have strict parents and excel in mathematics.[2]

1 http://www.socialindicators.org.hk/en/indicators/internationalization/22.10;
2 http://groups.psych.northwestern.edu/uttal/documents/chenanduttal1988_000.pdf

"The community that I live in is full of Western expatriates, so it seems like a very diverse place. But when you look at the rest of Hong Kong, 94% is Chinese. It's like living in a race bubble. In Hong Kong the expatriates are more wealthy, and as a result I feel privileged because I'm half-Canadian. People who are Chinese want to seem Westernized, so those who have relatives in the United States, Canada, Australia, or the U.K. will call themselves American-Chinese, Canadian-Chinese, Australian-Chinese, or English-Chinese even if they don't have roots there or have never lived there.

Being biracial means that I'm able to choose to experience the best of both cultures, and I'm thankful that my parents are willing to compromise and learn about each other's traditions. It's taught me to be more open-minded of other people's cultures. Although my mom is Chinese, she grew up in a more Westernized environment. And as a result, some of the more traditional Chinese ways of bringing up children, such as using strict discipline, were not enforced. For example, when I was playing soccer with local girls, I was the only mixed, only White person there. They told me I would never be a good player on the team; at a training camp, my coach threw a plastic water bottle at my head when I was talking during training sessions. But everyone was talking. I had difficulty assimilating with the coach's training tactics and had to take more time to build my self-confidence and get used to my environment."

"When I shop, I walk into a store and it seems like the employees will not acknowledge me, but they will acknowledge others. When I walk in, they don't ask 'how can I help you?' But when other people walk in, they do. That's how I realize that okay, there is a difference. Maybe they don't acknowledge me because they feel like I don't have the money to buy anything in that store.

I also network a lot and I've met many people. There was a lady who I used to talk to on the phone. We had really hit it off since we were both people-persons, and we both worked in the hotel industry. We talked about her family, everything, and before we ever met in person, we had bonded on the phone. Eventually, we decided we were going to meet. She was so excited. She made reservations for me in Colorado, and told me that her and her husband were going to show me around and I wouldn't have to worry about anything. Our meeting point was a restaurant. I got there and she took one look at me, and I remember the look on her face. She then told me all these excuses on why she couldn't stay: 'I have to do something,' 'I have to go somewhere,' 'I have an appointment,' etc. It was very interesting, because we had really hit it off on the phone, but after meeting me, she tried everything in her power to come up with an excuse to leave. Maybe she hadn't expected me to be Black."

INTER-PERSONAL

Maybe they don't acknowledge me because they feel like I don't have the money to buy anything in that store.

Refer to the second discussion point on page 179.

It was very interesting, because we had really hit it off on the phone, but after meeting me, she tried everything in her power to come up with an excuse to leave. Maybe she hadn't expected me to be black.

Dr. John Baugh and Margaret Bush Wilson, both professors at Washington University in St. Louis, conducted experiments to test how different companies reacted to the linguistics of different races. They hypothesized that employment and real estate agencies are misusing the telephone by contacting customers and denying or limiting services to them based on their apparent race. The test involved three people calling each advertisement with a distinct Black, Hispanic, and White dialect. The results repeatedly proved "that the person using the ethnic dialect got no return calls. If they did reach the company, frequently they were told that what was advertised was no longer available, though it was still available to the Standard English speaker."[1] This discrimination is called linguistic profiling.

The experience mentioned by the interviewee is a similar case of profiling, but by appearance: Based on their phone conversations, the woman assumed the interviewee was White. However, upon discovering that the interviewee was Black, her perception changed, racism kicked in, and the way she interacted with the interviewee changed negatively.

1 https://source.wustl.edu/2006/02/linguistic-profiling-the-sound-of-your-voice-may-determine-if-you-get-that-apartment-or-not/

Race plays a big part in everything that happens in Alabama, which a lot of people don't see. Alabama, the "Cotton State" and "Heart of Dixie," has a long history of slavery and racial segregation. During the 1960's, numerous race riots and attacks occurred in Birmingham, including the killing of four African-American girls in a church bombing. This critical event in the Civil Rights Movement is described in Christopher Paul Curtis's *The Watsons Go to Birmingham–1963*.

I identify as a Nigerian. I do not identify as an African, that's too broad—Africa is a whole continent.

In an article entitled "Optional Ethnicities: For Whites Only?", Harvard University sociology professor Mary Waters details the contrast between the costless "individualistic symbolic identity" available to White Americans and the "socially enforced and imposed racial identity." While White Americans can choose how to identify ethnically—for example, which European nation to associate their ancestry with—minorities are often automatically labeled as "African-American," "American-Indian," "Asian-American," or "Hispanic-American." The belief that all identities are equal is flawed because it ignores the historically unequal treatment of different ethnicities.[1]

1 http://www.pages.drexel.edu/~jc3962/COR/Racism/Racism_1.pdf

" I just walked into the Vineyard Vines in Birmingham, and all these White people stopped what they were doing and stared. There was a little baby who ran back to his mom. They stared at me, because I am a Black person. Usually the people that you see there are White. Race plays a big part in everything that happens in Alabama, which a lot of people don't see.

To me, my Nigerian culture means that I have an identity outside of where I live currently. I feel like with African Americans, there's always that part of Africa that they want to find. I don't have to do that, I know where I am from. I know my history, so it gives me a sense of identity. I identify as a Nigerian. I do not identify as an African, that's too broad—Africa is a whole continent. I could be from anywhere. I am also Black, technically speaking. In the United States, I know there's a bad connotation with being Black, but that's what I am.

American culture—it takes away from Nigerian culture. I've learned to take the good parts of both cultures, but I have many friends with Nigerian backgrounds who don't identify with the culture. They don't have the values. I feel like American culture dilutes it, and it makes the things I value not okay in their point of view. But in the future, I want to open my own psychiatric hospital for inpatient and outpatient care in Nigeria. This field is overlooked in all of Africa. Nigeria is where I call home, so I will start from there. "

My Korean-American Story

by Matthew Kim

My name is Matthew Justin Moo-Jang Kim. I am a 17-year-old with black, spikey hair and dark brown, almond-shaped eyes. I am 5'7, with the slim build of a dancer and a foil fencer. My complexion is tan, or as my older brother prefers to call it, golden. I am a third-generation Korean-American born in New York City. My father was born in Seoul but came to the United States when he was three and my mother was born here. In this way I am a very Americanized Korean. I do not speak much Korean and have never been to Korea. This is the story of how what I looked like influenced how other people saw me and treated me growing up, how I became an outsider to both sides, Korean and American, and how all of these experiences shaped how I perceive myself.

Until age 11, I never really thought about race. Even when I looked in the mirror, I barely recognized that there was something that differentiated me from the White kids in my class. Maybe I was just too self-absorbed

> **❝ I'm sure kids asked me plenty of times if I was Chinese... but no experience sticks out to me about race until fifth grade music class."**

to be self-conscious. I'm sure kids asked me plenty of times if I was Chinese, to which I responded Korean, and then South not North, but no experience sticks out to me about race until fifth grade music class.

It was a very boring class. Our teacher had us playing a game in which we split up into two teams, listened to the teacher clap a rhythmic pattern, and then repeated it. Five rounds in, I decided to mess with the other team by clapping different rhythms while they were trying to repeat theirs. While I cracked up, two guys on the other team, Jamie and Harrison, got up and began to yell at me. I just yelled back that I wasn't doing anything. Then in the midst of our shouting match, Harrison went for the low blow. He started singing a song called "I Am Korean," a parody of the Black Eyed Peas song, "I Gotta Feeling," made by Rucka Rucka Ali, who is notorious for making controversial songs that revolve around ethnic stereotypes. "I Am Korean" is no different, referencing the usual "ching chang chongs," pronouncing "r's" like "l's," and small dick jokes. The only way to describe it was humiliating. It wasn't the first time I had heard the song. But it's completely different listening to the song in front of an entire class with everyone watching how you react. Harrison was singing. Jamie was shouting a variation of the song title, almost chanting, "You are Korean!" over and over again, pointing at me. With my face burning and the unbearable sound in my ears, everything else faded into nothingness and I ran full speed towards the two boys, not knowing what I was going to do, only that I wanted to hurt them the way they had hurt me. But when I was right in front of them, I was paralyzed, unable to do anything but stare at them while they continued to yell and sing. So I just broke down. In a vain effort, in between sobs, I shouted back at Harrison (who was half-Malaysian), that he was "a stupid Malaysian." It didn't seem to bother him, but looking back, I'm not proud of saying it. I just didn't know what to do when someone attacked me because of something I couldn't change. Finally the teacher stepped in and took Harrison and Jamie to the principal's office and me to an empty classroom, where I sat and for the first time, realized that there was something different about me that other people noticed and could attack—almost a weakness.

After that, I started noticing it a lot

> **❝ And there was always that feeling of power-lessness."**

more. I would look in the mirror and stretch my face with my fingers to see if I really did have squinty eyes. Comments like, "you're good at math because you're Asian" or "Sorry, I can't tell Asians apart" seemed to happen more often and stuck with me for longer. And there was always that feeling of powerlessness. You can't freak out at someone who makes those comments because oftentimes they're your friends and you don't want to overreact, so you internalize it and try to let it go. But in some cases, I couldn't do it.

Derrick was a tall White kid with long blonde hair whom I met at camp the summer before 8th grade. From very first moment, he went all out with the slurs. Some of my favorites were, "We're in America, we speak English," "You eat dogs," and of course, "ching chang chong." This was a few years after Harrison, so it was a different me. By the second day, I had heard enough, so while he was speaking "Asianese" to me for the eighth time, I threw him against a wall and told him that if he didn't stop, I would beat him up with my taekwondo. It worked and he stayed quiet from then on, but it was too late. That was my breaking point of dealing with Derrick and others just like him. From then on, I was just another "angry Asian man," with a chip on his shoulder.

Before, I just tried to roll with being Asian. The summer after the music class incident, I went to a movie-making camp at my school, and the older kids in my group wanted to make a parody of "The Karate Kid." Of course, as the only Asian in the group, I was chosen to play Mr. Miyagi/Mr. Han/the Sensei. It didn't bother me at the time because I was the youngest in the group and just wanted to be accepted. So for me, this was a great opportunity. I watched the film recently and cringed. Not only did I have long hair down to my neck, but I was also playing the stereotypical wise martial arts master that speaks in proverbs with an accent. At the time I didn't see anything wrong with it. And even now, looking at the actions themselves, I can still say that the jokes aren't that bad. But the motivation behind them, to please non-Asians by making fun of Asian culture, is what I'm ashamed of.

But in 8th grade, I started working towards a different approach to race relations. All the internalization finally built up and created a backlash in me, starting me on what I like to call my " Super Asian Pride Stage." It was a good time to be Asian that year. "Gangnam Style" had just become the most-watched YouTube video ever, and the hallyu wave was in full force. So naturally for Halloween, I dressed up as Psy. You might be thinking, "wait, didn't you just say you weren't going to make fun of Asian culture to please non-Asians anymore?" and you're absolutely right. Dressing up as Psy was an expression of pride for me, to show others that I was Korean just like him, and that Koreans could accomplish anything White people could and more. The only problem was I was still wearing my culture as a costume (literally) and perpetuating stereotypes about K-pop. Because to other people, it didn't matter why I did it, all they would see is a wacky Korean guy dressing up as another wacky Korean guy. But it was a start.

Then came the social shift. There were three other Asians in my grade, two Chinese boys, and one Chinese girl. We had been friends for a while, but I started to spend more and more of my time with them, not isolating myself from my other friends exactly, but still creating a noticeable change. We all played instruments, and one day we decided that the three guys should form a boy band. We called ourselves "Triple A," as a joke and spent our recess time jamming in the music classroom. Again, there was a bit of "flaunting of my Asian-ness" going on at that time, but it was all part of my coming to terms with my identity. I started to see my race less as something that others could exploit, and instead as something that I could use to my advantage, something that made me different in a good way. Unfortunately, this new perception came at the cost of also becoming a little too prideful and exploitive.

But when I reached high school, I was thrown into a completely new world that changed every idea I had about race and my identity. Growing up, the only other Koreans my age that I really knew were my cousins. So after deciding to come to Lawrenceville, I was excited to meet people who were like me and not be one of four Asians in my grade. But when it finally happened, it wasn't really what I was expecting.

It was easy to figure out who the other Koreans were; a few of us share the same last name, after all. It was fine for a while; I made friends and learned that most of the Koreans were not only racially Korean but were from Korea as well. But it started going downhill a few weeks into the year, when they started to learn more about me. To start, most of my Korean friends would ask me, "Is it true? Can you not speak Korean?" or "Have you ever been to Korea?" Every time, I would explain that 1.) I was third generation and though my par-

> **"... it hurt back then, to have part of my identity ripped from me like it didn't belong to me."**

ents understand Korean for the most part, they never spoke it and never taught it to me and 2.) When I was younger, my brother and I played a lot of travel sports, so during school vacations we always had to go to tournaments, which meant that we never had time to visit Korea. But even after I answered, a few days later, they would ask again like they forgot, forcing me to go through the embarrassment of having to explain again. Eventually, it turned into humor, where I got teased a little bit for my lack of Korean-ness. I've heard it so many times, and I still hear it a little: "You're not really Korean" or "you're not a real Korean." I was like the black sheep of the family, if I had been part of the family, because back in freshman year, I wasn't in Club Korea, which was known for excluding non-Koreans. I was reclassified as a banana and an ABK made to feel ashamed of where I was from. I'm not going to lie; it hurt back then, to have part of my identity ripped from me like it didn't belong to me.

> **"... it still created a self-consciousness in me that tore me apart from the inside."**

And at the time, I was so confused because I thought I was definitely Korean enough. I fit most of the qualifications of what I thought it meant to be Korean. I got good grades and used to play violin, the keys to being a model minority. I did taekwondo for several years and ate traditional Korean food all the time with my family. My blood is one hundred percent Korean. So the phrase, "you're not a real Korean" didn't even make sense to me. But whether it made sense or not, it still created a self-consciousness in me that tore me apart from the inside.

Sophomore year was a learning year for me. The summer before, I had resolved to learn Korean, but I learned that it's a lot harder to do when your teacher is the Internet. So now, I'm not fluent, but I'm better than where I was before. I also started listening to K-pop to try to help me learn the language faster. It didn't work, but I did choreograph a K-pop dance for a dance concert. One of the older Koreans that I had never talked to before told me how great he thought the dance was, and that definitely stuck with me. I also wrote my history research paper on South Korea and accumulated a lot of knowledge about its modern history. But this was all my trying to compensate, my attempt to reconcile my two sides and rediscover what it meant to be Korean. But I still felt like a banana and that was unacceptable to me.

And that's where I was when I discovered Asian Americans in hip-hop. Two words that could not be less related in the ears of most people are "hip-hop" and "Asian." But, Asians, a commonly ignored group, have struggled and still do to find their place in the culture, and now have contributed more than people realize.

The hip-hop scene in which Asians have had arguably the most important impact is dance. On the television show America's Best Dance Crew on MTV, which first aired in 2008, there was a significant number of Asians on the show that consistently dominated the competition. The third season's winner, Quest Crew, marked the first time an all-Asian crew took home gold on the show, but it would not be the last. I watched that season with my older brother in 2009, but I wasn't paying very close atten-

tion at the time because I didn't start dancing until high school. But sophomore year, I started watching them on Youtube and was shocked. These guys were all Asian Americans, just like me, and they were accomplishing incredible feats that I could only dream of, combining hip-hop dance with martial arts tricking. I watched one of their performance videos almost every day for six months, and I was so excited when after a hiatus for several years, America's Best Dance Crew came back last summer, bringing in an all-star roster that included most of the past champions and one new crew. This crew, The Kinjaz, a ninja-themed all-Asian crew, made it all the way to the finals, where they lost in a very close battle to Quest. The Kinjaz, similar to Quest, are a blend of Asian culture and urban movement, something that was mesmerizing to me.

Two Korean-Americans from the crews, Victor Kim of Quest and Mike Song of Kinjaz, both have performed across the USA and in Korea and were loved by both sides. It didn't matter that they were Korean-Americans; the combination was what made their art unique. I thought that if all of these dancers could reconcile their two cultures and be successful in something that combined the two, then there was hope for me too.

Though Quest and Kinjaz were close to what I was searching for, my greatest help for coming to terms with my identity was the rapper Dumbfoundead. Dumbfoundead, or Jonathan Park, was born in Argentina but smuggled by his mother into the United States through Mexico at the age of three. Growing up in Koreatown, Los Angeles, Dumb was introduced to rapping at the age of ten, when he start-

ed learning the art and history of freestyling. His first claim to fame was in 2008, when he began to compete on a battle rap circuit, where he was known for his comedic punchlines and his epic freestyling flow. His battle with Brooklyn rapper Conceited is the most viewed KOTD rap battle on Youtube, with over 4,000,000 views, and Drake himself complimented Dumbfoundead in a press conference about the KOTD event. Dumb is one of the most versatile rappers who might have the best chance of breaking into mainstream media, with his ability to clown around on a freestyle, or evoke deep emotions when he raps about repping Koreatown, or get an audience hyped when he goes hard to a trap beat. Like with Quest, my brother was the one who introduced me to Dumbfoundead, as he had opened for Dumb in a concert at his college. The first song of his that I remember listening to was "Korean Jesus." This was the song that helped me retake ownership of being Korean, with captivating, confident but playful lyrics rapped to a hard beat. It wasn't K-Pop, or even K-Rap: Dumb raps in English. He's not part of the hallyu wave; just by listening to his diction, it is easy to hear that he is very American. But, he is anything but the stereotypical Asian American model minority. I used to watch his opponents dish out every Asian joke imaginable in battles, but Dumb would play it off so easily and come back harder with jokes and disses that could turn the entire audience against his challengers. He redefined what it meant to be an Asian American for me and helped me reclaim some of the pride I had lost. I realized I didn't have to fit into the box of what society called "Asian-American;" I knew Dumb definitely didn't and that was okay. I knew it was okay to be Korean-American.

> " I thought that if all of these **dancers could reconcile their two cultures** and be successful in something that combined the two, **then there was hope for me too.**"

> "**Asians in America are still treated like a joke and second-rate citizens; we are still outsiders. But I know that to effectively combat what I'm fighting against, I need to know who I am first.**"

Matthew (left) with Mike Song.

But through this process, as the saying, "once burned, twice shy," goes, I lost the arrogance that I used to have through being broken down and rebuilt in a better way. When I was invited to Club Korea this year, I was ecstatic, but cautious. I had most of the identity emotional garbage figured out, but there was still a little part of me that would always remember being an outsider to Korea and America. My second meeting was last week, and I realized: all of the Koreans put each other down. The kids who went to international schools got called out for not being real Koreans. One of the seniors asked a junior who had been in the club since freshman year if she even spoke Korean. Another junior forced a sophomore to eat spicy ramyeon, and when he grabbed a water bottle, the junior simply beckoned with his finger and the sophomore handed it over, only for a senior to curse out the junior, smack him upside the head, and hand the bottle back to the red-faced sophomore. It's part of the culture; even the language has different levels of respect that are to be used with people who are seen as above or below you. It's all about hierarchy, which means lots of competition, which means lots of "ragging." It was nothing personal against me; if anything, the teasing made me even more a part of the group. And though it's awkward when someone speaks in Korean and I don't understand, I can deal, especially because I know I'm not the only one.

The exclusiveness started to make sense to me too. They've never really been discriminated against because they've always been the majority back home, so they don't even know what it truly means to be Korean in the United States. One of

photos courtesy of Matthew Kim

my friends is on the football team, and though he's huge for a Korean, I saw him get more teasing from the team than anyone else. And though I had that experience growing up, it must have been a shock for him. So who would want those football players to come to a Club Korea meeting? Club Korea is a place for Koreans to go, a retreat almost, to speak in Korean and eat Korean food together. But I won't deny that it also felt good to be on the inside, to be a member of the rare "elite," and I'm sure that factored into how Club Korea became the way it is. So hopefully when I have more power as a senior, I'll try to make a push in a more accepting direction, so the half-Koreans (who still have trouble entering) don't have to go through the same identity crisis that I did.

After reflecting, I've come to realize a few things. The first is how fortunate I am. I've been exposed to so many other stories about people who have suffered so much more because of their race, and what I've described here doesn't make up one billionth of the total pain that people have felt because of their race, so I don't want to give the impression to whoever reads this that I think that it does. However, though I've made my peace with the Koreans, there is still work to be done on the American side. Asians in America are still treated like a joke and second-rate citizens; we are still outsiders. But I know that to effectively combat what I'm fighting against, I need to know who I am first. No one can make me ashamed of what I look like; I am proud of my golden complexion and diamond-shaped eyes. No one can make me believe I'm not Korean enough; my blood makes me a Korean American in my own right. And most importantly, no one can make me question my identity because these experiences shaped who I am today and every choice I will make tomorrow. This is my Korean-American story.

CURRENT EVENT

originally a CHOOSE Facebook post
graphic credit: Ayesha Qureshi

November 26th, 2015

Celebrate Thanksgiving by uniting as one people—we are thankful for the efforts of all advocates around the world who are part of the movement to achieve harmony. On this day, also take the time to recognize our national history of mistreatment of Native Americans. Uniting as one people means advancing in a direction that does not appropriate and ignore a culture, but embraces it by learning and teaching. #harmony #movement

CHOOSE to join our movement

❝ When me and my brother were walking home one time, we were walking past the Nassau Inn, and then—you know the restaurant on the other side, Teresa's? One of the waiters came out and started yelling at us for looking inside the Nassau Inn, [saying] that he was going to call the police on us. That's racism in Princeton, [New Jersey]. It is [a problem], but it's not a big issue because people are just going to keep low-key and not be outward with it... I do get that feeling [that people discredit my success] occasionally 'cause, as minorities, we are looked down upon. Even those as African-American are thought as not really overachieving and [without] anything good coming from us. One instance would be a teacher not really expecting much from me. From other people, she would expect so much more—perfect stuff. She definitely thought more of other students and held them to a higher esteem, while I would still try to have the same work ethic as them and put in the same effort and process. For other [minority students], it would definitely have a negative impact. They would be like, 'why doesn't this teacher think I'm as good as other students,' while for me I didn't feel like that because I knew I am capable for doing all this other stuff. ❞

From other people, she would expect so much more—perfect stuff. She definitely thought more of other students and held them to a higher esteem, while I would still try to have the same work ethic as them and put in the same effort and process.

In this interview, the teacher's actions are rooted in stereotypes about this interviewee's ability and work ethic. For example, Black students are often assumed to prioritize athletics over academics (refer to page 85), or to be poor and uneducated (refer to page 110).

CHOOS

"[Where] I live... we see a lot of people, and they go to run in the park that is by John Witherspoon Middle School. This year, my friend was running at about 5:30 in the morning, and three people came out, and they hit him. It was very ugly. That is racism towards the Hispanics, because the man was doing no more than what was told to him by the doctor, who sent him to do exercise because he was high in cholesterol. And so the kids hit him, and they took his money, and they went running. And he got up and looked at them, and he said that that was wrong, and that those people who treat the Hispanics badly treat us like an ATM. They always come to us asking for money, thinking that we have lots of money because we can't open bank accounts, and because sometimes one carries around all his money. And the police now have deserted us."

Those people who treat the Hispanics badly treat us like an ATM.

In the 21st century, multiple major American banks including M&T Bank, PNC Bank, and Bank of America have been accused and/or indicted of discriminatory practices toward minorities. For example, in 2011 Citigroup charged Blacks interest rates that were 3.38 times higher than other borrowers, with Wells Fargo at 2.28 and J.P. Morgan & Chase at 2.21 for the same demographic. As with Blacks, Hispanics were also charged higher interest rates twice as often across most investigated banks.[1] Here, the interviewee may also be referring to assumptions about undocumented status among some Hispanic immigrants, which would prevent access to bank accounts.

And the police now have deserted us.

After being hit and mugged—the possible result of community silence, immigration fears, and/or targeted racism by other ethnic groups, among other reasons—this man's friend was unable to find help from the police. This man believes this is due to racial injustice in law enforcement. In a nationwide survey, 51% of Hispanics agreed that police are biased and unfair, as opposed to 37% of Whites.[2]

1 http://www.marketwatch.com/story/do-banks-play-the-race-card-with-your-loan-2012-04-03?reflink=MW_news_stmp; 2 http://www.pewsocialtrends.org/2013/08/22/chapter-1-i-have-a-dream-50-years-later/#treatment-of-Blacks-by-the-courts-police-seen-as-less-fair

"One time, this guy came to our school who worked with this group called In-sight Photography on Pine Ridge Reservation in South Dakota. He talked about how these native children showed all these symptoms of cancer and diseases that stemmed from this poisonous interaction with the government. On Pine Ridge Res-ervation, there were campers, and they were affected with things that led to cancer and other diseases. The government sold them to [the natives] knowing they were not habitable. They did not even use them in New Orleans after Hurricane Katrina, so they gave them to the native groups. It's crazy.

I think social justice education is so key. If we want a generation that is more woke and progressive, it is vital that they have the resources. A lot of history is White-washed, and may be not as true. I feel like before I came to my school, it was like, 'Native-American people were there, they were oppressed.' It was glanced over. The thing that most people accepted when they were teaching me was that oppression was necessary in order to establish America, and therefore we should just ignore that it happened. If it didn't happen, you would not be here, so you shouldn't fret on it too much. It is like the all-time cultural appropriation, that we live on their land but don't recognize it. And historically, a lot of the land that Native American groups have been put on have not been fertile because the US government did not need that land. That land is hard to farm on. A lot of times, it is hard to feed a lot of people. A lot of the donated food is processed in cans, subsidized foods. It's not very nutritious, so there is an obesity problem... there are still health issues."

On Pine Ridge Reservation, there were campers, and they were affected with things that led to cancer and other diseases.
The Pine Ridge Oglala Lakota (Sioux) Indian Reservation in South Dakota is the second largest reservation in the United States, roughly matching the size of Connecticut and home to 40,000 people. According to the American Indian Humanitarian Foundation, most Indian American families in the nation lack access to basic needs: 59% of housing is inadequate while an average of 17 people live in a two or three room home, the unemployment rate is 85–95% while lack of infrastructure and industry prevents an increase in jobs, and schools receive the lowest 10% of federal government school funding while the dropout rate is above 70%. Health is a significant issue: there are few preventative health programs, much of the land and water is contaminated, the cervical cancer rate is 500% higher than the U.S. average, the tuberculosis rate is 800% higher, and nearly half of adults have diabetes. In addition, alcoholism affects 80% of families.[1] These factors all contribute to a 95% poverty rate, compared to a 14.8% national average in 2014.[2]

It is like the all-time cultural appropriation, that we live on their land but don't recognize it.
Cultural appropriation is the stealing of elements of one culture by members of a dominant culture. One example is White people turning traditional native headdresses into a trendy, hip Halloween costume of feathers and beads. While Native American culture is largely forgotten by most Americans and romanticized on media, the reality of huge disparities on native reservations is also ignored.[1]

And historically, a lot of the land that Native American groups have been put on have not been fertile because the US government did not need that land.
The 1830 Indian Removal Act forced thousands of natives from their homes and into unsettled territory west of the Mississippi River, a pattern which continued throughout the territorial expansion of the next few decades.[3] To this day, much of the land and water is polluted by nearby mines, military sites, farms, open dumps, etc. Government treaties to provide medical care in exchange for land have proved broken promises, too ineffective to match the need on most reservations.[1]

1 http://www.4aihf.org/id40.html
2 http://www.census.gov/library/publications/2015/demo/p60-252.html
3 https://www.loc.gov/teachers/classroommaterials/presentationsandactivities/presentations/immigration/native_american2.html

RESI-DENTIAL

❝ I just think it's very subliminal, it's everywhere, you don't notice it all the time, it's always underlying. But people do assume things if you're Asian. I'm from New York, and New York is more diverse, so more problems happen and it's more pronounced. It's less obvious here, but you see it especially with the housing [in Princeton]. There's that section of Princeton where only Hispanics live, and they're not given the opportunity to leave. And that's considered the bad part of Princeton—that's inherent racism. ❞

But people do assume things if you're Asian. Common Asian-American stereotypes include high intelligence, Chinese ancestry, musical prowess, and ability to play karate but not sports in general. While these may apply to certain individuals, they cannot be assumed for all Asian-Americans.

There's that section of Princeton where only Hispanics live, and they're not given the opportunity to leave. Wealth inequality is an intergenerational issue, particularly centered around housing. Evidence shows that Black and Hispanic people, for example, are less likely to own a home and more likely to experience inequity than White people (see pages 181 and 144). Segregated neighborhoods also impact the racial compositions of and disparities between schools.[1]

1 http://www.jstor.org/stable/4120744?seq=1#page_scan_tab_contents

36

❝ I hear racist comments all the time, especially during my freshman year of high school. There have been a lot of stereotypes about Hispanics and how they aren't well-educated and how they're stupid. That was hard for me because when teachers would put me in groups with others, most of the time they would give me less work to do in the group... Some teachers don't push minorities to do things outside their comfort zones... it can be hard for most of the minorities who don't have a voice in the community. **❞**

There have been a lot of stereotypes about Hispanics and how they aren't well-educated and how they're stupid. Refer to page 98 or 153.

EDUCA-TIONAL

CURRENT EVENT

originally a CHOOSE Facebook post
graphic credit: The New York Times

November 27th, 2015

"She ends up telling me, 'Oh wow, in the city where I'm from, we have so few Black people. The police are actually called nig*** knockers.'"

"I've been called a nig*** at least once or twice. I'm a student in chemical engineering here on a scholarship, but yet everybody asks me what position I play or what's my 400 meter time."

"'What does your father do—or is he not around?'"

Students protest racism toward Blacks at Purdue University in Indiana, leading marches and social media posts inspired by #Mizzou.

Read more: http://www.nytimes.com/video/us/100000004045468/black-on-campus.html

CHOOSE to support #BlackonCampus

"I'm a lot of things. Mostly I'm half-White, half-Black. My dad is Jewish and Moroccan, and my mom also has a lot of Native American on her side. I get mistaken as a Latina a lot, but none of that in there, unfortunately. I tried to learn Spanish so I wouldn't be a complete embarrassment when people asked me where something was [in Spanish]. Being biracial is interesting, because you always feel like you're not White enough, or you're not Black enough, and you're just this in-between mix. When I'm with my dad's family, they're always commenting on how tan I am, how cool my hair is. But when I'm with my mom's family, I'm always the Whitest person there, or the palest. I don't feel like I belong to either side, really. So I just have to create my own way of being, and not ascribe to either stereotype. My sister also looks Asian, and people think she's from Thailand. We both look pretty ambiguous, and it's interesting to hear what people say. But now there are so many people who are multiracial that it's not as big of a thing. You still come across people that are like, 'What are you?' as if it matters so much. It's still a big part of who I am, though. And it's also a weird in between feeling because both sides have such strong identities. Being Black in college is such an important part of the community, but I would never try to go into an African-American student group because I would feel so out of place."

"The most I thought about my race was when I was applying to college. I didn't think I could get into any Ivy League school, being an Asian, because I didn't think I was as smart or achieving as the other Asians in my school. And there's a defined 'Asian group' which I don't feel like I belong in, but I don't really belong anywhere else either. So it's interesting."

"Being as White as I am, recently with a lot of the racial tension that's going on in the country, I definitely try to be as politically-correct and respectful as possible. Especially in large groups of intolerant or racially-insensitive White people, others assume you're racist or insensitive or uninformed because you're White."

But now there are so many people who are multiracial that it's not as big of a thing. According to a 2015 investigation by the Pew Research Center, 6.9% of U.S. adults are multiracial. Out of this percentage, 60% feel proud of their multiracial background, 59% feel open to other cultures, and 55% have personally experienced racial slurs or jokes. Currently growing three times as fast as the overall U.S. population, the population of multiracial babies alone was 1% in 1970 and 10% of all babies in 2013. However, different patterns emerge among multiracial adults; for example, 69% of those with a Black background say they are most often viewed as Black or African-American, while only 22% of those with a Native-American background say they share commonalities with other Native Americans.[1]

Being Black in college is such an important part of the community, but I would never try to go into an African-American student group because I would feel so out of place.
According to an article by the social justice group ThinkProgress, difficulties of Black students at majority-White colleges include facing racial bias, "struggling with the psychological pressure of proving yourself," learning with Eurocentric teaching focuses, "being targeted by campus police," and failing to obtain administrative support.[2] According to Harvard University professor Mary Waters, Black students on college campuses feel the attraction of sharing cultural elements with other Black students, as well as "the need to band together with other students in a reactive and oppositional way in the face of racist incidents on campus."[3]

1 http://www.pewsocialtrends.org/2015/06/11/multiracial-in-america/; 2 https://thinkprogress.org/5-things-that-make-it-hard-to-be-a-black-student-at-a-mostly-White-college-33ef44abe034#.4jrapopsy; 3 http://www.pages.drexel.edu/~jc3962/COR/Racism/Racism_1.pdf; 4 http://repository.uchastings.edu/cgi/viewcontent.cgi?article=1845&context=faculty_scholarship

I didn't think I could get into any Ivy League school, being an Asian, because I didn't think I was as smart or achieving as the other Asians in my school.
The use of affirmative action in many colleges seeks to address a racial and ethnic inequality of opportunity by ensuring diversity on campuses. However, some Asian-Americans—primarily people of Chinese, South Korean, and Indian ethnicity—feel that they have been rejected from colleges because of their race, despite credentials higher than those accepted. This interviewee feels that college admission is a race against other Asian-Americans, because affirmative action creates a cap on the number of Asian-Americans who can be enrolled.

According to University of California professor Frank Wu, legal scholar John Hart Ely and the Supreme Court have agreed that "it is acceptable for the majority to disadvantage itself to benefit a minority, but it is not acceptable for the majority to disadvantage a minority, nor to disadvantage a minority in the course of benefiting another minority." In this case, he references the use of the model minority myth to claim that Asian Americans suffer just as much in the college admissions process, if not more than Whites, in order to benefit African American student enrollment. Stating that Asian Americans should be "considered on their terms, rather than as honorary Whites or constructive Blacks," Wu believes that Asian Americans should not be disadvantaged or used to defeat the concept of affirmative action, but rather honestly considered so that minimum but not maximum quotas are specified for certain racial groups, and Whites and Asian Americans can compete equally and fairly for college admission.[4]

CURRENT EVENT

originally a CHOOSE Facebook post
graphic credit: Ayesha Qureshi

January 13th, 2016

Redlining—a discriminatory practice by which services are either restricted or denied to residents of certain areas based on its racial or ethnic make-up—began with the National Housing Act of 1934 and is still practiced today.

"The practice was known as redlining because red ink marked out the minority areas. As Kansas City-based historian Bill Worley explained to me, these policies continued right into the 1960s, and excluded African Americans from one of the greatest motors of wealth in the 20th Century - home ownership."

Redlining in 2016 — BBC News

Read more: http://www.bbc.com/news/world-us-canada-35255835

“ En Brasil, hay una mezcla de razas muy fuerte. Tenemos los europeos, los africanos, y los indígenas. Entonces, en general no hay problemas de racismo. A veces pasan porque hay un desnivel social muy fuerte—los blancos piensan que son mejores. Pero esto no pasa tan seguido. Algo que nunca ha pasado en Brasil; por ejemplo, es lo que paso en Los Estados Unidos en los sesentas. Nunca hemos tenido el apartheid, como en Sudáfrica. Sabemos del racismo por lo que leemos en libros, y lo que vemos en la tele, por ejemplo, sabemos que en Los Estados Unidos hay algo pasando con las poblaciones negras.

Brasil fue el último país de Sudamérica que fue parte de la liberación de los esclavos. Esto fue en 1888. Fue el país que más recibió esclavos en toda América del Sur. Y por eso la economía estaba toda montada en este sistema de esclavitud. Fue una lucha muy grande.

La persona principal quien fue parte de la liberación de los esclavos era un intelectual: se llamaba Joaquim Nabuco. Era un diplomático, quien había venido a Londres, y fue inspirado con la lucha que estaba pasando en Inglaterra. Y después fue como diplomático a Washington... y dijo, 'bueno, esto es algo que necesita pasar en Brasil.' 'Necesitamos hacer algo, no una revolución, porque eso involucra sangre y muerte, pero tenemos que hacer un cambio en la mente de los Brasileños' dijo Nabuco. Trabajó con el congreso, poco a poco, año por año. Con el modelo de Inglaterra, especialmente de William Wilberforce, ha implementado la liberación de los esclavos en Brasil. **”**

Translation:
“ In Brazil, there is a strong mixture of races. We have Europeans, Africans, and Indians. So, in general, there are no problems of racism. Sometimes they happen because there is a very strong social gap—Whites think they are the best. But this doesn't happen very often. Something that has not happened in Brazil, for example, is what happened in the United States in the 60s. We have never had the apartheid, like South Africa. We know of racism because we read books and watch TV; for example, we know that in the United States there's something going on with the Black population.

Brazil was the last country in South America to liberate slaves. This was in 1888. Brazil was the country that received the most slaves in all of South America. And so the whole economy was mounted on the slavery system. It was a very big fight. The main person who led the abolition of slavery was an intellectual: Joaquim Nabuco, a diplomat, who had come to London and was inspired with the fight that was going on there in England. And then he came as a diplomat to Washington... and said, 'Good, this is something we need in Brazil.' We need to do something—not a revolution because that involves death and blood, but we need to change the minds of the Brazilian people. He worked with Congress, little by little, year after year. With the model set by England, especially of William Wilberforce, he implemented liberation of slaves in Brazil. **”**

CHOOS

Special thanks to Valeria Torres-Olivares for interview editing

Brazil was the last country in South America to liberate slaves.

From 1530 to 1888, four million enslaved African were forcibly brought to Brazil—40% of the total population brought to the Americas, compared to 10% for the United States. The growth of slavery was stimulated by the need for cheap labor to mine or produce coffee, gold, sugar, and diamonds. The abolitionist movement, which did not gain prominence until the 1860s, succeeded on May 13 with the passage of a "Golden Law" which stated that "from the date of this law slavery is declared extinct in Brazil."[1]

1 http://liberalarts.utexas.edu/hemispheres/_files/pdf/slavery/Slavery_in_Brazil.pdf

❝ [The amount of people who support a Muslim ban] is shocking, but there is a lot of fear these days and people are motivated by fear. People like Donald Trump play on this fear of the people [and] create a virtual enemy. And then they try to to make people vote against that enemy, which is not the actual enemy that people are facing."

"[The potential ban of Muslim immigration] is something that the American people should work in order to not allow. There is a lot of hypocrisy in such a thing, because American-Muslims are part of the American community and [potentially] banning people based on their religious backgrounds is making people feel like they're not Americans in an unequal way."

"There is also a difference between immigrants and refugees. So immigrants, some of them come and they have an education and work and help. They come in a normal, legal way. There [are] also the refugees who are fleeing the war. So these are different cases.**❞**

[The amount of people who support the Muslim ban] is shocking, but there is a lot of fear these days and people are motivated by fear.

Islamophobia, cultural racism against Islam or Muslims, has heightened after recent terror attacks and the Afghanistan and Iraq Wars. In a recent poll, 48% of all Muslim Americans felt they had experienced racial discrimination—more than any other religious group.[1]

After a rampage at an Orlando nightclub, where 49 people were shot by a man who pledged allegiance to the Islamic State, the 2016 Republican presidential nominee Donald Trump stated that he planned to "suspend immigration from areas of the world where there is a proven history of terrorism against the United States, Europe or our allies, until we fully understand how to end these threats."[2]

CHOOS

Trump argued that Franklin D. Roosevelt used similar strictures after Pearl Harbor, when a ban was placed on some 120,000 Japanese and Japanese Americans in 1942, along with forced internment.[3] During times of "fear," such as periods of war and economic instability, there has been similar systemic discrimination in the United States. Examples include the 1882 Chinese Exclusion Act, 1890 Jim Crow laws, Department of Interior's declaration in 1883 that many Native American rituals were "offenses" punishable by 30 years in jail, and anti–Semitic beliefs (such as the radio addresses in 1938 by Father Charles Coughlin, a Catholic priest who defended Nazi violence and the Klu Klux Klan).[4]

There is also a difference between immigrants and refugees.

An immigrant's legal status depends on the jurisdiction of his or her adopted country, however, refugees depend on that of the United Nations. Refugees also typically move to camps and later to a third country, unable to return home, while immigrants usually choose where to travel.

In February 2016 the United Nations identified approximately 13.5 million Syrians in need of humanitarian assistance.[5] 34% of the refugees were children and 20% were women. Racist backlash against the refugees, largely founded in fear that Islamic extremists are among them, has prevented millions from finding homes. Politicians, especially in Europe, are attempting to create seals against an "invasion" by these Syrian refugees—a complete ban on entrance. Furthermore, after the November 2015 Paris attacks, at least 27 state governors in the United States have questioned the vetting process or declared their refusal to accept Syrian refugees.[6]

1 http://www.gallup.com/poll/157082/islamophobia-understanding-anti-muslim-sentiment-west.aspx; 2http://www.nbcnews.com/politics/2016-election/his-words-donald-trump-muslim-ban-deportations-n599901; 3 https://www.ourdocuments.gov/doc.php?doc=47; 4 http://content.time.com/time/photogallery/0,29307,2011978_2179331,00.html; 5 http://syrianrefugees.eu/; 6 http://edition.cnn.com/2015/11/16/world/paris-attacks-syrian-refugees-backlash/

CURRENT EVENT

originally a CHOOSE Facebook post
graphic credit: Ayesha Qureshi

January 18th, 2016

I say to you today, my friends, that in spite of the difficulties and frustrations of the moment,

have a DREAM one day this NATION live out the true meaning of that will rise up and its creed: "We hold these truths to be self-evident: that all men are created equal." I have a dream that one day on the red hills of Georgia the sons of former slaves and the sons of former slaveowners will be able to sit down together at a table of brotherhood.... children will be able to sing with meaning, "My country, of thee, sweet land of LIBER-Y, of thee I sing. Land where my fathers died...let FREEDOM ring." And if America is to be a his must become true.

ring from the prod of Martin Luther King, Jr. Day ng from the

Three decades have passed since Dr. Martin Luther King Jr.'s birthday became a national holiday, a day that represents the formidable leaders of the Civil Rights Movement. In the crusade for racial justice, these individuals were the people's voice of anguish.

Today, and everyday, aspire to be like them— speak out against racial slurs in the workplace, stereotypes at school, and violence on the streets. Never forget the power of unified speech and outcry.

"How do you teach your students about diversity?"

"I think the number one way to address diversity in the curriculum—and it's going to sound silly—is to have a diverse curriculum. So if everything we're reading is by a dead White dude, that's not good. So texts that are still of high literary matter [and] by a diverse range of authors are going to give us a diversity of perspective. As good as a White author can be at depicting a non-White experience, they're never going to be as good at depicting that experience as someone who's had that experience... The next way I think is, within texts that are written by dead, White, heterosexual, cis-gendered, able-bodied males, finding the elements about diversity, or that maybe even are problematic about diversity, and addressing them rather than not talking about them."

"Would you say you create an atmosphere that makes students comfortable talking about these themes?"

"That's my intent—having and building a community where everyone feels as though they can contribute. And [making] it an academic environment, which means it isn't just who can shout the loudest. I want my students to feel like they will not be attacked for their opinions, but they'll also need to support them. It isn't okay for somebody to say, 'This is dumb, I just don't agree with this and I'm not willing to talk about it.'"

"What would you do in that situation?"

"I would remind the person that we're here to talk about the ideas in the text and whether or not I agree... isn't part of it. But also [I] would talk to them about standards of behavior, and probably not at the time because that really runs the risk of putting the person on the spot. Most people in the class would be put off by that. Even if I think what the person is saying is morally problematic, I wouldn't want it to be a situation where we all are metaphorically inching towards them and leaning in and bearing our teeth. But in a two-person discussion it's much easier to talk about that. Or asking them to offer support, so explicitly reminding them."

"How important would you say it is to teach about diversity in classrooms?"

"I would say it is certainly [one of the] top five most important things—so very, very, very important... part of what I want to do as a teacher isn't just teach people how to dissect a book for meaning, although that's a part of it. And it isn't just how to write clearly and effectively about literature, although that's a big part of it. I think the how to read is important and the why to read is important. I think seeing diversity and having diversity in what we read reminds people that not everything is a book by the same kind of author. Not everything is the male hero... not everything is The Great Gatsby or Huck Finn. It helps everyone know that there isn't one universal human experience. There are certain things every human experiences. Every human experiences loss. Every human experiences love. Every human experiences joy and fear and all of those emotions, but there isn't an American experience. There isn't this-category-of-person experience. Literature forces us to engage with the complexities of life, and that's what makes people. There's a study about how the more literature you read the more empathetic you are. It does not necessarily [have to] be literature, it can be talking to people... the idea of moving towards understanding

the spectrum of life rather than a good-evil, male-female, or right-wrong, all that sort of stuff. The more we can see the gray the more understanding we'll be, the more engaged or even interesting we'll be."

"Are there dangers of not seeing this gray?"

"They're significant. If I don't see the gray, everything that I believe is right, it's the only right. That moves us away from diversity. What's right for the communities that I'm in is going to be different from the communities you're in or any member of the state, the country, or the world is in. Which isn't to say that there aren't some things that are just wrong. But not seeing those complexities leads to a lot more conflict. On a personal level, I think not understanding the complexities of the world is painful, because then if your best friend does something bad, if it's Black and White, than now my best friend is bad. Everyone at some point is going to disappoint you. Nobody is going to get everything right all the time, and the danger of that binary thinking is you are all good or not. Or thinking you have to be all good to be good. You can screw up colossally on a thing or two and still be an overall good person. Understanding that complexity helps us to be more compassionate to people when they do screw up, but also help them to be better and foster [ourselves] to be better as well."

—Dr. Douglas Levandowski, English teacher

"I was born in Sri Lanka."

"Wait, you were born there? I thought your parents immigrated here."

"Nope! When my family immigrated here we first lived in a really diverse town, but then moved to a town with a lot of White and Hispanic people. There were sometimes divides because people were more comfortable with people with similar background. Now, I'm an engineer, and there are just so many perspectives. You wouldn't really think that it matters—we're all trying to do the same thing—but there are so many ways to approach a problem. So it does matter to hear differences, like where you grew up. You also need an interdisciplinary background. You can't just be an engineer without knowing the community you're impacting. You have to learn about all these societies. You have to know social justice."

You wouldn't really think that it matters—we're all trying to do the same thing—but there are so many ways to approach a problem.
Research shows that diversity leads to innovation. A study conducted by Margaret Neale of Stanford University in 2006 showed that racially diverse groups were able to problem-solve more quickly and effectively than any other homogenous group.[1] Furthermore, an American Sociological Association study found that for every 1% rise in the rate of ethnic diversity, there is a 9% rise in sales revenue.[2]

1 http://www.scientificamerican.com/article/how-diversity-makes-us-smarter/; 2 http://www.ft.com/cms/s/0/4f4b3c8e-d521-11e3-9187-00144feabdc0.html#axzz4lL1l-Gklq

" What do you think about the representation of Native-American contributions, histories, and abuses [in U.S. History curriculum]?"

"For the most part of the last decade or so, historians have gone back and tried to incorporate it much more fully and acknowledge the wrongs done to them, but also have acknowledged their contributions. I think that the U.S. 1 curriculum lends itself a little bit more heavily to their influence with the colonization of the new world. We go over quite a bit about the development of their tribes and colonies, but we also stress that just because their lifestyle was different than the Europeans' lifestyle, it doesn't mean that it was a bad thing or that it was inferior. I think that has been the perception of the eurocentric mindset: because they were not living the same lifestyles as the Europeans, they were somehow inferior

and that was how they were viewed for a long time. So what we have been doing as U.S. History teachers is trying to correct that and to show that they had many advantages that the Europeans did not have, like the way they planned out their cities and the agriculture and the development. In the present day United States, the Native Americans are really responsible for the success of Jamestown with their knowledge of how to cultivate tobacco. We still try to bring it in and kind of show how history doesn't just have to be the victor or the White male.

We also have Black History Month where we talk about a lot of Black 'firsts,' if you will—I think we could definitely do that [for Native Americans]. You can highlight more of the first Native Americans to deal successfully with the U.S. government or breaking through different barriers in terms of discrimination and prejudice. We can definitely do a better job; there's always room for progress. We always want to highlight that diversity and the accomplishments they had in spite of all the obstacles they faced. But There's definitely room to bring more into the curriculum. **"**

That has been the perception of the Eurocentric mindset... they were somehow inferior.
Throughout American history, the dominant culture of the colonizers has largely opposed native customs. Cultural assimilation was fueled by racism, as European settlers forced Native Americans to conform to the cultural norms of Whites. Those who opposed these standards were viewed as "savages," and colonizers ultimately viewed our nation's "first inhabitants" as a threat to European success in the new land. Ethnic cleansing, which included violent invasions, brutal genocide, and seizure of Indian American property, was how many Europeans sought to resolve the "Indian problem."[1]

We have Black History Month where we talk about a lot of Black 'firsts,' if you will.
According to the U.S. History Content Standards for Grades 5 -12, "the only time content teaching requirements about African Americans shows up is when discussing slavery, the Civil War and the Civil Rights Movement, treating the Black experience as a separate entity—only worth noting in climatic moments of social change."[2] While these moments are important, a complete and true Black history must be taught.

1 http://scholarworks.umass.edu/cgi/viewcontent.cgi?article=1027&context=chc_theses
2 http://www.theguardian.com/commentisfree/2015/jul/10/black-history-slavery-civil-rights-education

IDENTITY & FAMILIAL

But when I was there it was always gang wars and people disrespecting me.
The National Gang Center found that approximately 49% of gang members are Hispanic, 35% are Black, 4.6% are Asian or Pacific Islander, and 1.4% are American Indian or Alaskan Native, with increasing numbers of White and multiracial members in recent years. Factors that contribute to increased gang membership include "poverty, immigration, discrimination, and social isolation, while consequences involve substance abuse, limited educational and job opportunities, family stress, and neighborhood crime."[1]

I don't get much of that anymore, but I know it's still going on because every time you turn on the TV...
Refer to page 123 to read about bias in the media. In addition, it is important to note that media coverage on racial issues often reflects the views and biases of target audiences. For example, a 2011 study stated that 46% of Americans think discrimination against White people is just as prevalent as discrimination against people of color.[2] However, among people who said they trust Fox News Channel, which has challenged the notion of white privilege in the past, that number rose to 70%.[3]

1 https://www.ncjrs.gov/pdffiles1/nij/243474.pdf; 2 http://www.npr.org/sections/codeswitch/2014/12/06/368713550/four-lessons-from-the-medias-conflicted-coverage-of-race; 3 http://www.brookings.edu/research/reports/2011/09/06-american-attitudes

❝ I've had a lot of experiences. I'm from Philly, so when I came here it was nice. But when I was there it was always gang wars and people disrespecting me... My father was 100 years up from slavery. He died at 59, and I used to see him always hidden in the corner somewhere crying. He was a good man and he was well-loved by his family, but other races were hard on him just because of slavery. I got tired of seeing him like that so I asked him what was wrong and he said, 'people disrespect me all the time.' I don't get much of that anymore but I know it's still going on because every time you turn on the TV, [there's a] Black person getting killed by police. I think it's very disrespectful that they do that, but that's the way they are. ❞

Sumaiyya Stephens, Princeton High School Class of 2016, discusses racial discrimination within the predominantly White public school system she grew up in and how her parents shaped her understanding of identity.

" When I was younger, my parents kinda noticed I didn't like who I was. I would always want to do the things that the White girls would do. Like my hair is very nappy; I have a different texture. I wanted to be on the street with that silky, flowy hair, so I would have my mom perm my hair a lot. And looking back on it, I regret it a lot because it would have been better for me to stay natural, to embrace who I was. My mother always told me that she was happy with who I am, so I'm starting to realize things and appreciate myself. I guess it would upset her that I didn't appreciate my true beauty; I didn't like having dark skin initially. I've been taught that White is right. It's not fair to live in a society like this where they teach you that having lighter skin is ideal. You shouldn't have to change yourself so that you're more appealing to a man or to everyone else, so you can look like everyone else.

I like my skin now; it's different. You would always see people getting tanner so their skin would be darker and they could achieve this look. But they can't.

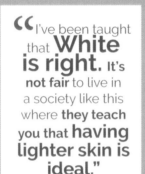

" I've been taught that **White is right.** It's **not fair** to live in a society like this where **they teach you that having lighter skin is ideal.**"

You see people getting plastic surgery because they want the features that us Black women have—bigger butt, bigger lips, all that other stuff that was naturally given. But they're also taking our hairstyles and stuff like that, making it their own and getting credit for it. When people see us with braids and stuff, we're ghetto, we're this and we're that. But it's a statement when people of other races do it.

It's so sad; I'm looking at myself now and I really hate that I used to be that way. I just didn't love myself and I feel bad I did that to my parents also. They always try to make me love myself more, but I just couldn't because of the environment I've been raised in. I'm not saying Princeton's a bad place, but it's not the best either. I'm not the type to sugarcoat with the things that go on in this school: they go so unnoticed and it's horrible.

***

One of my African-American friends has been suspended multiple times over the past

couple of years. She was a freshman or sophomore, and there was a [Caucasian] upperclassman she was having some ongoing issues with. There was one instance when my friend had stared at the girl, and got suspended by that because the girl went to the administration and said she felt intimidated. There was also another instance where she called a girl the b-word and got suspended for that. Yes, it's an offensive term, but she never should've gotten suspended for something so petty.

There was another time when there was a kid who was a freshman, and another kid pulled a knife out on him. I don't know what happened to the kid with the knife, but the African-American kid got suspended for defending himself against the knife. But that's self-defense, and that shouldn't have happened. What would you do if someone pulled out a knife on you? You're not gonna stand there and let it happen.

I remember there was a kid I had my first kiss with. I'm pretty sure he's Hispanic, but he doesn't say that he is, which is sad to me. I'm sure he is [ashamed]; people tell me he says he's White. He basically told me that I couldn't tell people that we kissed, because I was Black and he didn't want people to know.

He was basically sexualizing me the whole entire time, saying that Black women have more to them body-wise, saying what I had that White girls don't have. I didn't feel like that at the time though. I was excited that a non-Black boy at our school was actually acknowledging my presence. But after a while, I thought about it, and I was like 'wait—what? That wasn't right.'

I know for a fact that if I were to sit at a table full of White girls, they would look at me like I was crazy. I would not feel welcome at all. It would be uncomfortable for a White girl to sit with us too. Nobody's told me that, but you can always look at someone and tell when they don't feel right.

The general thing is the way people speak to me. Everyone's always like, "yo yo waz up Sumiayya.' They always have to speak to me in slang, and every time they speak to me you can hear the struggle in their voice as they try to mimic African-American people. I don't like that at all. When they speak like that, I just look at them back and don't say anything, because to me that's disrespectful and I don't speak like that. Why can't you come up to me and say, 'Hello Sumai-

yya, how are you doing?' like a normal person. You have to be like the angry, shafty, Black one. I am sassy, but that's not because I'm Black, but they say it's because of that. They don't expect m[...] fire back at them when they say things to me they know they shouldn't be saying. So every time I do stand [...] for myself, I'm always sassy. But if a White girl stands up for herself, she's not sassy, she's just like a girl gone wild. I don't appreciate the labels they try to give us.

I played basketball for four years, and every time we would play Trenton High at their court, other girls would always ask, 'are they gonna hit me? are they gonna shoot me? are they gonna jump me?' Why you gotta assume that, just because they're Black? I know it's a bad neighborhood, [...] that doesn't mean they're just gonna shoot you if you're playing the game. It's just sad, it's just ignorant to me.

They hide behind me because th[...] I'm strong and can protect them from other Bl[...]k people because I'm Black. But I'm like, 'No [...]t's just not how it works.'

This is everyday for me. People who are White at the school expect me, as a Black female, to be ghetto and loud and obnoxious and always trying to fight. And there have been a few fights that have broken out amongst the African-American kids at school, but I hate how they all put us in the one category of oh, she's Black, shes' gonna be like that.'

There's a couple of Black kids in our school who are White-washed, and that's all to fit in. They probably don't think nothing of it, don't think of the racial side of it. I thought the same way growing up. That's the first thing they do when you enter the school system: they strip you of your identity.

The other problem is, the administration doesn't say that.

We've been trying to get an assembly going for Black History Month; we had that all planned out and went to [the district superintendent] about it. He approved it. Then we went to [our principal], but basically they bullshitted us; they tried to give us the excuse that it wouldn't work because we wouldn't be able to fit all the kids in the auditorium. We had zero help. The principal tried to make it seem like he was really excited about it, like he was gonna help us, but he did nothing. We kept trying to give [the administration] options, but they just kept saying 'I don't know, I don't know.' I was really upset about that

because it was so just so crazy how quick and easy it was for them to conjure up a whole assembly for the Holocaust after the [Jews vs. Nazis] beer pong event. And I honestly don't think they had that assembly to educate us; I think it was really just for [the school's] bad name. It's all they're concerned about, making us look good. It's so sad.

The administration is definitely not open to change. [An administrator] wanted a school choir to sing, and I wanted an African-American choir. I wanted to have African-American people showcasing their talents. I wanted to have outside guests so people could see what we were doing, but I don't think she wanted people to know. I don't want to say this, but I think it's the truth. I just don't think they want to shine, you know?

As soon as we start proposing ideas about racial justice, they try to create a little group. They would never do it without [student activists]. The principal took down our emails and then we never got an email. I don't think [the principal] was truly concerned about it. He was all like, 'oh, I

was waiting for someone to propose this idea.' Well, if you were waiting for it, why wouldn't you propose it yourself? And even after I proposed, he didn't do anything.

I don't wanna blame it solely on administration because it also comes from what's going on at home, what parents teach about what's right and what's wrong. Honestly, most of this racial stuff comes from students, not so much the administration. But most of the time I don't even bother to go to administration, because I know nothing is going to be done about it. What am I gonna waste my breath for, you know?

I can honestly say that I don't know a lot about my people because we don't learn anything about them. The only thing we were taught was the fact that we were slaves. Then we learn about Martin Luther King Jr. and Harriet Tubman and Rosa Parks, and that's it. You can ask anyone in the school and they wouldn't know who Malcolm X is.

Along with the assemblies and stuff, I don't think we should only do something during Black History Month. Assemblies and curriculum are the most important. There are so many issues going on around right now about

> "That's the first thing they do when you enter the school system: they strip you of your identity."

> "I can honestly say that I don't know a lot about my people because we don't learn anything about them. The only thing we were taught was the fact that we were slaves."

51

racial justice, that it would be good to speak about it in history classes.

I take a human behavior class, and the teacher asked us in the beginning of the year what we wanted to learn about. I told her psychology and statistics of African-American women and men, but we didn't do that. We kinda went over what everyone else proposed. Like I'm not saying she was trying to avoid it, but it kinda seemed like she was. When I gave the idea, she was like 'did she just say that?' and was kinda surprised.

And I noticed every time we talk about African-American people, she always looks at me, and 'I'm like why y'all lookin' at me? Why you makin' it awkward? You shouldn't be awkward. When we talk about Caucasian people I don't look around at y'all.' We just need to talk about racism, because the thing is people don't think racism exists, and that's not true.

I have a lot of issues with race with teachers. One teacher, I don't want to call her racist, but she seems that way. She's always singling me out and I do not like that, so the other day I called her out on it. She had decided to call me out for talking when I wasn't the person talking. Another teacher, he was the substitute, and there was a whole bunch of kids running in and out of the classroom, being obnoxious and really, really rowdy. And I walked out of the room to get breakfast like I normally do—I didn't think it'd be a problem. I come back five mins later with my stuff, being quiet, not being rowdy. The teacher just starts raising his voice and going off at me like, 'hey! down! sit!' I was like, 'excuse me sir, you can lower your tone with me; that's not necessary," and then he continues to yell. I just sat down; I was respectful and didn't argue back. But then there were these other kids blasting music, and he was just like 'can you please turn that down?' And they're yelling and screaming and everything, and he's so calm with them.

I don't look at it like a rude gesture. [A friend] and I took chemistry one year and had a really good teacher who made sure I got my grade up and wouldn't let me mess up. But one day, we wanted to get a tutor for finals, so we talked to him after class. He wanted to help us find a tutor, so he got us an African-American man. I don't know what he was trying to say, but he said it would feel weird if it were someone else of a different color, and

he wanted us to feel more comfortable. But I don't think I'd feel any different if it were a White or Hispanic tutor or something.

In elementary school, the teachers would always give me free money to go to the book fair. It never really occurred to me that they were giving the money to the minorities, and they weren't giving it to the Caucasian people. When I was younger, I was just taking it, you know, thinking it's nice of them to do. I took it not knowing what it was about, but they were probably assuming that my finances weren't right at home, which wasn't the case. I took the money, but I didn't know. All the time, they would do that. I would be so confused. And even now, at the middle school a friend of mine goes to, a Caucasian kid said to her that [Donald] Trump is gonna win [the presidency] and that she's gonna have to go back to Mexico. Obviously nobody paid attention to it, but that wasn't cool.

There's this kid in my class who is constantly making racial slurs, but he tries to be low-key about it and probably thinks I don't pick up on it. He just makes comments like, 'of course you're gonna do that, because you're Black.' And once I told a teacher I was going to college in Philly. I said the school was in a

> " ... they were probably assuming that my finances weren't right at home, **which wasn't the case."**

> "**People use the n-word as a joke.** They think nothing is wrong with it."

hood and she was like, 'oh, that'd be the perfect environment for you.' And I didn't know what to say.

With the principal, we also talked about use of the n-word. People use the n-word as a joke. They think nothing is wrong with it. That just goes to show what we're being taught. I think the issue with race definitely needs to be brought to people's attention at a young age.

At a Stand Against Racism event in Hinds Plaza, I read:

School was an interesting experience for me. In elementary school I was assigned a book report. As a requirement, we had to take a headshot and place it onto a character's body. The book I chose to read was the Wizard of Oz. The main character was Dorothy, who happens to be a White girl with brown hair. However, I drew a White girl with blonde pigtails. I traded her White face with my brown face. In that moment, I did not realize who I was. At that point in my life, I wanted to be White. I had nappy hair; I wanted straight hair like hers. My hair is black. I wanted blonde hair like hers. I had full lips; I wanted thin lips. I wanted to be someone other than myself. As I reflect on it now, I realize that I did not want to be Black. That has not been the only time an assignment has made it easy for me to reject or even disguise who I am. I have been taught that White is right. This has affected me in multiple ways, including in relationships. What became easy in elementary school became hard in high school. It's easier to make friends when you assimilate; however, I am no longer willing to do it blindly. Stand Against Racism is accountability to a racist system. It means having real conversations in intimate settings, publicly and privately. I am beginning to understand this now. I continue to build relationships across racial boundaries—we're all better for it.

***

There's always this song that my father would play for me; it's called Black Pearl and I'm actually quoting it in my graduation speech. He never really wanted to call me a diamond because I guess that's basic, everyone uses that to refer to themselves. A black pearl represents my dark skin. And pearls are pretty unique, they're hard to find, they're rare. So I guess that kinda helped me see that in myself. Every time my father sees me—he no longer lives with my mother and me—he would always tell me how magnificent I am. And every time I would say thank you, he would say, 'no, thank you.' And that kinda builds up my confidence a lot more. My mom is more blunt and she'd be like, 'you can't be like them, you have to be you.' She was more honest, while my dad would sing songs to me to help me realize who I am. When I was younger though, my mom would always dress me and put myself together to make me feel better about myself, and that did help too.

My junior year, that's when I started feeling confident about myself. I had never really felt beautiful before. People would always comment about me having darker skin, people are always saying 'oh, I love dark skin, it's so beautiful." You see it all over the media. But I don't feel like it's genuine, it's just like a trend. People don't genuinely like us for our dark skin. They praise us on social media, then bash us in real life. Nobody wants us, basically, and that's just sad.**

> "**They praise us on social media, then bash us in real life. Nobody wants us, basically, and that's just sad.**"

... we couldn't do anything because he would threaten to call the cops and tell them that we were undocumented, or "illegal."

As of 2014, there were 11.3 million unauthorized immigrants in the United States, making up 3.4% of the nation's entire population. Although their numbers have recently been declining, Mexicans have been the largest group of unauthorized immigrants (49%).[1] Despite common belief that unauthorized immigrants are dangerous to our nation's well being, they actually have a positive impact. For example, from 1990 to 2007, undocumented workers increased legal workers' pay in complementary jobs by up to 10 percent.

1 http://www.pewresearch.org/fact-tank/2015/11/19/5-facts-about-illegal-immigration-in-the-u-s/; 2 http://www.nytimes.com/2013/02/17/magazine/do-illegal-immigrants-actually-hurt-the-us-economy.html?_r-0

Special thanks to Valeria Torres-Olivares for interview editing

"Crucé la frontera. Era caliente, triste, y espantoso en el desierto. Lo peor de todo es que había dejado a mi familia. No he visto a mi esposa, o mi hija desde que me fui. Mi hija acaba de cumplir un año de edad, y me mata. Mi sueño americano es un poco al revés: sueño de reunir con mi esposa y mi hija, pero el costo es demasiado alto.

Aquí, mi vida tiene muchos problemas. No tengo dinero para pagar la medicina, educación, etc.—y aquí todo esta muy caro. Ni siquiera sé mucho inglés, pero quiero aprender. Quiero aprender, pero no hay posibilidad para lograrlo. Tengo que trabajar largas horas, y entonces nada esta abierto cuando termino de trabajar, y aparte, nada es accessible.

El viaje para cruzar la frontera fue indescriptible. Había sangre. Muchas personas murieron. Recuerdo, cómo podra olvidarlo, que una mujer embarazada murió. Perdimos cuenta de ella, y pensamos que un animal la habia matado. Al día siguiente, otro grupo que intentaba a cruzar la frontera se reunió con nosotros y confirmó que animals la habian matado. El bebé no sobrevivió.

Cuando llegué por primera vez a los Estados Unidos, me puse a buscar trabajo el primer día. He trabajado en muy malas condiciones. Tuve un jefe Italiano que no nos pagaba. Él nos pagaría al final de la semana, así que trabajaríamos todos los días sin que nos pague. Cuando él nos pagaba, él sólo nos daria $15 por semana. Muchas personas gritaron en señal de protesta, pero no podriamos hacer nada porque nos pondría en peligro, el llamaria a la policía y les decia que éramos indocumentados, o 'ilegales.' Trabaje unos meses para ese tipo, y me fui quando ya habia acumulado $1,400."

Translation:
"I crossed the border. It was hot, miserable, and terrifying in the desert. Worst of all, I left my family behind. I haven't seen my daughter or my wife ever since. My daughter just turned one year old, and it kills me. My American dream is a little backwards: I dream of reuniting with my wife and child, but the cost is too high. Here, I have many problems in my life. I don't have money to pay for medicine, education, etc.—and everything here costs so much money. I don't even know a lot of English, but I want to learn. I want to learn, but there's no way of that happening. I have to work long hours, then nothing is open when I'm done, and nothing is accessible.

The journey to cross the border was indescribable. There was blood. Many people died. I remember, how could I forget, that one pregnant woman died. We lost track of her and thought an animal must have killed her. The next day, another group that was trying to cross the border met up with us and confirmed that animals ate her. The baby didn't survive.

When I first came to the United States, I looked for work the first day. I worked in very poor conditions. I had this one Italian boss who wouldn't pay us our money. He would pay us at the end of the week, so we would work everyday with out being paid. When he paid us, he would only pay us $15 per week. Many people screamed in protest, but we couldn't do anything, because he would threaten to call the cops and tell them that we were undocumented, or "illegal." I worked for a few months for that guy, and I had saved up $1,400."

❝ 70 years ago in New York City, if you were Jewish you experienced discrimination all the time. We would worry when we walked home from school because there were people who wanted to beat us up. That was a long time ago, and while I have no doubt that anti-Semitism still exists, it's no longer acceptable for it to exist out in the open where everyone can see it. A taxi on 110th street and Park Avenue wouldn't pick up Barack Obama if it was dark out. **❞**

70 years ago in New York City, if you were Jewish you experienced discrimination all the time.
Anti-Semitism is defined as "hostility toward or discrimination against Jews as a religious, ethnic, or racial group." While anti-Semitism has plagued the United States since colonial times, hostility toward Jewish people rose dramatically in the 20th century following major immigration during the decades before and after the turn of the century.[1] During this dark period of American history, people of Jewish ancestry were subjected to brutal violence and widespread prejudice, simply due to their religious identity.

That was a long time ago, and while I have no doubt that anti-Semitism still exists, it's no longer acceptable for it to exist out in the open where everyone can see it.
Although it has decreased greatly in the past 70 years, anti-Semitic hate crime has begun to resurge. According to the New York Post, anti-Semitic hate crimes in 2015 are up 27% from 2014.[2]

A taxi on 110th street and Park Avenue would not pick up Barack Obama if it was dark out.
Celebrity television personality, weather forecaster, actor, and author Al Roker was refused service by a New York City taxicab driver due to the color of his skin. His story was rapidly picked up by social media, and it raised the issue of how Black males are racially profiled as dangerous, no matter what their achievements are.

In a tweet following the incident, Roker notes that incidents similar to the one he experienced "[happen] to folks of color every day," and adds that "while most cabbies do their job, there are those ignorant, racist ones who hurt the others."[3]

1 http://www.merriam-webster.com/dictionary/anti-Semitism
2 http://nypost.com/2015/06/28/hate-crimes-against-jews-and-muslims-surge/
3 http://www.nydailynews.com/entertainment/tv/al-roker-yellow-cab-snubbed-black-article-1.2442923

"As long as one people sit on another and are deaf to their cry...

CHOOS

Afghan Refugees in Iran

by Shadi Tahvildar-Zadeh

There are 2.4 million Afghans living in Iran now, and around two-thirds of them are illegal immigrants. Every year, thousands more enter Iran illegally, as living conditions in Afghanistan keep deteriorating. The Iranian government routinely takes measures to limit their movement and restrict their residence to certain areas. Thousands of them have been summarily deported from Iran without a hearing of their right to remain. According to the U.S.-based advocacy group Human Rights Watch (HRW), Afghan refugees in Iran are often discriminated against, subjected to "physical abuse, detention in unsanitary and inhumane conditions, forced labor, and separation of families." Many undocumented Afghan children cannot go to school, and migrant workers recognized as refugees are limited to dangerous and poorly paid manual labor jobs.

As an Iranian, I am disheartened by the plight of Afghan refugees in Iran. Many of these people have nowhere else to go, and work very hard to earn an honest living, often supporting a large family on a single income. The Iranian people are proud of their history and their ancient civilization. As a child growing up in Iran I kept hearing about the Persian king Cyrus the Great, who is supposed to be the first person in history to have paid attention to human rights, and passed laws protecting those rights. At the same time I could see evidence of racism all around me, in the way various ethnic groups were put down, made fun of, and slighted in various ways, but most particularly how people of Afghan origin were subjected to verbal and sometimes physical abuse, and were generally treated as second-class citizens. I remember the atmosphere of suspicion and fear surrounding them, that they are up to no good, and are always plotting to kill you or rob your home. This despite the fact they have the same skin color, the same religion, and speak the same language as the majority of Iranians. That's why I believe racism knows no color, or religion, or nationality.

Racism is a disease of the human mind. It takes minute, insignificant differences between people, and magnifies them until it becomes possible to blame the targeted group for all the ills of the society. I am hopeful though, because I don't think it is an incurable disease. You can beat it back and become healthy again, if you want to. I do believe that acknowledging it and talking about it openly helps to diminish its power.

> "At the same time I could see evidence of racism all around me, in the way various ethnic groups were put down, made fun of, and slighted in various ways..."

> *...so long will understanding and peace elude all of us."*
> —Chinua Achebe

> **"** Race relations is very Black and White. But there are stories of all different races that we can't ignore. I'm Hispanic, and the fact that it's just become Black and White makes me annoyed. When people talk about racism, that's what it has become. It gives me mixed feelings about all these different situations that are going on, like [in] St. Louis, because it's become more about violence and less about racial relations. **"**

POLITICAL & LEGAL

Race relations is very Black and White.

The United States has a long history of racial conflict between Black and White Americans. More recently, extensive media coverage has been given to the issue of police brutality against Black Americans. The incident that the woman in the above interview refers to is the shooting of 18-year-old Mansur Ball-Bey, who was shot in the back by police in St. Louis.[1] The event occurred less than two weeks after the anniversary of the killing of unarmed Black teenager Michael Brown by a White police officer in Ferguson, Missouri.[1] Both incidents received widespread media coverage. In contrast, the killing of an unarmed Mexican man named Antonio Zambrano-Montes by police officers in Pasco, Washington did not receive very much media coverage.[2] It is important to recognize that racism in the United States does not exclusively affect Black Americans, and other racial and ethnic minorities, including Hispanics and Muslims, are also affected.

It's become more about violence.

While police brutality and violence against minorities should be exposed, racially-motivated violence is just one manifestation of racism. Other incidents of hate speech and discrimination should also be covered by the media, so that all perpetrators of injustice can be held accountable.

1 http://www.reuters.com/article/us-usa-police-missouri-idUSKCN0QQ1GD20150821; 2 http://www.cnn.com/2015/06/09/opinions/reyes-police-brutality-latin

CURRENT EVENT

originally a CHOOSE Facebook post
graphic credit: Ayesha Qureshi

January 13th, 2016

"Things like this are the reasons we keep fighting. To think that someone actually took the time to make the DO NOT JUMP into "DO JUMP BLACK PEOPLE" is absolutely disgusting. Nobody should have to deal with this in a school, and until something is done about this behavior at Tech, we will keep going strong."

Read more: http://www.nbcnews.com/news/nbcblk/blackin-brooklyntech-students-call-out-racism-brooklyn-tech-n494206

❝I was raised to have friends outside my race. Therefore, I am more worldly when it comes to knowing about different topics. I was always raised to have Black friends, Hispanic friends, different types of Hispanic friends, different types of everybody. Poor, rich, and all that. Having diverse friends makes you stay well-rounded and knowledgeable, I guess you could say.❞

Having diverse friends makes you stay well-rounded and knowledgeable...
Refer to the discussion point about some benefits of diversity on page 45.

Talk Teacher

❝My classes here are much more diverse than I originally thought they would be. Kids come from different backgrounds, work ethics, and ways of learning. You want to make all of your students comfortable. Everyone learns differently, and we think we have a way to teach our kids, but we don't have just one type of kid.

Kids have lived in different places, are different races, so it's important to reach every kid in the classroom. The best way to do that is adjusting the style of teaching. For example, we have some kids that don't speak a lot of English, and so we may do more hands-on activities as opposed to more verbal teaching.❞
—*Ryan Walsh, math teacher*

"When you look at us, we don't scream that [we're] Muslims. So maybe that helps. I wonder if we wore headscarves, if we would find out how we're actually looked at [as Muslims]..."

"We're normal, regular citizens like everyone else, and we shouldn't be part of a list or anything else that would profile us in any way."

"Having lighter skin has helped me dodge racism, but I'm not shy of telling people who I am."

CHOOS

I wonder if we wore head-scarves, if we would find out how we're actually looked at [as Muslims]...
Refer to page 115.

Having lighter skin has helped me dodge racism, but I'm not shy of telling people who I am. Active contemporary colorism, or skin-color stratification, is a manifestation of systemic racism and the deep historical legacies of colonialism and slavery. The ideal, internalized white aesthetic represents civility and beauty, while darker skin is often equated with savagery and ugliness. While the effects of colorism are often overlooked, its insidious and pervasive nature divides our society into color hierarchies, unfairly privileging the lighter-skinned.[1]

In addition, colorism is often ignored within a racial group, when in reality, human variation mostly falls within rather than between populations. Around 85% of all genetic variation is found within a local population, and 94% within a continental population.[1] And, among approximately 30,000 human genes, not a single one separates individuals of one race from another.[2] In fact, the concept of "race" itself is a social construction based off lived experience rather than genetic difference, and similarities within populations largely exist because of differences in social treatment, ancestry, etc.[3]

1 Margaret Hunter, The Persistent Problem of Colorism: Skin Tone, Status, and Inequality ; 2 http://newsreel.org/guides/race/quiz.htm#answer; 3 Larry Adelman, Race and Gene Studies: What Differences Make a Difference?

Take this day to honor the legacy of the many presidents who have advanced this country on a foundation of equality for all races. From the Emancipation Proclamation to the passing of the Civil Rights Act of 1964, we have taken significant steps against racial injustice.

As we consider the upcoming presidential elections, it is important to look back into history and take note of the consequences of presidents who did otherwise, as well as the racist legacies that they have left behind. Nevertheless, although much work still needs to be done, we are grateful to our leaders who have chosen and to advance rather than set back truth and justice.
#StepForward #PresidentsDay2016

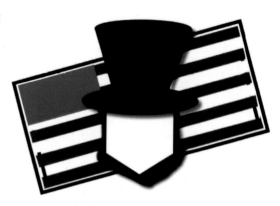

Presidents' Day 2016

INTER-PERSONAL

Frequently I'm told that my dance moves are bad and [that] I'm too "White" to dance to music I like.

The New York hip-hop dancer, Wendy Zamora, wrote a reflection on her experience of being rejected from dancing roles because of her race. She argues that most dancers are chosen because of their physical appearance rather than their talent, noting that dancers who fit an "all-American sexy" or "exotic; i.e., ethnic" description were casted more often, perhaps to appeal to men.[1] Nevertheless, it is important to note that being rejected from traditionally Black styles of dancing as a White person—an individual's experience—does not compare to the structural racism Blacks have endured for centuries.

For example, in the ballet industry, Black dancers and the expression of Black heritage have been historically unwelcome. Raven Wilkinson, one of the industry's first Black professionals, was not allowed "to let the public know that this light-skinned young woman was actually Black." Often, she was even required to whiten her skin with makeup. From ballet's beginnings in France in the late 17th century, Black ballet dancers were held back because of low quality training and fewer career opportunities.

Well-known Black ballet dancers include Misty Copeland, Janet Collins, and Virginia Johnson.[2]

❝ I'm a very outgoing and extroverted person, so I'm not afraid to speak my mind or even dance in front of people. At parties and other social gatherings, I tend to dance. Frequently I'm told that my dance moves are bad and [that] I'm too "White" to dance to music I like. However, I don't think my race plays any part in my inability to dance. I was born with two left feet, just the same as any other race could be... And I'm planning to dance off all future ignorant comments like I always do. ❞

1 http://www.xojane.com/it-happened-to-me/it-happened-me-i-was-too-White-not-white-enough-hip-hop-dance; 2 http://www.nytimes.com/2015/07/15/opinion/black-dancers-White-ballets.html?_r=0

"I was socialized in a high school back in the 80's. At that point I thought it was possible to ignore race and still thrive, however awkward it was to be denied that as an explanatory factor for anything that was racially-charged. Needless to say, as I grew older I realized race is like ethnicity and gender—all of these are identity markers that we use to define ourselves, that others use to define us as well. Unless we are willing to accept this is a marker for who we are and embrace that, we then become a prisoner to other people's perceptions.

There then becomes this conversation I had in my twenties about the difference between a filter and a lens, when [I understood] I could use other people's perceptions of me and allow them to be transformed by their bias, or I could react to it negatively, or I could do nothing. Very early in my career as a teacher, I said 'I'm just going to allow it to pass through me, and when necessary I'll confront it,' but for the most part just let random things pass. I started seeing that that was not good, so then I said, 'okay I'm gonna use this.'

And I was gonna put it into context. It's impossible to think about equity without thinking about difference. So I started adopting activities that would allow me to really explore what I call a range of diversity texts in my science classroom. Identity is definitely a diversity text, and it's varied: we think about who we are in our gender roles, which are social; our racial roles, which are social and cultural; the languages that we use, [which are] social, cultural, economic. We can think about our ability. Are we able-bodied? Are we not able-bodied? Are we identified in the Black community as the 'talented tenth'? Are we not? We could think about our class or our religious practices. We can think about all these various ways that are really used to shine a light or be a lens for everything that we experience. Now, if you're in my science class and you see me, probably your only Black teacher that you've had in a content area, you're like 'woah' right there. If I'm going to act like I'm not a Black person and try to not be who I am on an everyday basis, that's going to not only hurt me, but it will also hurt you.

But anyway, when I said I develop activities, I put things in context for students to see even if they don't recognize it in the moment. Years later, perhaps they will, but there's so many other things going on in the high school classroom. There are gonna be days when what I have to say and what we have to do as a chemistry class are gonna be so inconsequential. So, I'm free to accept that I don't teach chemistry. I teach humans. And in teaching humans I recognize there are going to be days when they say 'I don't want to,' and I'm going to give them that opportunity because again that's a social dynamic that is also cultural. Some people and places don't value traditions and elitists and education in the same way.

So I've been a teacher for over twenty years. I've looked at examining the Won Su, which

is a symbol of peace that has been perverted to become a swastika because of difficult social and historical context, because people historically have not wanted to deal with the impact of their fear. There's xenophobia. Or their racist habits. I looked at how the Won Su became a symbol and how it took its role as that symbol, and I used that as an opportunity to engage conversation with the 114 symbols that make up the periodic table. That there is a defining characteristic and purpose for the use of symbols. We need them; symbols adapt meaning. I allow that to be the basis of my discussion. Can you imagine how now you'll look at the periodic table and say 'what?'

When I get ready to teach scientific method, since you all hear about it for 10 years before, I say let's talk about social science. Instead of describing "what is the hypothesis if I take salt and grind it first," I show a clip from Brown Eyes-Blue Eyes, which is a Jane Elliott experiment that was conducted in 1968 with a homogenous group of students, on the surface. Very quickly she exposes diversity around class and gender, and uses that to adapt conversations about rest. She said, 'I was not going to allow this moment to pass without these children having these conversations, because perhaps their parents would not.' I realized that, as a teacher, I spend quite a bit of time getting to know humans that may not have opportunities to have these conversations with their families. It does not mean every conversation should be without familial context. I think some conversations you need to have with your parents, especially if it triggers some emotional response in you. But I do think teachers have the responsibility to help families have difficult conversations.

So that's [another] thing—I developed a Wiki so students could explore what I call 'Unsung Heros of Science.' We talk about Vivien Thomas, who was a custodian for Johns Hopkins for years... he was unable to become college-educated, and in spite of his skills [as a technician], he was treated like a custodian for his entire life. However, he and his colleague ended up transforming surgeries we do on the heart, especially in babies. I also use popular media and resources. I am often challenged by the question, 'is this an example of life imitating art or art imitating life'?

I firmly believe it's necessary to have race and identity education in every class. It should be done in ways that are thoughtful, by people who are caring. And I think all teachers have a shared value of human care—we want to see the human race be improved."

—*Dr. Joy Barnes-Johnson, science teacher*

Long Interview
Born in Ethiopia to Indian parents and raised in 7 nations, **Kalpana Peck** shares her views on her international upbringing, her interracial marriage, and the impact she had on her children.

"My father was in the diplomatic service, so we moved every two to three years. I was born in Ethiopia during a period of political unrest, when a military coup attempted to overthrow the emper-[or]. [I] was a really little baby then, and my family had to take shelter in our neighbor's basement. It's funny because I'm in [New] York right now visiting the family who sheltered us!

We moved to Delhi, India, for a year, and then to Russia, where we lived for three years. I went to school in a Russian kindergarten. That was an amazing experience—I didn't feel any racism there. But then again, I was so young, and I feel younger children just want to have fun.

From there, I went to Germany. And there I did feel... I felt something. Yeah, it wasn't a very positive experience... there was a lot of bullying, and I'm not sure if it had to do with my color, ethnicity, or what. But it was just there. One experience I have from Germany happened a long, long time ago. I was 17, or something like that, and I went with a group of my friends to a club. There was a sign outside the door saying, 'No Colored People Allowed,' but we went in anyways. I ended up being asked to leave in a very subtle and quiet way.

Then we moved to the Fiji islands, which was uneventful in terms of racism. After Fiji, we went back to India, and I lived there for two years during middle school. My dad was then sent to Boston for a year, where I attended a public school in Arlington. My time there was not pleasant since I was a minority, and there was a group of girls who were quite nasty to me. After that, we moved to DC where things were fine because I was in a very international environment. Following graduation, I went to a university in Damascus, Syria, and midway, I spent a year in Geneva studying French.

Soon after college, I married an American originally from Texas who was living in Damascus while I was studying there. When we told our families that we were planning to get married, there wasn't really a reaction, but rather just curiosity. Curiosity of whether there would be any problems due to our cultural differences. He is Catholic and I am Hindu, but his family has always been very open and very welcoming to me. I felt—and still feel—no negativity from them. They were just happy to have me in their family.

Being in an interracial marriage is a good thing. My husband's father, who was in the Air Force, used to say that the only way we could have peace in this world was through interracial marriages. Being in an interracial marriage, mixing things up like that, brings people together. It makes people more tolerant and understanding, and it encourages the feeling that everybody is the same. After all, our needs, wishes, goals, and emotions are all the same, except for our wonderful cultural differences.

Children born into interracial marriages benefit from an objective perspective that transcends racially biased beliefs. Biracial children also have a choice of how they want to identify themselves. On the other hand, their voices are sometimes not considered valid because they don't necessarily fully belong to either community. The issues of identity are made even more complex when their backgrounds are culturally and ethnically varied. I gave my children two names that reflect their two cultural backgrounds so they would have the option to assimilate more comfortably to their surroundings."

> "My husband's father, who was in the air force, used to say that the **only way we could have peace** in this world was through **interracial marriages.**"

It's how you respond to the comment that is really important. In communities where racial progress appears to be stagnant, the importance of being an upstander is imperative in order to start the path toward progress.

People who just make an off-the-cuff statement when they're trying to be funny need to be addressed. According to research by Thomas Ford, racist jokes serve to affirm the biases and prejudices of listeners.[1]

When comments are ever made in class about a group, they're usually addressed and made by the people of that group and not outside the group. Internalized racism occurs when the racist attitudes of the majority are accepted, both marginalizing the minority group and advancing inequality. Examples include trying to "act White" rather than retain self-identity and perpetuating stereotypes of one's own race.[2]

1 https://www.psychologytoday.com/blog/humor-sapiens/201107/does-racist-humor-promote-racism; 2 http://www.div17.org/TAAR/media/topics/internalized-racism.php

" People take on stereotypes, and if you don't ever talk about it, you can't really address it. Hearing people say something doesn't make it right; it's how you respond to the comment that is really important, and how you handle things that come up. People who just make an off-the-cuff statement when they're trying to be funny need to be addressed, because it's not always funny, whether it's coming from that person talking about themselves and their situation, or from someone else. Everyone sees races, you can look at someone and say this is the general race that the person classifies as. But it's different to look at someone and identify them by race, then turn around and be a bigot. Being a bigot and pigeonholing someone is unacceptable. Talking is the only way to solve it. If you don't talk about it, it continues to happen. People who mean well but don't want to talk about it, because they don't want to offend [anyone]—their heart is in the right place, but they need to speak out."

"Have you ever had an experience with a student who made derogatory comments without being stopped by others?"

"In my experience, when comments are ever made in class about a group, they're usually addressed and made by the people of that group and not outside the group. I once had a student who was really derogatory about her own ethnicity and race a couple years ago, and it was really interesting to see how she changed her opinion once she went to college. She was saying how a lot of the own stereotypes that she was basically saying in Princeton High School about herself and her ethnicity were what other people in college were actually saying aloud to her. She became an advocate for that and realized it's really important to start having the conversation and talking about it, not necessarily being part of the problem. "

" I'm originally from Philadelphia, so I saw a lot of racism growing up. I went to an all-girls private school right outside of Philadelphia on the ring line. I remember when I was younger, in 12th grade, one of my professors there told me that I just needed to go to a little community college because I will never be anything but a secretary. I was too embarrassed to tell my parents... I actually started to become a little depressed about it. The school that I went to was predominantly Caucasian and [even though] I was African-American, the kids treated me no differently... but to actually have another adult tell me this was kind of interesting. It wasn't until after I graduated that I told my parents and I just moved on with my life. **"**

I'm originally from Philadelphia so I saw a lot of racism growing up.

According to a 2013 Pew Research survey, "Adults who live in urban areas," including Philadelphia, "are much more likely than those living in rural areas to see racial inequality" in all seven areas of community life discussed—the police, the court system, the workplace, stores and restaurants, public schools, the health care system, and elections. Furthermore, while 29% of urban dwellers perceived racial inequality, only 16% of rural dwellers did.

When the data was classified further by both community-type and race, gaps in perception appeared even larger. Although accurate data was not available for rural Black adults, the proportion of both suburban (49%) and urban White (43%) adults who did not perceive racial inequality in any areas of community life was much higher than the proportion of suburban (15%) and urban (10%) Black adults who did not perceive racial inequality anywhere.[1]

In 12th grade, one of my professors there told me that I just needed to go to a little community college because I will never be anything but a secretary.

According to a 2016 John Hopkins study published in the journal Economics of Education Review, there is a discrepancy in the academic expectations held by White and Black teachers for Black students.[2] For example, the researchers found that when evaluating the same Black student, White teachers were almost 30% less likely than Black teachers to predict that the student would complete a four-year college degree. According to the study's co-author Nicholas Papageorge, this discrepancy in teacher expectation could negatively impact student performance, particularly among disadvantaged students who may not have positive role models present in their home life to counteract low teacher expectations.

1 http://www.pewresearch.org/fact-tank/2013/08/28/the-black-White-and-urban-rural-divides-in-perceptions-of-racial-fairness/; 2 http://hub.jhu.edu/2016/03/30/racial-bias-teacher-expectations-black-White/ http://www.sciencedirect.com/science/article/pii/S0272775715300959

EDUCA-
TIONAL

Graphic Credit:
Keri Zhang

SOUTH AFRICA
Stories

From 1948 to 1994, the all-White National Party of South Africa enforced a system of legal segregation called apartheid, forcing Whites and non-Whites to live in and use separate facilities. Under White minority domination, Black, Asian, and "colored"/ mixed people were deprived of basic rights and freedoms such as access to jobs, healthcare, housing, and education. In 1994, under the leadership of Nelson Mandela, the African National Congress took political power, ending the apartheid era after over 20 years of protest and establishing a national democracy. However, 22 years later and despite its progressive Constitution, South Africa is still plagued by the lasting effects of inequality.

INTER-
NATIONAL,
POLITICAL
& LEGAL

Graphic Credit: Ayesha Qureshi

The White people called you monkey, k*****. During the apartheid era in South Africa, the k-word was used as a common neutral or derogatory slur to refer to Black individuals, similar to use of the n-word in the United States. In Mark Mathabane's autobiography Kaffir Boy: An Autobiography—The True Story of a Black Youth's Coming of Age in Apartheid South Africa, he describes the violence, poverty, and hopelessness of his childhood amidst apartheid and his journey to the United States

I still like Nelson Mandela, because once the African National Congress took over they didn't just push the White people away like Idi Amin did.
Idi Amin, notorious for his violent rule as the president of Uganda from 1971-1979, expelled all Asians (not Whites) from Uganda in 1972.[1]

1 http://www.biography.com/people/idi-amin-9183487

❝ There was no electricity. If you go to buy something there was a line for only Black people. In the front was for White people. If you go deposit your money in the bank, you must go to the back of the bank. You couldn't just go to town, and walk like other people. They stopped you, searched you. They looked for ID's and told you you cannot pass here. White people used to give you a tin; you couldn't use their cup. You had to sit outside. You were not allowed in their house, only when they were cleaning. Even in churches. The White people called you monkey, k*****. But you can't say nothing. They stopped you in the street, and said "Aye, k*****, where is this street?" and you'd have to answer them. They wouldn't even say thank you. They called you John. We grew up like that. White people treated us very, very badly. They treated the Black people like animals. So, we just forgot because we knew God was there. Now today, they have no choice but to live with us, but they can't accept that we are the same. They think they are better than us, and we don't see what is different. Anyway, I still like Nelson Mandela, because once the African National Congress took over they didn't just push the White people away like Idi Amin did. ❞

*Interview conducted by
Treniya Bronaugh*

CHOOS

Sometimes violence can be related to race. Maybe if you get mugged, the Black person is always a suspect. Just because there was apartheid and Whites didn't care for Blacks, Whites always wanted to remove Blacks from the way—they wanted to own everything, take everything into their hands—they had the power. But right now, since apartheid ended, it's much easier to go out. I'm in a school right now that, in the olden days, a Black person could never be in because [he or she is] Black.

Now it's just foreigners versus Blacks, because many foreigners bring drugs and turn teenagers my age into prostitutes. Sometimes it happens that a foreigner kills a Black child and puts a drug in the child's body, transporting the body to Nigeria or Mozambique or other countries to people they work with in the drug trade. Sometimes they take just body parts and transport them to sell in another country, leaving the body where it is. It creates a lot of money in that country, but there's less teenagers in South Africa. They're killing only Blacks, people from here, Africans, just us because we're Black. They're Black too. You know people from here, Africans—they're very stubborn and don't want to accept that foreign people are just like us, that they just don't speak the same language. They don't accept that there's no need for violence. The [foreigners are] getting the South Africans angrier and wanting [the foreigners] to get out of the country. It's not understandable.

While you're walking, as a teenager, maybe on your way back from school, a person can just kidnap you, hold you hostage; he can rape you, then kill you after that, then open up your body and put drugs in your body and sew it. Once there was xenophobia, with foreign people and Black people beating each other up. You couldn't go to school because you were scared you were also gonna get beaten up. Lots of people thought that I was a foreigner because of my complexion, my skin color. It's very dark, and I know it. I was also scared to go walk to school, because they could just kill me, because I look like the foreigner. The people who would kill me are people from South Africa. They want to take revenge and kill foreigners, so they use teenagers. Lots of people are dying.

My fear [to go to school] ... has gotten less because the President spoke on a live TV show that we should stop what we're doing because violence is not an answer, and that it's very irritating when you're walking and you see a body laying down. The people stopped for a little while and then it went on again. But they're doing it undercover so the President won't know. Sometimes we hear in the news that another foreigner is dead, another teenager is into prostitution, another South African teenager was found dead or transported. A lot of stuff is happening that is disturbing South Africa's rights.

It's stupid because Blacks are killing Blacks, foreigners are Blacks just like us. It started off right when Nelson Mandela passed away, when South Africans killed foreigners, and vice versa. And then on social media, a White woman named Penny Sparrow posted a letter dedicated to the Blacks that they're monkeys, that they can't do anything; that they're lazy, ungrateful, will never be anything great in life. A White woman said that. Another White man commented on that and said yes, it's true. He's a judge on Idols—Gareth Cliff.

Apartheid is coming back. Slowly but surely. And this time it's much stronger, because in the olden days if Black people had weapons to fight the Whites, it would've been worse. But the Blacks didn't have any weapons to fight back, and Nelson Mandela went to jail for 27 years to fight for our freedom, and then he came out and apartheid stopped. Now that he's dead, it's just coming back, slower and slower. There is going to be a lot of blood, a lot of people dying. I might not go to the school I'm going to currently; they're gonna say 'Whites only.' I'm going to have to go to school with lower education, I might not get to be the person I wanted to be in the future. I want to be an electronic scientist, but if I go to that school I can't because there are no materials, and teachers won't show you the way... If apartheid comes back, things are gonna get tough. **

SOUTH AFRICA
Stories cont.

Now it's just foreigners versus Blacks, because many foreigners bring drugs and turn teenagers my age into prostitutes.

Cases of xenophobia in the post-apartheid era have led to numerous deaths of foreigners, people from different nations or smaller ethnic groups. Some local South Africans have attributed this violence to the claim that foreigners are taking away their jobs by accepting cheaper wages, committing criminal acts, and spreading diseases. The interviewee also discusses drug trafficking. In South Africa, nearly nonexistent use of drugs other than tobacco and alcohol at the end of apartheid drastically increased by the end of 20th century, partially due to the vulnerability of the new democracy amidst political, social, and economic change.[1]

It's stupid because Blacks are killing Blacks, foreigners are Blacks just like us.

This interviewee echoes a similar controversy in the United States surrounding the prevalence of Black-on-Black crime as a justification for or comparison to police shootings in Black communities. According to the Black Lives Matter website, 93% of Black murders are by other Blacks, and 84% of White murders are by Whites; disproportionate poverty, targeted police arrests, and lower quality education for Blacks can perpetuate violent crime but do not mean that Black people are innately more violent than other races.[2] In his novel Between the World and Me, Ta-Nehisi Coates explains that "to yell 'Black-on-Black crime' is to shoot a man and then shame him for bleeding."

1 http://www.sahistory.org.za/article/xenophobic-violence-democratic-south-africa
2 http://blacklivesmatter.com/11-major-misconceptions-about-the-black-lives-matter-movement/

EDUCA-TIONAL, INTER-NATIONAL

“ I live in Chesterville, and the education is very bad here, I won't lie. Some kids don't go to school because they're poor and don't have the money… or the shoes. Some parents are working or they're trying to get them to school, but it's hard. I remember when my mom wanted to take me to college, and she asked how much and they said, 'ten thousand rand,' [or 718 U.S. dollars]. She said, 'oh, we can't go here.' It's very expensive. I had to just stay home, because she doesn't have money to take me to college. I wish there was a free college, then maybe I would go. Free college! Free school! Free education! That would be nice.

What happened with the apartheid was that the White schools were richer; they would be the greatest, most beautiful schools. The Black schools didn't have paper or pencils to write with. Sometimes you see them on television—kids with no seats to sit on. One hundred children in one class. The school [building] is little. They complain about water. They complain about electricity. We are still living with it even right now, we don't even know. The White schools are still getting much more than we are getting. I just wish that we were getting great schools like the White people. We should do 50/50, it doesn't have to be about race, it shouldn't be, 'because I'm Black, I can't get that.'

I went to a great school, but it ended in 9th grade, then you have to [pay]. They should've given us money, and then later I would pay. They gave us a paper without even explaining. It was bad, I won't lie. It's a bad situation when you're staying at home doing nothing and you wish that you could stand up and do something, but what can you do? The only thing you can do is find a job. Even if I find a job, how am I gonna find a college that can take me to where I wanna go? Right now, I'm just messed up. I'm twenty years old, and seven years I've been at home, wishing I could do something. It's very bad when you see people going to school, and they say, "Wow, I did this, I have this homework." I wish I could help you—I'm not even in school. ”

I live in Chesterville, and the education is very bad here.

Chesterville is a low-income neighborhood designated as part of a Black township during the apartheid era in South African. According to research by the Umkhumbane Schools Project in 2014, 26% of Chesterville students were able to achieve the passing rate of 30% in mathematics, and 7% had scores above 50%. Among the 761 senior class students in the five public schools of the district, only 24 achieved 50% or higher in mathematics. These numbers are just one example of the huge disparities in South African public education, caused largely by a shortage of competent teachers and administrators, lack of funding and resources, overcrowding, low expectations, and student poverty.[1]

She asked how much and they said, "ten thousand rand," [or 718 U.S. dollars].

According to the 2011 national census, the average South African annual household income for Blacks was 60,613 rand, or $8,700 by the exchange rate at the time. The same figure for White households was approximately 6 times higher.[2]

I just wish that we were getting great schools like the White people.

Only a few miles away from Chesterville lie wealthy White neighborhoods, evidence of the lasting effect of apartheid and a common juxtaposition of wealth and poverty in South Africa that often falls along racial lines.

1 The Umkhumbane Schools Project
2 http://www.pewresearch.org/fact-tank/2013/12/06/chart-of-the-week-how-south-africa-changed-and-didnt-over-mandelas-lifetime/

"I look at an ant and I see myself: a native South African, endowed by nature with a strength much greater than my size so I might cope with the weight of a racism that crushes my spirit."

— Miriam Makeba

"There is no easy walk to freedom anywhere, and many of us will have to pass through the valley of the shadow of death again and again before we reach the mountaintop of our desires."

—Nelson Mandela

"I believe that here in South Africa, with all our diversities of colour and race; we will show the world a new pattern for democracy. There is a challenge for us to set a new example for all. Let us not side step this task."

—Albert Lutuli

Talk Teacher

"How do you teach sensitive or touchy topics in history?"

"Experience. Trying to gather the facts is the first way to attack it, and then hopefully creating a relationship with the student population. If I get something wrong and they tell me, then I can have a conversation with them and ask them to help me out. The facts are the facts, but some of the little intricate details can be important and might not be interpreted correctly. I've had students in the past of certain religious affiliations guide me and give me more information. Those personal relationships with the students—making them feel like they can come to me—is something I really try to strive for. Outside of that, just trying to be as well-informed as possible and trying not to promote anything more than the other. To give everything its due, especially in a world history class."

—*David Roberts, history teacher*

Written Reflection

Lines Drawn in Blood
by Isaiah Anagbo

We are supposed to be living in a highly sophisticated society. It is amazing to me that people still find ways to divide themselves across borders that are not limited to their own humanity. Humans are just one species and there is no scientific justification for our ability to separate ourselves through something as simple as skin color. I myself am of mixed race. I am both Black and White, with Lithuanian and African blood running through my veins, yet I am divided into a category of people with dark skin color. Identifying with my dark skin color exposes me to an array of dangers and difficulties that would not be met by my White counterparts who simply possess a little less melanin in their skin than I do.

The scientific and rational explanation for race falls well short of being sound yet this is not an excuse to label oneself as "colorblind." Every race alike now has to face the fact that we have created for ourselves generations of structural segregation

> We have made **murder a staple of American society** and used the advancements in human, social, and technological evolution to **create death and regression** rather than **diplomacy and progression.**

so great that it cannot simply be broken by will. We must accept the fact that a White cop will find a Black teenager more threatening than a White teenager, and that we have been hard-wired to accept race as an integral part of our divisions. We cannot work toward being "colorblind" until we stop thinking about ourselves along these borders and create true equality for humans of all skin colors. To be "colorblind" now is to deny the inequalities that exist between races. Saying that "all lives matter" is a good principle to accept as a core value, but one that is used inappropriately as a response to "Black lives matter." At this moment in our history, Black lives are being taken at a more targeted rate than other races in this country, and to say Black lives matter is not to suggest that other lives do not matter, or that Black lives matter more than other lives, but that the devaluation of the Black life in our society pushes us to say that these Black lives matter as much as any other human lives.

And this is not even addressing the main problem in the death of officers and Black men alike: we have accepted murder as a way of life. Murder has even been stipulated as a necessary part of our culture, and we have perpetuated it through the creation of various weaponry and institutions that educate to kill. We have made murder a staple of American society and used the advancements in human social and technological evolution to create death and regression rather than diplomacy and progression. By accepting retaliation as necessary, we leave room for aggression. Instead of remedying the problem of murder and creating less options for its perpetuation, we encourage violence with violence to create a vicious cycle that is almost impossible to stop.

This means that when a Black life is taken we are taught to retaliate by taking a cop's life, and being pro-Black lives becomes anti-police, race becomes war, and we become our own worst enemy. We have to realize that being "pro-Black lives matter" is not "anti-police," and that by even focusing on the racial component of police brutality and murder, we are positioning the importance of human life below that of our own social divisions.

We are devaluing the beauty that is lost in this world when a person is senselessly and unfairly sent to his or her death.

Graphic Credit: Barry Deutsch. leftycartoons.com

CHOOS

“ The benefits of being in an inter-racial relationship are the same as any relationship. If you don't see race as a barrier, you're good. If you're just open to any kind of person, I think that opens the possibilities—the possibilities of the kinds of people you meet, the kinds of people you interact with. So if you do see race as a barrier, then there's a rare possibility of finding someone. I love when Ethan introduces his culture to me. I love watching Bollywood movies, eating spicy food—I'm working on my spice tolerance—and, honestly, just being part of his family.”

“And merging two different cultures can be hard because, at least in my family, traditional Indians are more strict. My parents are fine with our relationship, but my grandparents would not approve.”

“That sucks. I really wanted your grandparents in India to like me.”

“Yeah, last year I was studying abroad in India. There you see how everyone is fixated on having lighter skin, and girls feel really pressured—”

“Wait, I have light skin, but how come your grandparents still don't like me?”

“I guess they like light skin, but also Indian culture. So if you dressed up in traditional Indian clothes, spoke the language, etc, they would love you because you would have the White aesthetics but the Indian culture at the same time. Does that make sense? I guess that goes back to British rule and how they enforced the White beauty standards as the only beauty standards. ”

I guess that goes back to British rule and how they enforced the White beauty standards as the only beauty standards.

In India, fair skin is glorified pervasively in society. British colonialism equated higher castes, and therefore higher power status to White skin. This aesthetic standard has larger implications than just beauty—having light skin is commonly associated with wealth, intelligence, poise, and power. Post-colonial Indian colorism has led to the celebration of White skin by celebrities and is heavily advertised in the media. Each year, over 233 tons of skin-Whitening and skin-bleaching products are consumed in Indian society.[1]

1 http://nytlive.nytimes.com/womenintheworld/2015/05/12/another-african-nation-bans-popular-skin-Whitening-creams/

CURRENT EVENT

originally a CHOOSE Facebook post
visual credit: The New York Times

February 26th, 2016

On February 26th, the New York Times published an investigation by Haeyoun Park, Josh Keller, and Josh Williams of 503 of the most powerful people in American culture, government, education and business. Out of the 503, only 44 were minorities.

Read more: http://www.nytimes.com/interactive/2016/02/26/us/race-of-american-power.html?smid=fb-nytimes&smtyp=cur&_r=1

The New York Times — White Faces of American Power

After the shootings of Philando Castile and Alton Sterling.
The killings of Philando Castile and Alton Sterling in early July were only two of over 120 police shootings of Black men in 2016. Video footage and interviews with loved ones were released on social media shortly after the incidents, prompting protests and calls for justice. Refer to pages 108–109 to read more statistics and stories regarding police brutality in the United States from 2014–2016.

Interview conducted by Katie McCarthy, CHOOSE Chapter @ Hun School Founder

"How do you think we can reduce stereotypes?"

"In my opinion, most stereotypes aren't completely true, but they also aren't completely made up. Each stereotype, whether it be all Black people play basketball or all Hispanics eat tacos, aren't true but undoubtedly originated somewhere. Therefore when trying to combat stereotypes we can't just say 'no it's not true,' because the person's own experience might very well contradict that. Instead what we need to do is explain the origins of the stereotype. We need to explain the misconception or series of events that caused this assumption to be so prevalent. In doing so you can reconcile anyone's personal experience with the facts. And instead of that person continuing their belief without thought, they can now consider the factors that went into that belief, and hopefully in doing so realize that the stereotype they believed in isn't completely true."

"Have you ever had an experience in which you were proud of your race?"

"After the shootings of Philando Castile and Alton Sterling. Like many, I was mad and grieved when I heard about the shootings back-to-back. I expected that the emotions I was feeling were the same that other African Americans were feeling. I thought that, like after the death of Freddie Gray in Baltimore, there would be some peaceful protests and also some riots. I figured that like other times the anger would cause a few to act out negatively and that the media would again focus on those few and the positive message would be lost. However, in the aftermath of both shootings, the messages for peace were so high. People, including both families, wanted change but also didn't want violence or deviance. I was proud how Black people from all over stood up and were unified for change and for peace. I was proud during those few days of peace and unity. However, of course that was cut short by the Dallas shooting and the Baton Rouge ambush. Nevertheless I feel the most proud of my race when we are united and working together peacefully for a cause. **"**

Amir Latif, Rawalpindi renowned Dermatologist, shares his father's experiences migrating from Kashmir to Pakistan in a time of death and discrimination. Interview conducted in Urdu.

"میرے والد کی کہانیوں سے میں کشمیری ہندوؤں اور مسلمانوں میں رہنے والے دو مختلف کمیونٹیز تھے کہ یاد۔ انثقافتوں اور طرز زندگی سے، یہ بتانے کے لئے کہ وہ کو لگتا ہے کہ کے طور پر طور پر اسی طرح میں نہیں تھی آسان تھا۔ مثال کے طور پر، مسلمانوں کے لئے عید کی طرح ایک چھٹی کے دن بھی نہیں تھا جب بھی، کشیدگی میں دونوں کے درمیان میں پیدا ہونے والے شروع ہو جائے گا۔ عید منانے کے لئے مسلمانوں کے لئے کوئی کھلے قبولیت ہو گی، اور یہ مسلمانوں کے لئے ایک بہت ہی خاص دن ہے کیونکہ، آپ کو اس کے منانے کے لئے نہیں کر سکیں کرنے کی ہوتی ہے کہ کس طرح پریشان کن تصور کر سکتے ہیں۔ دوسری طرف، ثقافت کے لحاظ سے، ہندوؤں کا گوشت کے کسی بھی طرح کے کھانے کے لئے مسلمانوں کو خوشی سے خاص طور پر مقدس دن پر،

جانوروں کی قربانی دی جبکہ انکار کر دیا.

ان کی سماجی زندگی کو بھی بہت مختلف تھی. انفرادیت پسند نقطہ نظر سے، بلکہ مجموعی نقطہ نظر سے نہیں دیکھ، میرے والد کہ دونوں فرقوں کے بزی مشکل سے ایک دوسرے کے ساتھ رہتے تھے کہتے تھے. اس وقت کے ارد گرد لڑائی کے ذریعے واضح ہوگئی جب مسلمانوں کے بہت سے نقل مکانی شروع. یہ ایک چھوٹی سی آبادی تھی، اگرچہ، قتل، جس میں طویل کہانیوں کے سینکڑوں سے دوبارہ تعمیر کر رہے ہیں کی ایک بہت تھا.

میرے نانا جموں سے تھا. اس وقت کے دوران، گزشتہ مہاراجہ *، ہری سنگھ حکمران رہا تھا. اور ہ ایک ہی، اقتصادی، تعلیمی، سیاسی، اور ہ ہی مواقع باقی آبادی کو فراہم کیا گیا تھا کہ بات سے انکار کر رہے کے کے پر اس آدمی مسلمان جبر کا ذمہ دار تھا. یہ ہی نہممکن ایک مسلم صفوں چڑھنے اور ایک باختیار بنانے کی ملازمت حاصل کرنے کے لیے بنایا ہے تاکہ ہندوں تقریبا تمام سہولیات اور وسائل پر اجارہ داری تھی.

ان تفاوت کے ساتھ ساتھ اب تک پاکستان یا بھارت یا تو کے ساتھ شمولیت اختیار نہیں کیا تھا کہ کشمیر کے کچھ حصہ سے کی وجہ سے بدامنی کی وجہ سے، یہ ہے کہ مسلمانوں کو احتجاج شروع ہو جائیں گا ناگزیر تھا. مسلم کمیونٹی کے زیادہ تر، حقیقت میں، جموں میں فعال طور پر، مسلم لیگ احتجاجی مظاہروں میں شرکت کری گے کہ وہ سیالکوٹ کا سفر کرنا پڑے گا کا مطلب ہے یہاں تک کہ اگر. اگر میرے والد کے بڑے بھائی، میرے چچا، ایک بار سیالکوٹ، جس میں ۲۸ کلومیٹر کے فاصلے پر تقریبا تھا میں ایک مسلم لیگ کے جلسہ * میرے باپ لیا. اور صرف آج کے لیے ہم راولپنڈی اور اسلام آباد "جڑواں شہروں" تصور کیا جاتا ہے کی طرح، جموں اور سیالکوٹ میں بھی اس وقت کے "جڑواں شہروں" تصور کیا گیا تھا. (لیکن تقسیم کے بعد، سیالکوٹ کا حصہ پاکستان کا حصہ جموں بھارت کا حصہ بن گیا ہے جبکہ بن گیا.)

لٹھ ہ اس ٹرین پر واپس سیالکوٹ سے جموں، جموں پولیس سوار جانتا تھا مسلمانوں کو نشانہ بنایا تھا. خوش قسمتی سے، میرے چچا اور میرے والد کی شوٹنگ فرار ہونے میں کامیاب ہو گئے اور محفوظ طریقے سے گھر واپس آئی، لیکن کچھ ہے جو ایسا کرنے کے قابل تھے میں سے تھے.

لیکن آخر، وہ کوئی چارہ نہیں تھا لیکن اپنے دور کو چلانے کے لیے اس بات کا احساس. یہ ان کی ہوم جگہ وہ انہائی ہوئی تھے، وہ دوستی کی جگہ، وہ تعلیم یافتہ تھے، لیکن وہ کہاں سے وہ ہر روز اپنی زندگیوں کو، جہاں وہ مساوی حقوق کی تردید کی اور کے طور پر علاج کیا گیا کے لیے خدشہ ہے ایک جگہ میں نہیں رہ سکتا دوسرے درجے کے شہری. کوئی بھی اپنے گھروں کو چھوڑنے کے لیے چاہتا ہے لیکن آپ کو اس طرح کی صورت حال ہے جب، یہ اب کسی ایک کا انتخاب نہیں ہو جاتا.

وہ تمام اجتماعی قتل کے بیچ میں چھوڑنے پر مجبور کیا گیا تھا جب میرے والد نے نہیں جماعت میں تھا. اس نے ہمیں بتایا کہ وہ اپنے گھروں، ان کے سامان، اور کچھ نہیں کے ساتھ اپنے پیاروں لیکن کپڑے ہے کہ وہ اس دن پہنے ہوئے تھے چھوڑنے کے لیے مجبور کہ کس طرح. بہت بہت افراتفری خاندان میں جلد پر تقسیم کیا گیا تھا کہ ہ نہیں تھا. میرے والد کے بڑے بھائی سب سے کم عمر ایک آٹھ سال کی عمر میں لاہور میں ایک کیمپ میں ختم ہوا جبکہ سندھ ہجرت ختم ہوا.

مجھے خاص طور پر میرے والد سے بیان کس طرح سے کس طرح ان ہوں نے اپنی بہن، میری چاچی کھو یاد. وہ چل رہا تھا مگر میرے دو چاچیوں، سات اور دو سال کی عمر سے اوپر، پانی کا ایک جام حاصل کرنے کے لیے بند کر دیا اور وہ اپنے سروں جھکی، میرے والد ان ہوں نے اپنی سات سالہ کہ تلاش کرنے کے لیے ان سمتوں میں براہ راست گولیاں سنائی کہ بہن جاں بحق کر دیا گیا تھا.

میرے والد اور کیا ان کے خاندان کے باقی سیالکوٹ کے دوسرے رشتہ داروں تھا جہاں کے فرار ہونے میں کامیاب ہو گئے ہیں تھے. کچھ وقت کے رہنے کے بعد، ان ہوں نے آخر میں راولپنڈی جہاں میں آج ہوں ہجرت.

ایسی، مجھے نہیں لگتا کہ اس موضوع کے لیے کافی بیداری ہے. ہزاروں اور بچوں اور خواتین سمیت لوگوں کی ہزاروں اگرچہ، اس تنازع کے دوران ہلاک ہو گئے تھے اور اب بھی ان کے پرامن احتجاج کے لیے قتل کیا جا رہا ہے، میڈیا کے مغربی چترن دنیا کے اصلی ہوسکتیں کو احاطہ کرتا. تاہم، مجھے لگتا ہے کہ یہ ان بدسورت تنازعات، اور ان کے تمام لرز ہ خیز تفصیلات کے بارے میں جاننا ضروری ہے. میرے والد بھی لوگ درختوں، عمارتوں، اور لائنوں سے منسلک، اور ان کے مذہب کی مشق نہیں میں ان کو ڈرانے کے لیے سب کے سامنے موت مارا پینا گیا تھا کہ کس طرح کے بارے میں مجھے بتاؤ گے.

لیکن ہمیں غصے سے دیکھنے اور اعمال دو کرنے اور الے نہیں ہو سکتا اور نفرت کسی کا دھیان نہیں کی طرف سے جانا. ہم میڈیا جیسے نہ ہو اور بحث کے معاملات کی طرف ایک نظر تبدیل کر سکتے ہیں. یہاں تک کہ چھوٹے چھوٹے کہانیاں، یا چھوٹے جملوں کا سب سے بڑا اثرات ہو سکتے ہیں. میری نسل کے لیے کم سے کم، لوگوں کی کہانیاں اشتراک اور زیادہ براہ راست اور حقیقی طور پر کا تجربہ کرے گا. لیکن اب نئی ٹیکنالوجی، ذرائع ابلاغ، اور حقیقی مواصلات کی کمی کے ساتھ، ماضی اور حال کے درمیان ایک پوری ہونی لگتا ہے. ہم سب پڑوسی ہیں اور انسانوں، کوئی بات نہیں نسل، رنگ، قومیت، یا مذہب کے طور پر ایک دوسرے سے قبول کیا جائیں چاہیئے. اور تم اشتراک اور کہانیاں سننے نہیں ہیں تو، آپ سب یہ لیتا رفت دکھانیں کرے لیے ایک کہانی ہے کیونکہ انسانیت انصاف نہیں کر رہے ہیں. کس طرح کسی لوگ کھو زندگی کی اقدار معلوم ہوگا؟ وہ کبھی بھی پتہ نہ چل جائیں گا اور کبھی بھی ہے کہ کس طرح ایند دی ذیتھلی امتیازی سلوک؟

اشتراک اور سننے کی طرف سے، ہم معاشرے کو پیغامات اور سبق پھیلا رہے ہیں. اور یہ کہ کیا ضروری ہے."

CHOOS

Translation:

" From my father's stories, I remember that there were two different communities living in Kashmir— the Hindus and the Muslims. From their cultures and lifestyles, it was easy to tell that they were not as similar as you would think. For example, whenever there was a holiday like Eid for the Muslims, tensions would start arising in between the two. There would be no open acceptance for the Muslims to celebrate Eid and because it's a very special day for Muslims, you can imagine how upsetting it would have been. On the other hand, in terms of the culture, the Hindus refused to eat any sort of goat meat while the Muslims happily sacrificed the animal, especially on holy days.

Their social lives were also very different. Looking not from the individualistic perspective, but rather from the holistic perspective, my father used to say that the two communities lived together with great difficulty. It became evident through the fighting around the time when lots of Muslims started migrating. Even though it was a small population, there was a lot of mass murder, which hundreds of long stories are built off of.

My father was from Jammu. During this time, the last Maharaja[1], Hari Singh was ruling. This man was responsible for Muslim oppression as they were denied the same economical, educational, political, and social opportunities that were supplied to the rest of the population. The Hindus had a monopoly on almost all the facilities and resources so that it made it impossible for a Muslim to climb up ranks and earn an empowering job.

Because of these disparities as well as the unrest caused from the parts of Kashmir that had not been joined with either Pakistan or India yet, it was inevitable that the Muslims would start protesting. Most of the Muslim community, in fact, in Jammu would actively participate in the Muslim League protests, even if that meant they would have to travel to Sialkot. My father's older brother, my uncle, once took my father to a Muslim League jalsa[2] in Sialkot (1945), which was was approximately 28 km away. And just like today how Rawalpindi and Islamabad are considered to be 'twin cities,' Jammu and Sialkot were also deemed the 'twin cities' of that time. (But after the partition, Sialkot became part of Pakistan while Jammu became part of India.)

Little did they know that on the train ride back from Sialkot to Jammu, the Jammu police had targeted the Muslims. Fortunately, my uncle and father were able to escape the shooting and safely returned home, but were among the few who were able to do so.

Eventually, though, they realized that they had no other choice but to run away. This was their home— the place they were raised, the place they made friends, the place they were educated, but they couldn't live in a place where they feared for their lives each day, where they were denied equal rights and treated as second class citizens. No one wants to leave their homes but when you have a situation like that, it does not become a choice anymore.

***

My father was in ninth grade when he was forced to leave in the midst of all the mass murder. He told us how they were forced to leave their homes, their belongings, and their loved ones with nothing but the clothes that they were wearing that day. There was so much chaos that

> " Because of these disparities as well as the unrest caused from the parts of Kashmir that had not been joined with either Pakistan or India yet, it was inevitable that the Muslims would start protesting.

the family was split early on. My father's older brother ended up migrating to Sindh while the youngest one ended up in a camp in Lahore at the age of eight.

I especially remember how vividly my father described how he lost his sister, my aunt. They had been running but my two aunts, at the ages of seven and two, stopped to get a drink of water. And as they lowered their heads, my father said he heard gunshots directly in their directions—he found that his seven-year-old sister had been shot dead.

My father and what was rest of his family were able to escape to Sialkot where they had other relatives. After staying there for some time, they finally migrated to Rawalpindi where I am today.

Unfortunately, I do not think there is enough awareness of this topic. Although thousands and thousands of people, including children and women, were killed during this conflict and are still being murdered for their peaceful protests, the Western portrayal of the media hasn't covered the real horrors of the world. However, I think it's important to know about these ugly conflicts, and all their gruesome details. My father would even tell me about how people were tied to trees, buildings, and sticks, and beaten to death in front of everyone to scare them into not practicing their religion.

But we cannot be the ones to watch and let actions out of anger and hate go by unnoticed. We can't be like the media and turn a blind eye towards matters worth discussing. Even the small stories, or the small sentences can have the biggest effects. At least for my generation, people would share stories and experience them more directly and genuinely. But now with the new technology, media, and lack of real communication, there seems to be a whole between the past and the present.

> **"** However, I think it's important to know about these ugly conflicts, and all their gruesome details. My father would even tell me about how people were tied to trees, buildings, and sticks, and beaten to death in front of everyone to scare them into not practicing their religion.

We are all neighbors and should be accepting of each other as humans, no matter race, color, ethnicity, or religion. And if you don't share and listen to stories, you are not doing humanity justice because all it takes is a story to show progress.

How else will people know the values of the lives lost? Will they ever know how deathly discrimination really was and still is?

By sharing and listening, we are spreading messages and lessons to society. And that is what is essential. **"**

[1]Mahraja=great king
[2]jalsa=gathering for movement purposes (today, mostly political)

My Race is Beautiful Too
by Nina Sachdev

I identify as Asian, and more specifically, to the Indian sub-continent of Asia. I'm very proud to be Indian because I constantly discover new and exciting aspects of my ancestors' culture. I strive to embrace the Indian ideology that impacts me the most: Being open-minded and aware of others' disadvantages. Indian people are very humble, yet still motivated to succeed and find happiness in life.

I was actually born in New Jersey and have only visited India, rather than lived there. This means that I identify with other ethnicities, and although many might be quick to assume that I identify only with the Indian culture, I am made up of complex, multiethnic characteristics and experiences.

I never really registered what 'race' and its implications were until middle school, when I faced racial discrimination. I was living in an area where it was rare to encounter someone of Indian descent, so naturally, people my age were not exposed to people that looked like me. These recurring instances of discrimination led me to learn more about my own race, and why it is necessary to embrace where I come from. It took me so long—and still does today—to realize that my race and my ethnicity are beautiful, not inferior or worthy of prejudice.

Racial Injustice
by Shiv Sethi

On the topic of ethnic discrimination, I've always felt that there is a certain degree of euphoric ignorance on the part of young students at educational institutions—in particular regarding their verbal assertions. My earliest recollections of racial prejudice are from elementary school, however the majority are from my years at PHS. In the hallways, one will often hear people saying how smart somebody is because they're Asian or how great they are at sports because they're Black. These stereotypes are so embedded in school life that we often neglect the nature of what we are saying.

Psychologically, one of the fundamentals to our cognition is our formation of concepts, which in turn are based on prototypes. Prejudice is essentially a basal element to our mental capacity. Consequently, the issue of racial discrimination is not one that can entirely mitigated.

However, for me, the easiest way to minimize prejudices at school is to make people more aware of the repercussions of their statements. Whether that be through large assemblies or through a new class on the subject, I'm not sure. But what I do know is that through increased awareness regarding the emotional consequences of what we say on those around us, we can hope to reduce ethnic dispute.

“ I came from a refugee camp in Nepal to the United States in 2008. Upon my arrival, I faced language barriers and racism. At first, I felt as if the 'land of opportunity' was only the land for someone who was born here. I was somewhat made fun of for not being able to speak English properly, and was tagged with stereotypes that probably resulted from my inability to communicate my background with them. And now that I think about it, it would be more accurate to call them racist remarks.

I was born in the refugee camp, and I lived there for most of my childhood before coming here. My grandparents entered the refugee camps in Nepal as political refugees from Bhutan. I was raised there, but for my family and the other 100,000 refugees, life instantly became a struggle. They had to build makeshift camps for shelter from bamboo trees and plastic. The camps lacked proper sanitation, an education system, jobs, and food.

We decided to come to the United States when UNHCR and IOM gave us the option to choose between the first-world countries for resettlement. Almost every family from the 7 camps has been resettled in the participating countries, but some still live there as they are awaiting their immigration process, while some wish to return to their homeland, Bhutan. 'The land of opportunity' was not a common belief in the refugee camps. In fact, we pretty much picked a random country out of the list they provided, although the United States of America was well-known. However, we had no idea about the huge culture shock re-settlers were going to face.

I do share my story when people ask. I think the best way to educate people about race and culture is right when they start high school. We want to instill good values when students are developing their own sets of beliefs and outlook of the world— when they are teenagers. We should do anything to expand their knowledge about different race and cultures. **”**

ECONOMIC

I came from a refugee camp in Nepal to the United States in 2008.

Around 1890, the Lhotshampas arrived in Bhutan. As they grew in size, the natives felt they were a threat to the ethnic purity. Starting in 1991, the Lhotshampas were expelled from Bhutan. Some were removed by gunpoint in the middle of the night, and others separated from their families. More than 100,000 Bhutanese have landed in refugee camps in Nepal and, after decades in limbo, have begun resettling around the globe.

According to the International Organization for Migration, as of April 2014, around 75,000 refugees have been relocated to the United States. The transition has not been easy for refugees— often family members are left behind and there is a high rate of suicide. As Bhutanese refugees are being resettled globally, it is often difficult to preserve their cultural identity.[1]

However, we had no idea about the huge culture shock re-settlers were going to face.

Refugees often move out of fear—for reasons such as war, persecution, or natural disasters. Forced evacuation makes assimilating into another culture difficult, and for many refugees, relocating to a new country is disorienting. Culture shock is a key stress for refugees, and most governments do not take active steps to help.[2] Germany, however, has illustrated progressive methods of treating refugees. The German government has paid for refugee "integration classes," and many schools have "welcome classes" for refugee children, teaching them the language, life, and values in Germany.[3]

According to the Cultural Orientation Resource Center:

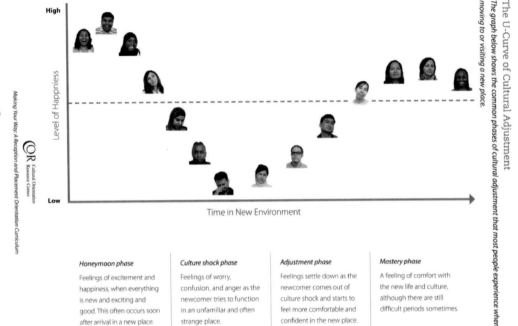

The U-Curve of Cultural Adjustment
The graph below shows the common phases of cultural adjustment that most people experience when moving to or visiting a new place.

Making Your Way: A Reception and Placement Orientation Curriculum

COR Cultural Orientation Resource Center

Level of Happiness — High / Low

Time in New Environment

Honeymoon phase
Feelings of excitement and happiness, when everything is new and exciting and good. This often occurs soon after arrival in a new place.

Culture shock phase
Feelings of worry, confusion, and anger as the newcomer tries to function in an unfamiliar and often strange place.

Adjustment phase
Feelings settle down as the newcomer comes out of culture shock and starts to feel more comfortable and confident in the new place.

Mastery phase
A feeling of comfort with the new life and culture, although there are still difficult periods sometimes.

1 http://pulitzercenter.org/projects/usa-asia-himalaya-bhutan-nepal-lhotshampa-nepal-migrant
2 http://therefugeecenter.org/culture_shock/
3 http://www.nytimes.com/2015/11/18/world/europe/migrants-germany-culture-shock-in-the-promised-land.html

CURRENT EVENT

originally a CHOOSE Facebook post
visual credit: NBC News

February 29th, 2016

The Peter Liang protesters gathered in Brooklyn on February 20th, a group of primarily Asian Americans who have been passionately making a stance against the 15-year sentence given to Peter Liang, an Asian American NYPD officer. Because Liang was the first New York City officer convicted for a line-of-duty shooting in over a decade, protesters argued that he was not given the same treatment as White NYPD officers who were also involved in the killing of unarmed Blacks.

However, some argue that Peter Liang's conviction is not an injustice but a precedent for increased awareness of justice for all.

Read more: http://www.nytimes.com/2016/02/12/nyregion/officer-peter-liang-convicted-in-fatal-shooting-of-akai-gurley-in-brooklyn.html?_r=0

 Steph Yin Reflection

"There's no 'Make America Great Again,' as Donald Trump says. We have never achieved the greatness that we think we have. Women were just allowed to vote, and they just recognized an entire race as human beings. So we got a xenophobic, misogynistic person representing the disenfranchised. It's similar to what happened in London, and if the sentiment stays the same, we could find ourselves in another Brexit situation.

I hope the Asian and Latino communities will overpopulate this place in the next 20 years so we can have a more even playing ground. I heard something earlier—someone didn't like the BET award ceremony because it was 'very Black.' They said there should be a White television network, too. And I'm like, 'There already is one. The White television network is *everything*.' "

It's similar to what happened in London, and if the sentiment stays the same, we could find ourselves in another Brexit situation.
Brexit is used to describe the 2016 withdrawal of the United Kingdom from the European Union. The issue of refugee immigration and "controlling our borders" was used heavily in the rhetoric of the Brexit campaign. Immigration was cited in polls as the second most common reason in voting for Brexit.[1] Refer to page 82-83 to read more about refugee migration.

I heard something earlier—someone didn't like the BET awards because it was "very Black." They said there should be a White television network, too.
Refer to page 123 to read about the White control of media.

1 http://www.theguardian.com/politics/2016/jun/29/frenzy-hatred-brexit-racism-abuse-referendum-celebratory-lasting-damage

Talk Teacher

"Teaching students about diversity in the classroom is essential for preparing young minds to understand the world they live in today. More importantly, exposure to different perspectives helps cultivate a sense of local, national, and global responsibilities that students will eventually adopt as adults.

From my experiences, the most effective way to teach students about different cultures is to help them reflect on the relevant aspects of their lives to create a foundation for comparison and understanding. Often times, I find that students can't gain an appreciation for conversations about race, sex, or poverty because they haven't reflected on their own lives in the context of the topic at hand. I always emphasize to my students that a lot of the things we discuss are 'how the way the world is, not necessarily how it should be.' This helps them objectively see situations for what they are and inspires classes to have dialogue about how things could be better. "
—Daniel Chung, history teacher

CHOOS

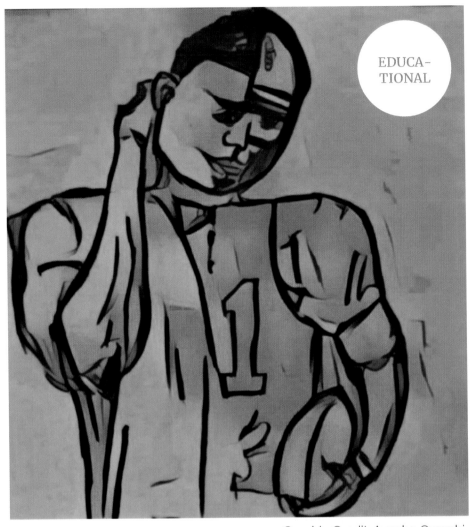

Graphic Credit: Ayesha Qureshi

"When I got accepted into Princeton University, my high school football coach told me I wouldn't fit in. He wanted me to go to another school, [which] was a bigger football school but nowhere near Princeton academically. My coach is White, and he told me, 'Those guys wear bow ties and stuff like that. You don't want to be like that, you want to be around your boys and I don't think you'd like it if you went to Princeton.' He tried to talk me out of it. He was wrong. I don't know what any of that had to do with me coming here. Not everyone wears a bow tie. Not everyone is from a certain background. I'd argue it's one of the most diverse campuses. I think it's a great place to experience different cultures."

He wanted me to go to another school, [which] was a bigger football school but nowhere near Princeton academically.
According to an analysis based on critical race theory called Theorizing on the Stereotyping of Black Male Student-Athletes, a "legacy of racial disparities and discriminatory policies and practices in the U.S. and a combination of social, economical, cultural, educational, and psychological factors influence Black student-athletes."[1] For example, individuals will tend to attribute White athletes' successes to superior strategy and skill, whereas Black athletes are often believed to be more physically capable but lacking in intellect. In addition, as in this example, it is often assumed that athletics and being an athlete are more important to a Black player than academics.

'You don't want to be like that, you want to be around your boys and I don't think you'd like it if you went to Princeton.'
In this interview, the White coach believes the football player wants to be around "his boys" rather than White or socioeconomically-privileged students. Despite his incorrect assumptions about this particular institution, the coach's judgement is based on the difficulties that minority students continue to face in predominantly White institutions. In a dissertation about Black college female student-athletes, Noël Suzanne Harmon argues that a lack of diversity in campus culture "can be problematic for students of color because these cultures can convey messages of unimportance, devaluation, and exclusion to those students."[2] Surveys demonstrate that, unlike White students, minority students often feel the pressure of representing their racial group. Likewise, racially marginalized college students at predominantly White institutions tend to rank their schools as less tolerant of diversity than their White counterparts.

1 https://cnr.ncsu.edu/wp-content/uploads/2014/04/StereotypingAthletes.pdf
2 http://ir.uiowa.edu/cgi/viewcontent.cgi?article=1561&context=etd

> **"** I'm from Viet-nam. I came here in '75 as a refugee. I was in the Air Force, fixing the airplanes, the fuel tanks, the machines. [In the U.S.], I worked by myself. I worked, and I moved on. Now it's over with, so I'm fine. **"**

I'm from Vietnam. I came here in '75 as a refugee.
The Vietnam War was a conflict in which the Communist government of North Vietnam fought against South Vietnam and the United States, among other allies. An estimated 2 million civilians died during the war.[1] The end of the Vietnam War in 1975 resulted in a large volume of Vietnamese migration to the United States, many of them refugees. Previously a small immigrant population, the number of Vietnamese roughly doubled every decade between 1980 and 2000, increasing by 26% in the 2000s. As of 2014, the sixth largest immigrant group in the United States is the Vietnamese (after those born in Mexico, India, China, the Philippines, and El Salvador).[2]

1 https://www.britannica.com/event/Vietnam-War
2http://www.migrationpolicy.org/article/vietnamese-immigrants-united-states

CHOOS

Graphic Credit: Barry Deutsch, leftycartoons.com

Although we should be celebrating all humanity all year round, take this month especially to recognize the central role of African Americans in U.S. history. This is a month to embrace the country's rich history and share the stories that deserve to be heard. Join the tradition and embrace all cultures alike by taking the opportunity to learn the positive contributions made to our diverse society.

Read more:
http://www.nbcnews.com/news/nbcblk/black-history-month-2016-your-guide-events-around-country-n508466

CURRENT EVENT

February 2016

BLACK HISTORY MONTH

"Wait... You're Black?"

by Zandra Campbell

"So, like, I don't understand your hair."

These were among the first words my blonde, straight-haired fellow advisee ever said to me.

"What do you mean, you don't understand my hair?" was my perplexed response.

"Well, why doesn't it look like mine?"

Shocked and confused, I responded, "Because I'm Black...?"

Even more shocking than the question was her reaction to my response. "Haha, no really, why?"

I realized that not only did she have no clue about my ethnicity, she would not even believe me when I corrected her misconception. Events similar to this occur frequently. Almost everyday, I hear the stunned, "wait, you're Black?" Although I am half-Black, people perceive me as White, leaving me with confusion about my identity.

My dad immigrated to America from Jamaica with his Black parents at nine-years old. Though light-skinned, as Jamaicans tend to be, they are all definitely Black. I have no doubt in my mind about my "Blackness." Unfortunately, not everyone at this school sees that. For example, last night, I got parietals in upper, and as we sat on a bean bag chair on the floor, someone walking past saw my ankle through the trashcan-sized crack in the doorway and said, "oh, so-and-so is getting parietals with a White girl?" This comment did not surprise me at all, but it proved that people recognized me as so White that, even just by seeing my ankle, they labeled my race. Not only do students not recognize my race, they tend to suspect me of lying when I inform them of my heritage. A girl once approached me at lunch and told me that someone had told her about my Black father, but she "totally didn't fall for it," and I just sat there, unsure of what to say. How do you tell someone that she did not fall for the truth?

If people only see me as White and do not believe me when I educate them on my true race, I must benefit from white privilege as much as any pure Caucasian. I constantly grapple with my identity between the White person everyone sees me as and I the biracial person I see myself as. On one hand, I do get white privilege. People do not stop me on the street and hand me money as they do my father, people do not refer to me as the "n-word." I certainly do not get excluded for certain opportunities because of the color of my skin. I do not share experiences of racism with my Black peers and family members. If I lived in the 1950s, I could have passed for White. Not being Black has many societal benefits, so it sometimes seems selfish and almost condescending to demand my biracial identity be acknowledged. Society gives me white privilege, so can I really ask to be included in the experiences of a less-privileged group? I do not feel I can use the "n-word" as my Black-appearing friends do because I do not experience racism. When I join in with my Black friends picking on my White friends for the paleness of their skin or their intolerance for spice, I feel slightly like an imposter—I definitely appear whiter than several of them. My white privilege makes me feel as though I cannot truly belong to the Black community.

On the flip side, I also frequently feel that I am not Black enough to feel uncomfortable with racism. For example, a blonde, White friend of mine will rap along to certain songs, and should she encounter the "n-word," she sings it right along with the song. Our friends who are "Blacker" than I am condone her behavior, and although I feel uncomfortable with it, I also feel that I can not say anything since racism really does not affect me.

On the other hand, I identify with my Black heritage. In my youth, my dad drilled my "biracial-ness" into me, and I have never been able to see myself as being completely White. My household recognizes Jamaican traditions, celebrating holidays that my dad celebrated as a child and eating typical Jamaican food. I have witnessed my dad struggling with racism; once, a man handed him a dollar, confusing him for a homeless man, despite his classy attire. In my middle school class, there were only two other Black kids, so my peers recognized my Blackness. When I came to Lawrenceville School and everyone declared my "Whiteness" for me, I did not know how to respond. Although I do experience white privilege, I do not appreciate my peers erasing my identity.

> "Society gives me **white privilege,** so **can I really ask to be included in the experiences of a less-privileged group?"**

> "I exclude myself from the White community because I identify as Black, but my Black peers exclude me from their community because I do not look Black, **leaving me with no sense of racial community."**

My Black peers illegitimizing my Black identity hurts the most. Most of them notice that I am half black and still actively choose to ignore it. My Black friends constantly tell me, "you're not fifty-percent Black. You must be twenty-five percent. There's definitely some more White in there." Although they do tend to be the ones who stand up for me the most when White students question my Black identity, they, too, discount me from their community because I am far too light-skinned for them. I exclude myself from the White community because I identify as Black, but my Black peers exclude me from their community because I do not look Black, leaving me with no sense of racial community.

Not having a community to turn to singles me out from every other student at this school. I am not the sole biracial student, but no one else's identity gets questioned as frequently as mine does, and I find it incredibly harmful to my mental health. So to all the people who have ever questioned by black identity: piss off.

Winners on Top

Anonymous

Whether it be a running race or a biking race, there is a finish line. For a brief moment in time, any number of people compete to get that revered first prize. Yet, the human race has been occurring for centuries, a competition in which humans have split into factions by race and attempted to 'win' first place as the most superior. As soon as a single race assumes some supremacy over others, it highlights it through suppressing others.

The most prime example lies within the very own history of the United States of America. Once the White, European migrants settled in the "New Land," they celebrated their discovery and claimed the land as theirs. The country built by these White migrants quickly acquired considerable amounts of land through imperialism and fully exercised its own authority among the "backward" island natives.

In the decades following colonization, the primarily economic gain to be sought from African Americans developed into slavery. Financially, the White settlers were a success—but they only did it through the unfair and oftentimes brutal domination of "lesser" races and ethnicities. But not even all Whites were accepted: they retained animosity toward Irish settlers—'a different kind of White.'

America then put somewhat of an end to its imperialistic days and focused on the people standing on its soil. The Native Americans were still treated as sub-humans. African Americans continued facing pressure, because with slavery gone, blatant segregation at any public or private institution was at an all-time high.

When immigration from below started to gain popularity, the Latinx coming in were certainly unwelcomed and denied rights, too. Furthermore, right through World War II, America had prided itself with degrading Japanese, sending one after another to concentration camps (similar to what America's opponent, Germany, was doing with concentration camps).

Throughout our history, one phase of racism just melted into another. Now, in the 2000s, all previous forms of racism have become diluted. But, unfortunately, it has come back in a stronger form with a new minority target: Muslims—literally, the "submitters to peace."

Currently, America is stuck in yet another phase, and in some time racism will pinpoint another group and go after them for a while. This cycle may never end, because as soon as one race (currently White people) loses power (however it is measured), another race will gain it immediately and repeat the same racism.

Humans, psychologically, have this desire and passion to be at the top, and the same carries through to a population of people who have a common tie by apperance. So, that desire to be the first-place winner in a race is inherent in human nature. However, despite all the efforts to be "Number One," is all the hassle really worth it when God sees us all as equal?

Graphic Credit: Ayesha Qureshi

The British had controlled Nigeria... and it was a remnant of that.
Racism is the psychology of imperialism. Racism is not only a by-product of an empire but an intrinsic part of it. When an empire conquers another group, racism emerges as a defensive ideology between the conquered and the conquerors, who seek to defend their ruling power. This ideological racism eventually roots itself into systematic racism which remains even after the conqueror leaves.[1] This can be seen in the Indian racial caste system and South African apartheid era, among other examples.

Except it was reverse discrimination. Despite being a minority, the interviewees were afforded similar privileges and deference as was shown to British colonizers, a result of white privilege rather than "reverse racism."

1 http://www.tandfonline.com/doi/abs/10.1080/10848779808
579862?journalCode=cele20#.VdKEc-vMG48

"Back when I was part of the army, I was stationed in Georgia. I got leave to go back to Wisconsin, and I had never been to the South before. I was around 19, and there was segregation: fountains that were for Blacks and fountains that were for Whites. When I walked into the railroad station, I had this funny feeling that everyone was looking at me. It dawned on me that I had gone into the wrong door and was in the section for Blacks. It was like I had done something terribly wrong. I got on the earliest train I could, and it moved very, very slow... it was not comfortable at all. I saw things I would never have seen. I thought it would be wonderful, seeing the backwoods all the way across, but I saw a lot of racism. On the train, there wasn't any White person except me. It's a different world [now]; you see remnants, but it's much better... on the surface."

"We stayed in Nigeria for a couple years, and the discrimination was similar to the South. Except it was reverse discrimination. When we went to the post office, everyone would move out of the way so I could get my stamp. I didn't want to cut the line. The British had controlled Nigeria for many years, and it was a remnant of that. That was how the British expected to be treated. Now it's changed."

"Those two years were interesting. We were treated very well. But we were a very small minority there. It was eye-opening, because we grew up in Wisconsin where everyone was White. [In Nigeria], we did not have the problems that minorities often do have, realizing that there weren't people that looked like us, which is very superficial... but there's that feeling of being different, of being a minority."

❝ How can you doubt somebody just based on their colors? That just pretty much shows that you got no class. You got to learn how to appreciate anybody. Doesn't matter what their race or color is. But anyway, people are just people. I can't change somebody, they got to change themselves. **❞**

Interview by CHOOSE Chapter @ Penn State Founder Papakojo Kuranchie

❝ My father came here twenty years ago. Now, he has a couple homes, and he has three or four businesses—yeah, he's pretty much living the American dream.

I mean, it was tough, it was really tough. I mean a lot of hard work, but he made it. He worked so much for his family, and now he's okay. [My parents] always tell me about the hard work. That's what we all come here for.

When he first walked in [the U.S], when he first walked out of the airport, he spoke only Spanish... then he learned English. Not too bad, not too good. And he made it, he's speaks really well to me now. **❞**

ECONOMIC

Now, he has a couple homes, and he has three or four businesses—yeah, he's pretty much living the American dream.

Latin-American immigration from Central America, Mexico, South America, and islands in the Caribbean has become a popular social issue explored by many media outlets in the United States. Extreme poverty, abusive governments, and lack of fair employment are often push factors that lead to migration to the United States; most immigrants generally aim to make better lives for themselves and their families.[1] The American dream, characterized by success regardless of status, attracts many immigrants. The United States has the highest total number of immigrants, receiving 19% of world immigration.[2]

1 http://digitalcommons.liberty.edu/cgi/viewcontent.cgi?article=1238&context=honors
2 http://www.telegraph.co.uk/news/worldnews/middleeast/12111108/Mapped-Which-country-has-the-most-immigrants.html

" We provide opportunities for year long fellowships [for] service-minded people, people who want to be in an immersive work experience. We have 21 posts in Asia. You hear it in the media, and we hear a lot of hate right now, in the news, about the elections, etc... It's so important for people to have that experience to create friendships with people from different cultures. We're striving to be as diverse as possible among our fellows. [For them], it's not only important on a personal level; people are gonna have such wonderful opportunities after this because so many companies see the value in people learning to adapt to a different environment and being culturally competent. There's fellows that come in with that can-do American attitude and then [they go] to another place where they have to depend on other people. It's important for [them] to ask questions, to listen, to understand... humility is really important in that way.

People of color definitely have a much different experience going to Asia. In terms of the expectations people have of them, for a Chinese-American to go to China, they're not as much of a novelty compared to their Caucasian co-fellows ... but they're more trusted; they are seen as having similar values. [We want to make] them conscious of their own identity here and how that's gonna be perceived going there. Obviously everyone is a multidimensional person; everyone has different aspects of their identity, but when you go to a different culture people are gonna see you in a more one-dimensional way. And a lot of our fellows who are African-American—there's a whole different dynamic. They're very exoticized—hair, skin—people take pictures with them, people associate them with being from Africa. Obviously they're not. Like [the recent laundry detergent commercial], that's pretty ridiculous. Many people in China have probably never met a Black person. Only what they see in the media, in the news. **"**

You hear it in the media, and we hear a lot of hate right now, in the news, about the elections, etc...

In the past few years, the shooting of Trayvon Martin in Sanford, Florida and numerous other instances of police brutality toward Black males have reignited a national conversation about race. A Huffington Post survey found that 37% of Americans think that the media has overreacted about misconduct concerning law enforcement, 31% believe it has given the issue the appropriate amount of attention, and 20% desire more coverage. However, 43%, 29% and 16% of White Americans fall in these categories, respectively, contrasted by 8%, 35% and 46% of Black Americans.[1]

People are gonna have such wonderful opportunities after this because so many companies see the value in people learning to adapt to a different environment and being culturally competent.

In an increasingly globalized world, a Harvard Business Review article calls for the necessity of adaptability, discussing how "those that thrive are quick to read and act on signals of change, "can experiment rapidly, frequently, and economically," and "have built up skills in managing complex multistakeholder systems in an increasingly interconnected world."[2] In addition, according to language expert Ryan McMunn in a US News article, learning a second language can increase wages 10-15% and provide opportunities to develop relationships and conduct business internationally.[3]

1 http://www.huffingtonpost.com/entry/media-police-poll_n_7259942; 2 https://hbr.org/2011/07/adaptability-the-new-competitive-advantage; 3 http://www.usnews.com/opinion/blogs/economic-intelligence/2014/01/29/the-business-benefits-of-learning-a-foreign-language; 4 http://www.chicagotribune.com/lifestyles/travel/ct-talk-glanton-china-blacks-20141226-story.html; 5 http://www.blackpast.org/perspectives/africans-and-african-americans-china-long-history-troubled-present-and-promising-future; 6 https://www.americanimmigrationcouncil.org/research/african-immigrants-america-demographic-overview; 7 http://www.manhattan-institute.org/html/why-im-black-not-african-american-0153.html; 8 https://www.psychologytoday.com/blog/black-womens-health-and-happiness/201110/black-american-or-african-american; 9 http://www.cnn.com/2016/06/02/opinions/china-racist-detergent-ad-opinion-yang/; 10 http://www.worldpublicopinion.org/pipa/pdf/dec08/WPO_UDHR_Dec08_rpt.pdf; 11 http://socialsciences.people.hawaii.edu/publications_lib/dalisay.howard.pdf

CHOOS

They're very exoticized—hair, skin—people take pictures with them, people associate them with being from Africa.

Dahleen Glanton, a Black columnist for the Chicago Tribune, wrote that she and her family were seen as a novelty in certain parts of China, surrounded by Chinese residents interested by their skin color and hair and requesting to take a few photographs. According to Glanton, "in a country where television and the news media are owned by the Communist government, it's not every day that residents get to see people from other parts of the world."[4]

However, in recent years, economic and educational opportunities in China have increased contact between the Chinese and Africans or African Americans.[5]

Obviously they're not.

According to the American Immigration Council, from 2000 to 2010 the amount of African Americans nearly doubled from 881,300 to 1,606,914, while African immigrants were 4% of the foreign-born population in 2010.

However, among African immigrants, it is important to recognize that under three-quarters are black, and approximately one-fifth are White.[6] According to Los Angeles Times writer John McWhorter, the identity "Black" is preferred over "African-American" because African-American "sets us apart from the mainstream... carries an air of standing protest, a reminder that our ancestors were brought here against their will, that their descendants were treated like animals for centuries, and that we have come a long way since then."[7]

According to a 2009 Barna Research survey, 78% of the Black American population agrees.[8]

INTER-NATIONAL

Like [the detergent commercial], that's pretty ridiculous.

In May 2016, an advertisement released by a Chinese laundry detergent company depicted the transformation of a mark-covered Black man into a clean Chinese man. While many Western media sources labeled the video "the most racist ad ever," according to former NBCUniversal Chief Diversity Officer Paula Madison, it is an example of "class-based skin-color bias" and "shadeism" rather than racism, stemming from ignorance rather than prejudice.[9] In a 2008 World Public Opinion survey, 90% of the Chinese population considered racial equality important, second only to Mexico (94%) and in comparison to 79% of the United States population.[10] In addition, a Washington State University and Towson University study found that negative portrayals and stereotypes of African Americans were more common in U.S.-based rather than Chinese media, while Chinese high school students had a more positive perception of African Americans than Americans in general.[11]

CURRENT EVENT

originally a CHOOSE Facebook post
graphic credit: TIME

March 16th, 2016

On February 29th, the first Black principal dancer at the American Ballet Theater, Misty Copeland, met with President Obama, the first African-American President, to discuss empowering oneself through fighting racial discrimination.

Copeland reflects: "I didn't want to pancake my skin a lighter color to fit into the ballet. I wanted to be myself,' she said. 'I didn't want to have to wear makeup that made my nose look thinner.'"

New York Times —Misty Copeland

Read more: http://time.com/obama-and-copeland/?xid=newsletter-brief

"It's Great to See Such Diverse Job Applicants"

Graphic Credit: Barry Deutsch, leftycartoons.com

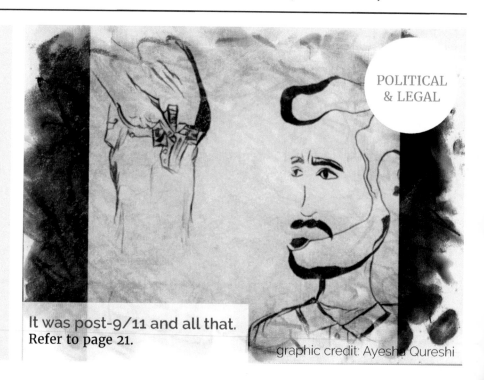

"One time I was [in] Pennsylvania, right? And I walk into a store, there was a police officer. As I walk in he grabs his gun and I was like, "Oh?"

I had a beard. It was post-9/11 and all that, but he grabbed his gun, which took me by surprise. That's why I'm sure racism is a prevailing thing entrenched in everything.

It was post-9/11 and all that.
Refer to page 21.

graphic credit: Ayesha Qureshi

POLITICAL & LEGAL

CHOOS

IDENTITY & FAMILIAL

People may get better with succeeding generations, right? According to a 2013 survey, 45% of Americans believe that a lot has already been accomplished toward racial equality. Approximately 8 in every 10 Americans believe that further progress needs to be made.[1]

Whether it's Indian society looking at us or American society looking at us. Bridging two societies, this interviewee struggles with her biracial identity. Biracial identity has become more fluid since the rejection of a "one drop rule," in which any African ancestry automatically categorizes an individual as being Black. This experience creates a unique conflict during one's growth and development. According to Poston's Biracial Identity Development Model, the stages include personal identity, choice of group categorization, enmeshment/denial, appreciation, and integration—emphasizing pressure to identify as one racial or ethnic group while also appreciating multiple identities.[2]

Racial stereotyping can happen on both sides of the fence there.
While stereotyping and bias can be a "two-way street," it is important to recognize that racism—implying the stereotyping or bias has the power to affect those involved—is not.

" I grew up on the borderline of the South, so I certainly saw some instances where certain people were not welcome. I was never taught that way myself, which was great; I applaud my parents for being that way, but I've definitely seen some things there along those lines. I think that even this generation's differences between people may get better with succeeding generations, right? But I think we've made a lot of strides, I really do. I think with each new generation, we definitely see racism as less of a threat. Her mother happens to be of Indian descent and I think there might've been times, certainly, [when] even different parts of society, whether it's Indian society looking at us or American society looking at us, [will] sometimes see us in different ways too. So I think that racial stereotyping can happen on both sides of the fence there. "

1 http://www.pewsocialtrends.org/2013/08/22/chapter-1-i-have-a-dream-50-years-later/#treatment-of-Blacks-by-the-courts-police-seen-as-less-fair
2 http://www.ncbi.nlm.nih.gov/pmc/articles/PMC2695719/

"Fellow-citizens; above your national, tumultuous joy, I hear the mournful wail of millions! whose chains, heavy and grievous yesterday, are, to-day, rendered more intolerable by the jubilee shouts that reach them. If I do forget, if I do not faithfully remember those bleeding children of sorrow this day, "may my right hand forget her cunning, and may my tongue cleave to the roof of my mouth!" To forget them, to pass lightly over their wrongs, and to chime in with the popular theme, would be treason most scandalous and shocking, and would make me a reproach before God and the world. My subject, then fellow-citizens, is AMERICAN SLAVERY. I shall see, this day, and its popular characteristics, from the slave's point of view. Standing, there, identified with the American bondman, making his wrongs mine, I do not hesitate to declare, with all my soul, that the character and conduct of this nation never looked blacker to me than on this 4th of July! Whether we turn to the declarations of the past, or to the professions of the present, the conduct of the nation seems equally hideous and revolting. America is false to the past, false to the present, and solemnly binds herself to be false to the future. Standing with God and the crushed and bleeding slave on this occasion, I will, in the name of humanity which is outraged, in the name of liberty which is fettered, in the name of the constitution and the Bible, which are disregarded and trampled upon, dare to call in question and to denounce, with all the emphasis I can command, everything that serves to perpetuate slavery—the great sin and shame of America! "I will not equivocate; I will not excuse;" I will use the severest language I can command; and yet not one word shall escape me that any man, whose judgment is not blinded by prejudice, or who is not at heart a slaveholder, shall not confess to be right and just."

—Frederick Douglass

Tick, Tick, Tick: A Timeless Fight for Freedom
by Winona Guo

"We will win our freedom because the sacred heritage of our nation and the eternal will of God are embodied in our echoing demands."
—**Dr. Martin Luther King, Jr., Letter from a Birmingham Jail**

The grandfather clock behind me ticks slowly but steadily—tick, tick, tick, never stopping. It's a staring contest between my mind and the Google Doc, both desperately blank. Suddenly, my mental search for inspiration is sabotaged by the ding of a new e-mail.

"It's not about guilt or blame," writes Roberto Schiraldi, a member of the local race advocacy organization Not in Our Town, in an essay about the need for dialogue and action. "It's about acknowledging and taking responsibility to work for change... we need to be change advocates."

My eyes are jolted into sharp focus. Race? The need for change... *still?*

Schiraldi's words are small on my screen, but echo the widespread efforts of mighty advocates nationwide in a movement towards racial justice. From #oscarssowhite to Peter Liang's conviction to Macklemore's White Privilege II, current national debate easily parallels historical American movements, together illuminating the timely and timeless issue of fundamental human rights.

In 1963, Dr. Martin Luther King Jr. scribbled his optimistic vision of peace, brotherhood, truth, and justice on newspaper margins. By doing so, he left behind hope that one day, his "we," oppressed African-Americans unfairly stripped of equality, "will win," through persistent and peaceful protest, the "freedom" that America has promised.

King justifies both direct action toward his vision and his optimism toward its fulfillment through "the sacred heritage of our nation and the eternal will of God," two forces "embodied in [his movement's] echoing demands" and inseparable from his mission. The former alludes to the very creation of our nation, of our full heritage—inherited values, traditions, and culture—and of a dedication to and fight for the civil rights of the Black man that began before American slavery.

> **❝** ... current national debate easily parallels historical American movements, together illuminating the timely and timeless issue of fundamental human rights."

King's words transport me even further backwards in history; more than a century earlier, in his speech "What to the Slave is the Fourth of July," Frederick Douglass compares the slave's necessity for revolution in the face of oppression to that of the founding fathers of the nation. Even while "the eye of the reformer is met with angry flashes, portending disastrous times," Douglass expresses hope "at the thought that America is young" and questions whether one may "not hope that high lessons of wisdom, of justice and of truth, will yet give direction to her destiny." Like King, his vision is shaped by the the promise of sacred moral values, polluted and ripped apart by men who "glory in the deeds of [America's] fathers" and "the saving principles" of the Declaration of Independence, yet ironically refuse to "to side with the right, against the wrong ... with the oppressed against the oppressor." Like King, he knows that the national values we avowed to had been neglected or even forgotten but could still be recovered with change and action to avoid becoming a "sad tale of departed glory."

These values, as King justifies in his latter point, are rooted in the higher law of the Bible. Here, King goes back to Henry David Thoreau's assurance in *On Civil Disobedience* that "it is enough if [the abolitionists] have God on their side," and in Walden that "our whole life is startlingly moral ... goodness is the only instrument that never fails." King, an advocate of many of Thoreau's ideas, brings this "instrument" a step further as an embodiment of his action, finding it God's will for it to be used, obtained, and thus guaranteed. For King, goodness and morality are not options, but the ultimate solution. And, according to Douglass, it is rooted in the founding of the nation, when "justice, liberty, humanity were 'final,'"— again supporting King's commitment to freedom.

Now, as I peruse Schiraldi's appeal to the responsibility of we, the community, I am reminded that the fight for these ideals centers around our movement and partnership. As I pore over King's promise of success, I am reminded that he speaks for we, not I, and that his demands cannot echo without the tireless fight of many, of people who, as Thoreau preaches, "let [their lives] be a counter friction to stop the machine" of injustice that is our polluted— yet not ruined— society. As I understand the power of the movement, I am reminded of an unending list of allies: Elie Wiesel firmly believing that "there must never be a time when we fail to protest," Mahatma Gandhi that he "[he] shall conquer untruth by truth," Robert F. Kennedy that "each time a man ... strikes out against injustice, he sends forth a tiny ripple of hope, and crossing each other ... those ripples build a current which can sweep down the mightiest walls of oppression and resistance." And,

as the grandfather clock continues to tick, tick, tick, I am reminded that, while I have traced American history back centuries, history is still being made, and the high vision monumental leaders such as King have set still remains unfulfilled. We cannot be satisfied or stagnant; it is our job to carry on his timeless legacy with full and open hearts.

For, so many decades later, as we celebrate King in the movie Selma, we nevertheless end on the lyrics that "movement is a rhythm to us/freedom is like religion to us/justice is juxtaposition in us ... the war is not over/ victory isn't won/ and we'll fight on to the finish/then when it's all done ... we'll cry glory."

We'll push forward, we'll keep ticking, we'll never stop—until the day we, together, will let freedom ring.

"and tick tick tick ...

EDUCA-
TIONAL

He automatically thought the Hispanic girl was asking for help from the White girl, but it was actually the other way around. Racial stereotypes and prejudice work hand-in-hand. Disregarding the dimensionality of members of one race and placing them into constrained boxes can cause harmful psychological effects. By abiding to the stereotype of the "uneducated Hispanic," this substitute teacher becomes blind to a reality in which the number of Hispanics between 18 to 24 years of age and enrolled in a two-or four-year college has more than tripled since 1993.[1]

1 http://nces.ed.gov/pubs95/95769.pdf

" In science today, my [subsitute teacher] caught two girls talking to one another. He automatically thought the Hispanic girl was asking for help from the White girl, but it was actually the other way around. "

INTER-
NATIONAL

" I'm from China, and there are no races—we call them minorities. We have 56 minorities; different minorities have different languages and cultures and live in different areas in China. A lot of people from other countries and cultures come to America because America has all these cultures together. Sometimes, people from other cultures don't understand me. Like, we don't expect you to know exactly what [our] culture or country is, but we want respect. If [I am not] familiar with something, you know the difference comes from the culture or country. It's not because I'm uneducated, just unfamiliar. "

We have 56 minorities. The Han ethnic group accounts for approximately 91.6% of China's population. 55 other ethnic groups—including the Mongolians, Tibetans, and Uyghurs—speak over 80 languages.[1]

1 https://www.case.edu/affil/tibet/moreTibetInfo/documents/Bilingual4.pdf

"I think it's great that they are adding more people of different races and cultures into the casts of [shows]. For instance, the new Annie. Disney princesses, for example, are portrayed as White and thin. I think that by seeing someone who looks like them, minority children can feel like princesses themselves. They wouldn't want to look into a mirror and want to be blonde, when they're not."

Disney princesses, for example, are portrayed as White and thin.

Disney princesses, starting in the 1950s, are predominantly White characters. They not only enforce the ideology of White supremacy, but they also affect the way girls treat their cultural background and racial group. If young girls do not see reflections of themselves in Disney princess films, or any other mass-cultural platform, they can "become disillusioned with their self-image and cultural heritage," and may assume that their background is not valued by society.[1]

1 http://dialogues.rutgers.edu/all-journals/volume-9/148-fairytale-dreams-disney-princesses-effect-on-young-girls-self-images/file

CURRENT EVENT originally a CHOOSE Facebook post **April 17th, 2016**
photo credit: Pixabay

"Chicago remains one of the most segregated cities in America, according to new studies by the Chicago Urban League and researchers at American University. But the city's segregation is not just the legacy of a racist past: Chicago-area governments continue to actively pursue policies that were originally intended to prevent racial integration."

Read more:
https://www.illinoispolicy.org/chicago-remains-a-segregated-city-by-race-and-income-and-government-deserves-much-of-the-blame/

Treniya Bronaugh, Cornell High School Class of 2017, discusses her search for family history, as well as the intersectionality between race, religion, gender, and class.

" I am an African-American woman, and I love it, I love it, I love it. I wouldn't want to be any other race. When I was younger, I might've been like, 'Oh my god, I'm a Black girl, I have dark skin, my hair is curly and it's nappy, and all these pretty White girls, oh my goodness,' but now I'm older and just like, 'You know, I'm bomb.' I couldn't imagine being any other color. And now there are all these Black women on TV and on commercials, and it makes me confident. I love being Black. I just love everything—culture-wise, how we walk, talk, dress, joke—I just love it.

I have a very close family, for the most part. My mom's side is closest, and my dad's side is more distant, but I've been working on them. My sisters used to be very distant; sometimes, I wouldn't see them for months at a time. I would just see them on the street and be like, 'Hey, sister," but now we're super close, almost inseparable. My two sisters who were arch-enemies for the longest time are now the closest of us all. It's amazing. Amen. My family is everything to me. Everything. Like, who am I without my family, you know?

And my religion, my religion is everything. If there was one word to describe me, I would say that I am a

> " If there was **one word** to describe me, I would say that I am a **Christian.**"

Christian. That's just who I am. I'm a Christian before I'm Black, I'm a Christian before I'm a woman. Because I'm a super religious person, I believe in God, and that everything I am is because I'm a Christian.

***

I feel like Black people as a whole wouldn't be who we are today without the struggle, you know? There's that cliché line: what doesn't kill you makes you stronger. You can kinda take that in the African-American community and say that with the oppression and hatred from other races, we have no choice but to fall on one another, because we have no one else.

I've always been obsessed with African-American history. Sometimes I feel like in my previous life, I was fighting in the Civil Rights Movement. Honestly. It's just something about it; I don't know how they found the strength to receive beatings, and be abused, and just stick with it. They just kept faith, marched peacefully without violence. It just worked, somehow. It's just so amazing and makes me so proud to be African-American. I'm so proud. It's a good feeling, to know that my ancestors, my grandpa and my grandma—they just fought for us.

But, sometimes we take it for granted today. We use the n-word so loosely, and they fought for it to stop. Black men today talk bad about Black women—like back then, Black men were fighting for Black women, and now they are fighting Black women. It makes me feel like we're going backwards, but we don't have to go backwards. It's like we're making ourselves go backwards.

Rappers, in music—it's just disgusting the way they talk about women. And it's not just Black women, it's women in general. There's this rapper named Kodak Black, who made a line like, "Where them yellow bones, I don't want no black b****." The Cavaliers player, Kyrie Irving, after they won the title, had a boat party that was a no-Black girl party. He had all White girls. But it's like, 'You're Black, your mom's Black, your sister's Black.'

And my cousins will come to me and say, 'Where your White friends at? Black girls are this, Black girls are that,' and it's just like, 'Really?' The whole team light skin, team dark skin thing—light skin is always better, dark skin always takes the backseat. It's like self-inflicted hate. Maybe it's because they hate themselves and the way they look; they can't love anybody that looks like them.

> " ... with the oppression and hatred from other races, **we have no choice but to fall on one another,** *because we have no one else."*

Black-on-Black crime is every racist White man's dream, because they don't have to do the work—their work is being done. I read online from the Ku Klux Klan that it's the Black population doing them a favor. The hate, I don't understand it. I think it's the hate for themselves that radiates to people who look like them. I feel like Black-on-Black crime goes back to slavery; it's embodied in the psyche of Black men. Back in slavery, they used to make it a sport for Black men to fight to death. White men would just be around with their beards and their hats, and watch two Black men fight to death. And [the Black men] had to, they didn't have a choice.

But I feel like a lot of attention comes on Black-on-Black crime. What's the difference between Black-on-Black and White-on-White crime? Black people kill each other every day, White people kill each other every day, why is it only a big deal for Black-on-Black crime, why is it so looked down upon?

Anyways, the struggle back then was more blatant, there was segregation with places that were 'Whites only.' It's not like that anymore, but that doesn't mean it's any bet-

> " **Black-on-Black crime** is every racist White man's dream, because they don't have to do the work—their work is being done."

ter, it's more of a systematic thing, with the whole mass incarceration and War on Drugs and how they put trash in impoverished Black neighborhoods to keep them down. You have to think and meditate on it—it's not like 'you're this, you're that.'

With the whole Ferguson thing, it was like, 'These thugs are rioting,' but weeks before with those White teenagers for some sports game, the headline was like, "White teens celebrate after something something."

Are you kidding? They literally set things to fire over something so simple, because a team won or lost or whatever, when these Black teens are just crying out for help. I don't agree with violence, but what else can they do? It was just a burst of anger, and Ferguson wasn't the first time. Why they gotta be thugs? They're angry, they're sad. It's so horrible, even with Black women. Say I'm in public with my mom. My brother does something wrong, my mother yells at him. The reaction will be that's she's ratchet, and loud, and this and that. But if a White woman did it, it'd be like, 'That's good parenting skills.'

My godmother told me to address myself as T. Bronaugh, not Niya or Treniya. I had to make a whole new email. She's a Black woman doing very well in DC, and knew that stereotypes would be laid against me. She didn't want them to know I was a Black woman on the spot. And her name is Jillian, so she didn't really have that problem, because when you hear her name, you think of a White woman. Like when she gets an interview or something, they'll be like, 'Oh, I thought you were Jillian, but you're actually Jillian.'

I feel like now people think names like Shaniqua and Laquisha have to be ratchet, that the name makes them ratchet. It's literally just the name, just letters pushed together. But because it's an average Black woman's name, it has to be ratchet. When my sisters were naming their babies, the first thing was they wanted to make sure they could get a job. Which is crazy.

I was kinda going through this thing, trying to figure out who my family is, what my background is. My sister was going through Facebook, and typed in the last name Bronaugh, which isn't a popular last name. All these people came up, these Black people, and we were like, 'Cousins, cousins, cousins.' We all connected where we came from. There was this White guy in particular, something

Bronaugh, and my sister was like, 'Are you our cousin?'

I was thinking no, that's impossible. He was like, 'I'm not sure, but we have mixed people in our family. I don't want you to get offended, but my great-grandfather down the line owned slaves.'

We didn't take offense, because it's not like he was a slave master or anything. But we thought it was interesting, looked in this book his dad kept, and found a slave name that was our great-great-great-great grandmother—Mary Bronaugh, or something. It was weird because it made me feel like this whole time Bronaugh was me, but it's not me. This isn't who I am. This whole time, I feel like my family took on this White man's name by force. Even now, I just want to know what my last name is, what it was supposed to be. If slavery never happened, who would I be? I'd probably look completely different, my hair would be different, where I would live would be different. I'd probably still be in Africa. It kinda made me ashamed, like I don't want this White man's last name. Especially a lot of African-Americans, they

have a lot of White, Westernized, British, English last names. So Africans, Haitians, Jamaicans—they come to America and you can tell because they have ethnic last names. I know that slaves' last names changed, but I guess I just didn't realize that they were passed on after slavery.

A lot of African-Americans, when they think of going to Africa, they think of returning to the motherland, of this beautiful thing, of reuniting with your people. But in South Africa this summer, I realized I'm not like them at all. I felt like I was kind of robbed from experiencing the whole culture. I listen to people who know where they're from, know how people from their culture act, but I'll never get to know that because that was robbed from me when my ancestors were stolen and brought here to America. I just want to know where I come from. But when people asked me to speak Zulu, I couldn't and I felt so American. I hate feeling like that. All these Black people know they're Jamaican, Trinidadian, Nigerian— when people ask me where I'm from, I'm like 'I'm from Pittsburgh.' It sucks, kinda. I don't know what I am. I'm just Black.

Being in Africa, I felt like I was appropriating

> " I listen to people who know where they're from... I'll never get to know that because that was robbed from me when my ancestors were stolen and brought here to America."

> " I'm not just a granddaughter of a slave, I refuse to be like that, to carry that with me."

POETRY

by Treniya Bronaugh

COCOA BROWN QUEEN

Defined by the curl in my hair, the slang in my voice, the
strut in my walk, and the shape of my hips.
Society called and said I wasn't it.
I'm nappy, ignorant, sassy, and fast.
I've become slaved to the fact that the average black wom-
an is nothing but a sexual figure with very little class.
Not much has changed from African American women
being raped after being whipped on slave ships, to African
American women being paid, to twerk for tips.

Black Girl booty and Black Girl breasts do not define me,
because without it I can not be the best?
I can't be like the modest women colored like the clouds I
dream in bed, walking into fancy meetings with shoulders
under her good head.

Pretty Cocoa Girls, twerking for work: Please open your
eyes, and realize; we come from Queens of royalty.
Women who fought, marched, and prayed for the very right
for us to see today.

But are we free? Is the job really done? Or are we still slaves
without the shackles around our new Jays or the chains
around our watch by Michael K?
We're not quite free, but Lord we are destined to be.
We stand alone in a world who has an image of us being
rude and full of attitude.
No matter how hard we try, we'll never be accepted.
Why?

Wipe your eyes little cocoa girl,
Our trials can only make us wise.

Being belittled by the world we live
Sometimes by the very black
men who claim to defend our honor.

To my sisters and future black daughters,
the curl in my hair, the slang in our voice, the strut in our
walk, and the shape of our hips.
Does not define me, WE. But the urge to continue the fight
that Ciecley, Winfrey, Parks, and Gwendolyn battled so one
day a pretty cocoa girl can hang up on society and say:

Not Today!

THEY BEAT AFRICA OUT OF US

"Sawubona Sisi" is what I hear as I
walk down these streets.
Unfortunately, I don't know Zulu,
so I have to open my mouth to
speak:
"I'm sorry sista, I can't understand
your words to repeat"
My upbeat sista suddenly becomes
meek
Her excitement to talk to me de-
pletes.
When I open my mouth, I am
nothing but a privileged sista,
touring the streets.
But sisi please understand, my
grandma and your go-go used to
make beads
They used to sing songs for the
mans, as they danced along the
lands.
Until one day, our history began
A White gentleman captured my
grandma like a lamb.
They burned her with a stamp, and
shipped her to a new land.
The hands she used to bead, was
now used to bleed
On the cotton that she kneads.
The voice that she sung with
Was now used to scream until her
agony was done with.
Her dancing body was now used to
satisfy the needs
Of the men whose future slave
children she would conceive.
They beat our culture out of her.
They beat Africa out of her.
They beat everything she was, and
I could be, out of her.
She was no longer African,
but she for dang sure wasn't
American.
She was nothing but a praying
property of Satan.
Sawubona became Hello
Sisi became Mrs.
Baba and buhti became Masta.
She had nothing left to give to me
That yours gave to you
I am You, You are Me.
I promise, Sisi,
Just with different life fatalities.

African, I'm from that continent, but where? What country am I from? I'm not just a granddaughter of a slave, I refuse to be like that, to carry that with me. A lot of people carry that with them, but you gotta think past that. We come from something, we were something before we became slaves. I come from a queen from a tribe somewhere.

Before, when I thought of Africa I thought of the stereotypical Africa, living with lions and struggling for food. You think of the skinny, skinny Black children crying with flies in their eyes. That's what I thought, but actually Africa is one of the richest continents resource-wise. It's just gorgeous, the tribes, it's just beautiful. I'm in the process of learning more, but Africa isn't just starving, and struggling, and needing.

I don't know whether I want to go back to Africa. I feel out of place. I don't feel that I have no right, but that I'm not them. I feel like I need to know where I come from, before I go back. They erased my identity, they burned documents, they made it rare for us to find out where we came from, what tribe we came from. It's just carried through stories, but if the slave was killed, the story just ended there. Hashtag, who am I?

On Google, I just typed in my family's names, always intrigued by the history. They came from a small town outside Pittsburgh, and there were a lot of Black people in the town, but now it's just White-washed. There were a lot of historical Black landmarks that are now gyms. So I would just Google everything, to a point when I could find my grandma's mom's mom's dad. And that's all I know, as far as it goes. He was Pittsburgh, 1800's. So I'm Pittsburgh, we're all Pittsburgh. I don't know anything else.

My neighborhood is predominantly White, but it's like connected and one. There's no White side and Black side. I think the majority of my school might be mixed, which is a good thing—there's definitely integration. Most of my teachers are White, but all the sports leaders are Black. I did go to a school for two years that was stereotypically White, you know, rich and snobby. I felt so uncomfortable, and moved right out.

I graduate this year, and I want to go to Howard University. It's calling my name. I've been in a predominantly White school all my life, and I want to go to an HBCU—a Historically Black College and University—I want to break out, I want to experience, I want to be around people who look like me, I want to be comfortable for four years of my life. I feel like there's nothing wrong with that, people say it's not gonna prepare me for life. But I feel like I won't have to hold back, they'll instill confidence in me and teach me how to be a Black woman in society. Because a White school can't teach me that, only a Black school. I want to minor in African-American studies, and major in Political Science, and then go to law school after that. It's a lot of school, but I want to be Dr. Bronaugh, you know. It's worth it.

Every Black person knows that being Black is like a family. I could walk into a complete Black stranger's cookout, and they would accept me. I don't know why, but it's just like we're all family. I could walk down a street to a Black person I've never met in my life, and just be like 'hey, sister!' It could be like people you think are brothers, but they're actually strangers. And church, Black churches are unlike a lot of churches. We just put our music and our dances, it's just lit, and especially in HBCUs. The way we talk, we speak, we cook—it's very family-oriented. And that goes back to slavery.

> " ... I want to be around people who look like me, I want to be **comfortable** for four years of my life."

> " But I don't want to say that all Black communities make me comfortable, because there are some in the hood and deep urban cities that don't."

But I don't want to say that all Black communities make me comfortable, because there are some in the hood and deep urban cities that don't. Those with drugs, poverty, and teen pregnancy. It's saddening to see people act like that, and they see me as being privileged because I didn't grow up like that. I always had the clear, pretty skin and the long, long hair when I was younger. It was an insecurity thing, so that made me feel uncomfortable. But at an HCBU, there will be people as motivated as me, people like me. I've never been around people like that.

About the hood and urban cities, I read something about people putting drugs systematically into ghettos and those communities to keep them in poverty and high and in jail. Even marijuana and alcohol. There's this cycle, there's no sense of escape or success. These kids are growing up and seeing their parents do this, do that. They drop out of school because they feel like they're not having a good education, and then they rely on sports, but you can't succeed in sports without an education because you got to keep your grades up. Then they fail from that, so they go to drugs, then go to jail, and then can't go to college, or sports, because they have a felony. The girls feel like they can't go to school—they get pregnant because they're insecure,

when someone shows them attention they think they love them, but no, they just want to get with them because they're cute and have hips on them. So he gets her pregnant, and now that's a cycle. And because you were damaged, your kid is going to be damaged, and that's a cycle. It's just all a cycle. A lot of people think Black people sell drugs just to do it, but to justify it, they just need money. They need bread, diapers, formula for their kids.

The majority of Black people aren't rich, but when you think of a Black person you automatically think of them as poor. Going back to slavery, there's a competition, when the one rich person in the Black community feels like they won't help the Black community because they can do better, or the poor community looks that them like they're better than them. So that provides mistrust. Another thing, if a Black person makes it rich, the rich Black family won't want to go back to where they once were, they often don't want to give it away—it's a mental thing. Which is understandable, but help your people, you know?

***

People ask me, 'Why do you love Jesus so much?' Why wouldn't I, you know?

> ❝I used to think White people were the Devil, I thought they were sent from Satan to kill people.❞

You can't really talk about it with someone who doesn't know, because it's kinda just like you talking to them. There's been so many incidents in my life where everything was supposed to go wrong, but didn't as soon as I prayed about it. When I was one, maybe approaching two, I would randomly start breathing in the middle of the night, my face would get purple and I would almost die. My parents would take shifts at night to puff air into my breath. They took tests that my White blood cells were down, and I was diagnosed with leukemia. They assigned me to do a spinal tap and my mom just went to church and took me to the altar. My pastor called everyone up to pray, and after when I went to the doctors office, they found my White blood cells tripled. That's just impossible, that's not a coincidence—they called me a miracle baby. I've never had a health issue after that. My mom prayed and it worked. There's just been so many instances. People have said I'm so angelic, that I have such an anointing on my life. I've just always had such a close relationship with God, I can't ever remember not knowing who he was. I just feel like he's sitting right next to me. It's like he's my imaginary friend. I remember walking to school at six or seven, th... Jesus, don't let me trip. I would pray to have a better relationship with my sisters, and now we're inseparable. He's just dope. God is my best friend. I definitely don't force my religion on anybody, but I feel like if I just stay true to who I am, people who want to find God will just find Him and come to me and ask me questions because they know I'm a super religious person.

There's a difference in religion when it comes to race and religion, with Catholics being mostly White and Baptists mostly Black. I feel like the Black community sings and shouts, while the White community is more traditional and follows the rules. I don't think that's a bad thing, it's more cultural. I was so confused when I read that slave masters were Christian. How are you Christian, and read the Bible, then treat your people that way, and not feel regret? I used to think White people were the Devil, I thought they were sent from Satan to kill people. But when I grew up, I realized not all White people were bad.

God is not White, God is not a race or color. But Jesus is Jewish and Middle Eastern. Angels aren't even White or people—the Bible describes them as ugly. Some even have four arms. Christianity was definitely White-washed. When you see a Black Jesus, people

flip. But why does he have to White then? When you see a Black Jesus, people flip. But why does he have to White then? I think if you see God as White, he's White, and if you see him as Black, he's Black. But he's neither of them. God is the most superior point, so it's just a political statement to say God is Black or White. Because if God is Black, Black people are superior, and if he's White, then White people are superior. You can't put a race on God. So I disagree with the beliefs of [Elijah Muhammad]—and God definitely wouldn't believe in the whole separatist thing either. It's the freaking color of your skin. I never understood that, are you really hating on me because I'm freaking brown? Are you hating on that couch because it's red?

I really don't think there is a solution to racism—it goes back too far. Prayer, maybe. My ten-year-old self was like, 'I'm gonna kill racism, I'm gonna end it.' But there's just too many people in the world, teaching their kids, and teaching their kids. There's just this mental stigma. If it is possible, it's a very low chance. We get to a point where it looks like hope, and then someone gets shot. It's like history repeats itself. I feel like it wouldn't be fair for me to say race relations isn't getting better, because we're no longer in shackles and picking cotton. And then the Civil Rights

Movement, and now the Black Lives Matter movement. I can't define what's worse and what's better, but once one era ends, another one starts. So once the Black Lives Matter ends, there will be something else—another movement, and then another movement, and then another movement, and then the world ends. There will be more movements, and more movements, because people are so stuck on their ways.

My hope is because I believe in God, and I believe anything is possible through Him. But then again, I know humans, and the pattern of history. You can't force people in believe in things. God is the only way. He is our only hope. Even Christians, they're doing things wrong racially. You can't be a freaking racist Christian. It's hatred, it's like a disease. God didn't let oppression happen to Black people, White people did that to Black people. God rescued us; he's been helping us the whole time. Look at where we started and where we came—that was on faith and prayer, that wasn't on our own strength. Without prayer we wouldn't have made it. They were in the cotton fields in agony, praying and singing Negro spirituals. It was peace through the storm. Black people weren't miserable their whole life—they had an inner peace, like joy will come in the morning, and it did come. Freedom will come in the morning... and it did come, kinda. "

April 30th, 2014

In Milwaukee Park, Dontre Hamilton, diagnosed with paranoid schizophrenia, was shot fatally 14 times by Officer Christopher Manney, who was not charged.

July 17th, 2014

Eric Garner, 43, was put in an illegal chokehold by a White police officer for allegedly selling loose cigarettes. He said "I can't breathe" eleven times as he was held down; still, Officer Daniel Pantaleo was not charged.

August 5th, 2014

At a Walmart in Beavercreek, Ohio, John Crawford, 22, was shot for holding a toy BB gun; Officers Sean Williams and David Darkow were not charged.

August 9th, 2014

Officer Darren Wilson shot and killed unarmed eighteen-year-old Michael Brown in Ferguson Missouri, and was not charged.

August 12th, 2014

A 36-year-old and father of five, Dante Parker, was killed by repeatedly being stunned by a taser during police custody in San Bernardino County.

November 13th, 2014

A 37-year-old, Tanisha Anderson, was killed in Cleveland after officers allegedly slammed her head on the pavement while taking her into custody.

November 20th, 2014

A 28-year-old, Akai Gurley, was killed when Asian-American police officer, Peter Liang, shot him while Gurley was walking with his girlfriend in a dimly lit New York City public housing stairwell. The officer was charged with second-degree manslaughter, criminally negligent homicide, second-degree assault, reckless endangerment, and two counts of official misconduct.

November 22nd, 2014

Mistaking a toy gun for a real weapon, Cleveland police shot and killed twelve year-old Tamir Rice, and the officers involved were not charged.

in 2015 alone:

police killed at least 102 **unarmed** Black people

only 10 officers were charged with a crime. Only 2 were convicted

while Black people make up 13% of the U.S. population, 37% of unarmed victims were Black

Blacks ... to be ki... Whites

fewer than 1 in 3 Black people killed by police were suspected of a violent crime and allegedly armed

CHOOS

Yvens Seide
Kajieme Powell
Tyree Woodson
Yvette Smith
McKenzie Cochran
Jordan Baker
Andy Lopez
Miriam Carey
Jonathan Ferrell
Carlos Alcis
Roy Nelson
Miguel Espinal
Tiara Thomas
Bettie Jones
Larry Eugene Jackson, Jr.
Deion Fludd
Kimani Gray
Johnnie Kamahi Warren
Malissa Williams
Timothy Russell
Reynaldo Cuevas
Chavis Carter
Shantel Davis
Keith Childress
Sharmel Edwards
Cornelius Brown
Chandra Weaver
Jamar Clark
Richard Perkins
Kevin Matthews
Leroy Browning
Tamon Robinson
Kris Jackson
Markus Clark
Lorenzo Hayes
Nuwnah Laroche
Walter Scott
Askari Roberts
Brandon Jones
Tiano Meton

A deeper look into
LAW ENFORCEMENT

Ervin Jefferson
Stephen Tooson
Michael Lee Marshall
Kendrec McDade
Lamontez Jones
... and so many more victims of police brutality 2014-2016

July 6th, 2016
32-year-old Philando Castile was shot and killed in Minnesota when he was allegedly being pulled over for a busted tail light. His girlfriend reported that he was reaching for his wallet when the officer fatally shot Castile four times.

July 5th, 2016
37-year-old Alton Sterling was shot and killed outside a convenience store in Louisiana after a witness claimed he was "brandishing a gun."

April 19th, 2015
25-year-old Freddie Gray was arrested in Baltimore for allegedly possessing a switchblade and died of spinal cord injury while in a police van. The officers have been criminally charged.

April 2nd, 2015
44-year-old, Eric Harris was killed in Tulsa, Oklahoma when a reserve deputy officer allegedly mistook his own gun for a Taser; the officer was charged with manslaughter.

March 31st, 2015
32-year-old Phillip White died in Vineland, New Jersey while in police custody, after a violent encounter in which a police dog bit White while he was on the ground. So far, the officers involved have not been charged.

ecember 2nd, 014
istaking a pill bot- e for a real weapon, Phoenix police of- cer shot and killed 4-year-old Rumain risbon and was not arged.

December 30th, 2014
36-year-old Jerame Reid, sitting in the passenger seat of a car driven by his friend, was shot and killed by Bridgeton officers when he was asked not to exit the car, but he did. The officers were placed on administrative leave with pay.

March 6th, 2015
Unarmed nineteen- year-old Tony Robin- son was shot and killed by a Madison officer for allegedly assaulting the officer. The investiga- tion remains ongoing.

"I was just going to the store to get groceries for my mom. I was turning left near Princeton High School, and my friend told me that there was a cop following me. I didn't do anything wrong. He pulled me over... first question was, 'Does this car belong to you?'

Of course, I told him it was my family car... Honestly, I tried so hard not to look at it from a racial standpoint, and [to] give the cop the benefit of the doubt. I'm from Princeton, but the fact that I was being chosen out of so many cars on the road, and that his questions just kept getting weirder and worse. He thought the car didn't belong to me. I was chosen in the dark out of so many cars, and it still makes me wonder why he chose me. Maybe he thought a Black guy driving a PT cruiser was too suspicious. It lasted 30–40 minutes—he had to check my license, my registration, see if my story was true. A part of me feels that I have no regret because I was being completely honest, and I had nothing to hide. I'm a slow driver, I don't want any problems with the cops. If I make a mistake, I'll take responsibility for it, but that did not feel fair. What the hell did I do wrong? All the stories I've heard, about Black people being pulled over, at that point I really believed it—them being pulled over due to them driving good cars. In Princeton, [racism of the police] is definitely a problem that needs to be addressed. But I can't say for sure because I've never had a criminal record. I don't want to give a reason to hate the cops. I don't want to hate the cops. I graduated, I won awards, I did this, I did that, but no matter how much [I did], they still pulled me over to ask if the car belonged to me. "

All the stories I've heard, about Black people being pulled over, at that point I really believed it. Studies show that police officers are more likely to pull over Blacks or Latinx than Whites. In New York City, 80% of the stops were of Black or Latinx people, whereas only 8% of White people were stopped.[1] This gap is largely due to the stereotypes associated with Blacks and Latinx, police power backed by discriminatory laws, and the systemic prejudice within the police force. Often cited is the disproportionate number of Black officers: in 2013, 12% of the U.S. police force was Black, while Blacks made up 13.2% of the U.S. population. However, while Hispanic police officers are increasing, making up 11.6% of the police force, the percentage of Black police officers has remained flat for the past few years.[2]

I graduated, I won awards, I did this, I did that, but no matter how much [I did], they still pulled me over to ask if the car belonged to me.

Stereotyping and racial profiling ignore individual characteristics under racially-based assumptions. For example, a common stereotype associated with Black males is that they are uneducated, poor, and therefore dangerous. However, more than 17% of Blacks have a four-year college degree and more than 80% have a high school diploma. Despite these statistics, some law enforcement officials inappropriately act on misconceptions of Blacks to make unjust arrests, actions that are often backed by law and support America's high rate of incarceration—the highest in the world.[3]

1 https://www.dosomething.org/facts/11-facts-about-racial-discrimination); 2 http://www.wsj.com/articles/percentage-of-african-americans-in-u-s-police-departments-remains-flat-since-2007-1431628990: 3 http://nobullying.com/stereotype

POLITICAL & LEGAL

❝ They [pit] immigrant workers against American workers, or Whites against Blacks. It keeps our community divided, so that people don't work together to make change for our causes."

"Do you think poverty or lack of opportunities is associated with race?"

"Absolutely. Those who benefit from poverty in our communities, [can also] promote racial differences, and it's just one way they keep the community divided. And that's the history of this country. We've got poor Blacks who were slaves, and then the poor Whites who were sharecroppers in the South. They pay the poor Whites a little more, so they don't organize with the slaves. They even pit the Irish and Chinese against each other to build the railroads.**❞**

They [pit] immigrant workers against American workers, or Whites against Blacks.
According to the Pew Research Center, 55% of adults say that there are "very strong" or "strong" conflicts between immigrants and people born in the United States, and 39% said there are serious conflicts between Black people and White people.[1]

They pit the Irish and Chinese against each other, to build the railroads.
The construction of the transcontinental railroad was largely the result of efforts by Irish and Chinese immigrants. Racism was rampant. The Chinese were labeled as "heathens" and "little yellow men," while the Irish were barred from certain public places. Separate companies hired them for exhaustive and dangerous labor, forcing them to compete and build the railroad from different sides of the country.[2]

1 http://www.pewresearch.org/daily-number/see-immigrantnative-born-conflict/;
2 http://cprr.org/Museum/Fusang.html

Ohio to Texas: Personal Growth of a Pakistani Muslim

by Arqum Bin Farrukh

I was always a shy kid, but I never had much difficulty making friends once I got to know someone. However, Proctorville, Ohio, is a small town which lacks much cultural diversity. As a result, when I, a Pakistani Muslim, moved there in the fourth grade, I stood out as being very different. This was the first time in my life that I was exposed to racism, and I learned that someone may not judge you for who you actually are, but rather based off their own preconceived notions about your ethnicity or religion.

My fellow students in Proctorville never let me forget this, as many of them either ignored me by excluding me from activities, or addressed me with racist remarks such as "terrorist." A group of kids went as far as making up a twisted version of tag called "kill the terrorist," in which one of my classmates would play as a terrorist who they "cleverly" gave my name. Even some of my teachers publicly denounced Muslims, which made it all the more difficult for me when people found out that I am one.

Because I was already shy, I completely stopped talking to other people, in fear that they would also ridicule me. However, my quietness only made matters worse, as others began viewing it as arrogance, making them even more hesitant to be friends with me. Because it seemed like so many people

> " A group of kids went as far as making up a twisted version of tag called **"kill the terrorist,"** in which one of my classmates would play as a terrorist who they 'cleverly' gave my name."

were against me, I began to believe that perhaps my failure to make friends was all my fault and that I was just a bad person. I became severely depressed and felt worthless for most of my childhood in Proctorville.

Four years later, I moved to Fort Worth, Texas and began attending Trinity Valley School. I was ecstatic to move because I felt like I was getting a new start. Due to the fact that Trinity Valley and Fort Worth are far more culturally diverse than Proctorville, it was immediately easier to fit in and be accepted by others. I began to realize that all the bullying I experienced was not my fault and that it stemmed from the ignorance of others. I understood that by appearing aloof, I was only inhibiting people from seeing the good in me. As a result, I stopped blaming myself and began trying to prove my denouncers wrong by displaying kind and respectable behavior. Even though the process was very slow, because I had become so socially withdrawn, I eventually became part of a culturally diverse group of friends, who I am still very close to.

Although my experiences in Proctorville were tough, they gave me the knowledge to deal with a very difficult situation, which could have been destructive to my relationships with others. By observing how other people's prejudices clouded their perception of me, I now have a chance to correct my own views and think more deeply about how my actions may affect others. I am now able to better identify my own strengths and weaknesses, as well as more properly judge other people for who they really are.

Graphic Credit: Barry Deutsch, leftycartoons.com

CURRENT EVENT

originally a CHOOSE Facebook post
graphic credit: Ayesha Qureshi

April 20th, 2016

"Welcome to 2016: A cemetery in South Texas has denied a woman's request to bury her husband there. Why? Because he's Latino."

Read more: http://www.latina.com/lifestyle/news/hispanic-man-denied-burial-Whites-only-cemetery

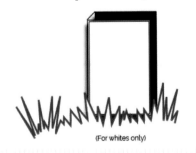

"A rattlesnake, if cornered, will become so angry it will bite itself. That is exactly what the harboring of hate and resentment against others is—a biting of oneself. We think we are harming others in holding these spites and hates, but the deeper harm is to ourselves."

—E. Stanley Jones

❝ In Princeton University, in the engineering department, there are very few Hispanics and African Americans. I'm Indian, and because of that I hear stuff a lot about how [that's why] I study sciences and engineering. That stereotype mostly just manifests itself in little things people say and hear.

I also see friend groups forming around race, and even though people don't do it intentionally, it's weird to see to how much of an extent it happens. I think most people do feel more comfortable with people of similar backgrounds, and often if you see people who are very similar in appearance and background hanging out, it feels more awkward to hang out with them and be part of that group. **❞**

EDUCA-TIONAL

I'm Indian, and because of that I hear stuff a lot about how [that's why] I study sciences and engineering.

A stereotype associated with South Asian Americans is their attachment to fields of engineering or science. However, in 2013, 19% of South Asian Americans were involved in science and 16% in engineering, while the most popular field was art, with 37% involvement by South Asian Americans.[1]

I also see friend groups forming around race, and even though people don't do it intentionally, it's weird to see ti how much of an extent it happens.

A 2013 poll found that around 40% of White Americans and 25% of non-White Americans exclusively befriend those of their own race.[2] This habit stems from a human desire to be around people of similar physical characteristics or backgrounds, and creates divisions between racial and ethnic groups along social, economic, cultural, and political lines.[3] In *Why Are All the Black Kids Sitting Together in the Cafeteria*, Beverly Tatum discusses the issue and necessity of communication about racial identity across differences and divides.

1 http://www.pewsocialtrends.org/2012/06/19/chapter-1-portrait-of-asian-americans/; 2 http://www.dreducation.com/2013/08/data-statistics-india-student-college.html; 3 https://www.pearsonhighered.com/assets/hip/us/hip_us_pearsonhighered/samplechapter/0205790615.pdf

" [Racism] is awful. It shouldn't happen. It hurts people's feelings. I've been through it. I used to wear the hijab and people used to discriminate me all the time. They used to call me stuff that I wasn't, and it really hurt. And it made me retaliate. I couldn't stand up for myself, because I was just one minority in the thousands of people that there are. It hurts, it impacts your life, and I couldn't resolve it. "

I used to wear the hijab and people used to discriminate me all the time.

Hijab, translated as "cover" in Arabic, is a type of head-scarf or veil worn by most Muslim women for religious, cultural, or personal reasons. However, since the September 11, 2001 Islamist terrorist attacks and the U.S. government's declaration of a global "war on terror," the hijab is often seen as a symbol of Islam and terrorism, leading to many cases of discrimination and violence toward Muslim women.[1]

1 http://arabsinamerica.unc.edu/identity/veiling/hijab/

Interview by
CHOOSE Chapter @
Penn State Founder
Papakojo Kuranchie

I saw a dent in your car so I thought it was stolen, and he wrote me a ticket...
Stereotypes and racial profiling are factors that cause Black people to be pulled over for crimes they didn't commit.

Is the crime rate of Black people higher than the crime rate for others? Yes, but only if we consider crime rate as equivalent to number of incarcerations. Both Blacks and Whites are incarcerated in similar numbers, although there are about five times as many White people as black people in the US.

The higher rate of crimes among Black people is not due to Black people actually committing more crimes, but rather to racial bias among police officers when selecting who to investigate. If a Black person and a White person each commit a crime, the Black person is more likely to be arrested. This is due in part to the fact that Blacks are more heavily policed. For example, Blacks and Whites smoke marijuana at similar rates, yet Black people are 3.7 times more likely to be arrested for marijuana possession. Furthermore, when Black people are arrested for a crime, they are convicted more often than White people arrested for the same crime.

Whether or not an arrestee is convicted is often determined by whether or not a defendant can afford a reputable attorney. The interaction of poverty and trial outcomes could help explain why, for example, while Black defendants represent about 35% of drug arrests, 46% of those convicted of drug crimes are Black.

In addition, when Black people are convicted of a crime, they are more likely to be sentenced to incarceration compared to Whites convicted of the same crime. One study found that in a particular region Blacks were incarcerated for convicted felony offenses 51% of the time while Whites convicted of felonies were incarcerated 38% of the time.[1]

When I got there and when he saw my skin, he told me his apartment was no longer available.
Racial discrimination exists in the housing market. A new report by the U.S. Department of Housing and Urban Development shows that real estate and leasing agents show minority homebuyers and renters less available properties as they do to White customers. For example, Blacks were told about and shown about 17% fewer homes than Whites in 2013.[2]

1 http://m.huffpost.com/us/entry/8078586
2 http://www.cbsnews.com/news/racism-alive-and-well-in-housing/

CHOOS

"Racist behavior is often learned behavior. It's always good to get to know somebody first before making any judgements about them; however, some people are closed-minded and don't take that time to get to know others. Instead, they go off based on what others have taught them.

I was driving to work one day on Route 206, and I had a little dent in the side of my car... I was pulled over, and then I asked the officer, 'What did I do, did I do anything, was I speeding?' And he said, 'Um, well, I saw a dent in the side of your car, so I thought the car was stolen.' His exact words. I saw a dent in your car so I thought it was stolen. He ended up writing me a ticket—not for theft, but for not having my insurance card in my glove compartment.

I was in Charleston for a family reunion, and my whole family was going out to lunch. We walked into a restaurant and my older brother and I heard a Caucasian man say, "Oh lord, we better hide all the fried chicken and watermelon" because there is a stereotype that Black people love fried chicken and watermelon... A lot of people love watermelon; however, to him, only African American people love watermelon and fried chicken. As for the "we better hide" part, he was saying that we were going to come and steal it. Like we wouldn't pay for our food.

I was looking for an apartment in Hamilton Township, where I grew up. I called the seller of an apartment and he told me that he had this unit available, its monthly cost, its amenities and everything else that went along with it. He said, 'If you can come at four o'clock today you can look at it. I'm tired of showing it to people, I haven't met anyone yet, and you sound like a nice young lady.' When I got there and when he saw my skin, he told me his apartment was no longer available. Over the phone, he was very receptive, very nice, very cordial, very friendly. When I got there it was a totally different story. Totally, totally different story...

Although I've had a lot of bad experiences, there's a lot of good people out there too... I work from home and do a lot of work over the phone. I was phoning a client and we hit it off really well. After two weeks, she invited me to her church. Over the phone, we would go back and forth like, 'Hey sister this,' and 'hey sister that,' and when we saw each other, she didn't change and it was all the same... I was one of two African-Americans in the whole church, but everybody was so friendly and so warm and welcoming. It was really, really nice. There are some awesome people out there, and I like meeting all those people!"

"To know what is right and not to do it is the worst cowardice."
—Confucius

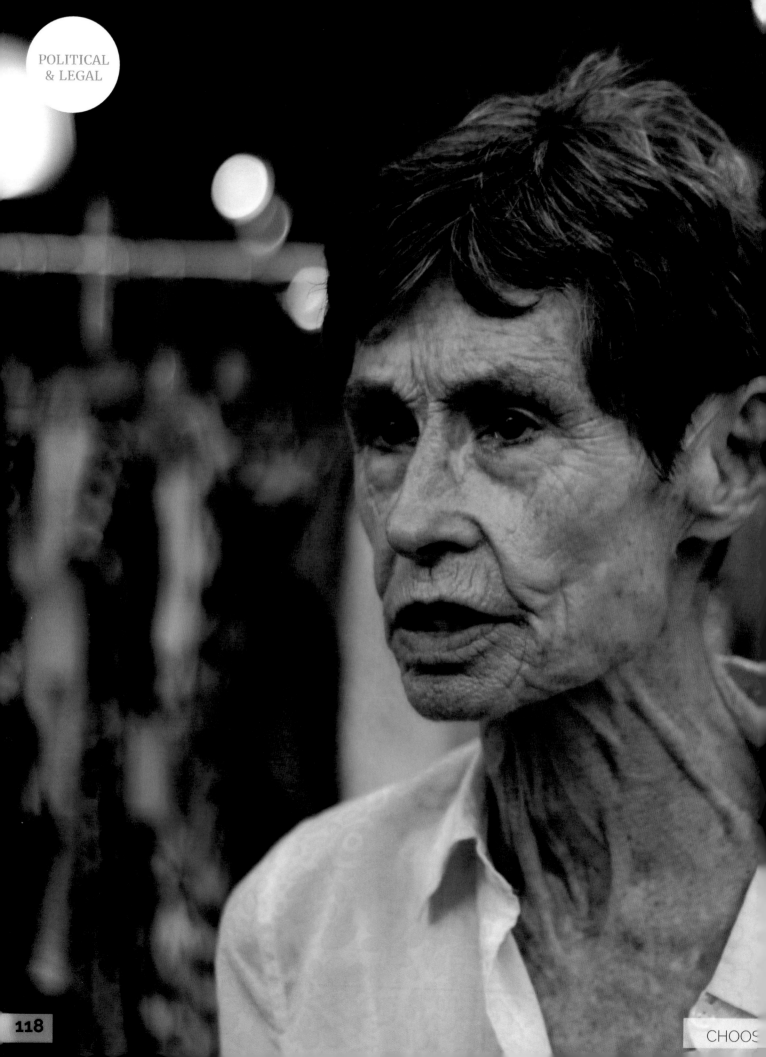

CHOOS

"Look at me. I'm a White WASP, a White Anglo-Saxon Protestant. Historically, I think of us as English, Nordic... I think of the Puritans and how the few of us WASPs didn't like the Church of England. We decided to come here and build our City of God on top of a hill. We fled the English church, but then they came to America and oppressed the natives. It's one of the horrors of our history. Literally, the genocide of the Native Americans. How does that happen? I think people with power—way back then, the weapons and diseases that evidently killed half the Native Americans—[they] can control the information [they] want. I think it's going on today with the government, like come on! Our newspapers! My sister is a professor at Columbia, and she really is quite brilliant, and as far as she's concerned, the U.S. news is so manipulated and biased. Whatever the currency, whatever it is that makes you powerful, if you've got it, you can call your shots it seems. This thing about being powerful is just that... once you're seeking that and fame, it's very hard to give up."

Look at me. I'm a White WASP, a White Anglo-Saxon Protestant.
WASP, sometimes used in a derogatory manner, refers to a group considered to hold the most power, influence, and privilege in American society.

I think of the Puritans and how the few of us WASPs didn't like the Church of England. We decided to come here and build our city of God on top of a hill.
The interviewee references John Winthrop, minister and future Governor of Massachusetts Bay, when he stated in 1630 that the Puritans had traveled to the Americas for religious freedom to "be as a city upon a hill—the eyes of all people are upon us."[1] Aiming to be a model of righteousness and morality, the colony wrote in their 1629 charter that they "maie wynn and incite the Natives of Country, to the Knowledg and Obedience of the onlie true God and Savior of Mankinde, and the Christian Fayth."[2] However, the outnumbered Puritans did not attempt missionary work until after winning the Pequot War of 1636 and 1637.[3]

I think people with power—way back then, the weapons and diseases that evidently killed half the Native Americans—[they] can control the information [they] want.
While advanced weaponry was an important factor in the quick dominance of native populations, the European colonizers also brought diseases such as smallpox, influenza, and measles that wiped out an estimated 20 million native people, or up to 95% of the American population.[4] This interviewee references Europeans as the "people with power," explaining that the mass killing of the natives—whether direct or indirect—is not reflected in the narrative they have created of colonization and American history. Her message is reflected in the common saying that "winners write history."

1 http://www.ushistory.org/us/3c.asp; 2 http://www.let.rug.nl/usa/documents/1600-1850/charter-of-massachusetts-bay-1629.php; 3 http://public.gettysburg.edu/~tshannon/hist106web/Indian%20Converts/the%20puritans3.htm; 4 http://www.pbs.org/gunsgerms-steel/variables/smallpox.html

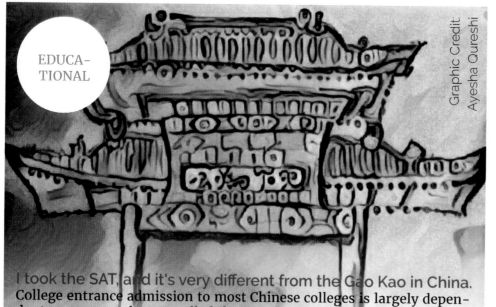

Graphic Credit: Ayesha Qureshi

I took the SAT, and it's very different from the Gao Kao in China. College entrance admission to most Chinese colleges is largely dependent on an annual exam called the Gao Kao. Compared to most U.S. colleges, greater emphasis in admission is placed on the test score.

It's becoming really high demand, especially along the coast, to come to the U.S.A. to pursue higher education.

Since its first wave in the 1850s—which ended in the 1880s after the U.S. government imposed immigration quotas and began again in the 1970s—Chinese immigration to the United States has been steadily increasing. The Chinese immigrant population was 384,000 in 1980, 1,195,000 in 2000, and 2,018,000 in 2013, currently forming the third largest foreign-born group in the nation.[1]

1 http://www.migrationpolicy.org/article/chinese-immigrants-united-states

" I took the SAT, and it's very different from the Gao Kao in China. It's becoming really high demand, especially along the coast, to come to the U.S.A.to pursue higher education. I come from the southern area and many of my friends are coming to the USA to study too. But I felt uncomfortable being with a lot of people [I didn't] know, so I kind of felt like I wanted to be surrounded by an Asian community. **"**

Teacher Talk

" I know I've had conversations about race in my classroom before, and I think it was after Ferguson that we had a big conversation in my [older] classes. We agreed that we need to have these conversations in order for things to change. But I think there's that issue of not being comfortable talking about it, and that's something I struggle with. To make everyone participate is a little bit tricky.

[Race] is really important to talk about because it's not just a possibility, it's a real thing that's happening. It's a touchy-feely thing that is not that easy to engage.

It depends on which end of racism you have been on. If you've been on the receiving end, if you've been oppressed, then you tend to be more sensitive about it. So if you happen to be Black and the teacher happens to be talking about Ferguson, it's a sensitive issue to your people, you're not sure if you want to contribute to the conversation because you don't know if someone is going to say something judgemental or painful.

That's where we fail—in saying it's not okay to talk about it. We want to talk about it, and we should talk about it, and hash it out. If you leave it there, it just brews and it turns into something else."

"Often times people who are racist don't intend to be that way, they just don't realize that they are being racist. But it's painful to be on the receiving end. You don't want to hear people making comments about the experiences you and your people have been through."

"But at the same time if you don't say it, they'll never know. If you speak up, that opens up a conversation and opens it up to thinking differently about it. Dialogue is really crucial to change something. **"**

—*Martha Hayden and Susan Richardson, world language teachers*

Jazz and many forms of music were started by African-American people. Several distinctive musical forms and styles created throughout American history are often uncredited to their original African-American roots, despite being common in mainstream American culture. During the slavery era, the 'Negro' spiritual was often welcomed by slave masters because it appeared to represent a conversion to Christianity and European-based ideology, despite its theme of freedom and escape from slavery. These spirituals later evolved into gospel music within many African-American churches. The post-Civil War era saw the rise of blues and early jazz, centering around "the disheartening realization that although slaves were granted emancipation, African-American equality was by no means also guaranteed." While complexities of African-American music were largely ignored and undervalued, musicians like Edward Kennedy "Duke" Ellington rose to prominence, still "[composing] pieces that were consciously grounded in the African-American heritage, in its rhythms, melodies, and harmonies, so that the musical essence arose from the hardships and triumphs of the African-American people," making music a valuable tool for social change. In the 1940s, blues gave way to rhythm and R&B, another precedent to disco, funk, and rock and roll, while jazz continued to evolve from swing and bebop. The emergence of rap and hip-hop expressed the discontent following the Civil Rights Movement and the "war on drugs" that led to the incarceration of disproportionate numbers of Black men, calling out social issues while empowering youth.[1] Meanwhile, before its American and international popularity, reggae grew in Jamaica during the late 1960s from traditional and contemporary Jamaican music and American R&B. As African-American music continued and continues to evolve, it nevertheless remains an undeniably crucial element of African-American culture, traditions, and history.[1]

1 http://www.arts.cornell.edu/knight_institute/publicationsprizes/discoveries/discoveriesspring2001/03sullivan.pdf

EDUCA-TIONAL

❝Jazz and many forms of music were started by African-American people. It's important to recognize and appreciate that. But if you're not African-American and you enjoy playing jazz, you should still go for it.❞

INTER-PERSONAL

❝I still feel like there is racism here, even though it is not that evident as in other places. I've never had one moment of racism that sticks out to me, but many. You know, as a minority I'm looked at differently. I've been walking down the street late at night, and people sometimes walk towards the other side of the street... stuff like that.❞

You know, as a minority, I'm looked at differently.
In the United States, Whites have historically been associated with superiority, privilege, and the "normal" standard, while people of color have often been labeled the "other."[1]

I've been walking down the street late at night, and people sometimes walk towards the other side of the street.
Statistics show a large disportionality between the lives of Black and White men, stemming from historical segregation. Examples include wages for Black men, which are on average three-fourths those of Whites, and incarceration, which Michele Alexander labels a redesigned racial caste system in *The New Jim Crow*.[2]

1 http://www.criticalmediaproject.org/cml/topicbackground/race-ethnicity/; 2 http://www.washingtonpost.com/wp-dyn/content/article/2006/07/01/AR2006070100462.html

I've certainly been paid less in my jobs and been offered less even though I may be just as qualified as my contender. The most frequent field claims that the U.S. Equal Employment Opportunity Commission receives are allegations of race-related discrimination or harassment. In 2006, over 27,200 charges for race-based discrimination were filed, which made up 36% of all charges.[1]

I went to a prep school in Princeton, and I found that that environment can be very marginalizing for a lot of people of color, even in academics. The achievement gap has been increasing over time, especially for Blacks and Latinx. In many schools, Advancement Placement classes are predominantly made up of White and Asian-American students. Black and Latinx students make up 37% of high school students, but only 27% of students taking an AP course. Additionally, between 1990 and 2011, Blacks and Latinx earned significantly fewer diplomas (48%) compared to Whites and Asian Americans (75%).[2]

1 http://www.eeoc.gov/eeoc/initiatives/e-race/e-race-facts.cfm
2 http://www.nationaljournal.com/next-america/education/the-race-gap-in-high-school-honors-classes-20141211

" It can be hard to pinpoint it, but that's the danger of racism. It can be really insidious, and sneak in in ways we didn't expect. I've grown up in Princeton, but I've traveled a lot, and now I study in Europe. There I've certainly been paid less in my jobs and been offered less even though I may be just as qualified as my contender. I see the same issue in Princeton. I went to a prep school in Princeton, and I found that that environment can be very marginalizing for a lot of people of color, even in academics.

I believe many are very aware of the inequalities in the school system. When I was 15, we were assigned a year-long research paper, culminating in a final paper. The paper's length was supposed to be between 12 and 15 pages. I wrote mine on the musical *RENT*. I worked very hard on it, and it was probably about 14 pages long. One of my friends turned in the paper past its due date, a few pages short of the minimum. When we got the papers back, I had received an A-. My friend received an A. Upon looking at his grade and then looking at mine, he apologized to me, saying that it was obviously an issue of racism. This astounded me. It certainly didn't help that there were only a handful of people of color in my class. A few years earlier, I ran for the middle school president position. The night before the election, when my mom came to pick me up, the principal stopped her. He told her that I should be very proud of the race I ran, and that it was a shame I wasn't going to win. I won the election. His comments just showed that the absurdity of racism and its inequalities were, in his world, commonplace. It's a system. **"**

" I think racism still very much exists in the United States. I actually think I'm racist. Not in a negative way, but in an actual way. Like, I worked at a Japanese department store in New York City, and because I had never been around Japanese people, I had to realize they were people. It sounds awful, but if you always grow up around certain types of people... And in the w, groups of people are portrayed certain ways, and it takes a lot of effort to reverse a lot of history. Especially in the U.S."

"Do you think it's important for people to interact at a young age with people of different cultures and different races?"

"Yeah. And people not just their own age, but older people. That's probably more important. If you have friends that are different races, you can still have prejudices of strangers of that race. I think the most important thing is interacting with strangers of all different races. "

Not in a negative way, but in an actual way. One way racism can be classified is into ideological and conditioned racism. Ideological racism refers to the belief that certain physical qualities render one person inferior to another, whereas conditioned racism refers to more subtle racial biases. There are two major factors that contribute to the biases of conditioned racism: predisposition, the tendency of the human brain to classify anything unfamiliar as a threat, and amplification and reinforcement, socially learnt processes that reinforces biases against certain specific racial groups.[1] Research has found that one of the most effective ways to combat conditioned racism (the racism practiced by the person in the above interview) is through exposure. It was not until he finally met and interacted with Japanese people that the person in the above interview was able to finally begin to reverse the conditioned racism that he had held.[2]

In the media, groups of people are portrayed certain ways. Due to its global influence as a primary platform for knowledge, the media is crucial in shaping how people percieve and are perceived. Bias and racism in media effectively perpetuate racial ignorance. For example, extensive research shows a lack of diversity in reporters and journalists, leaving what and how issues are covered up to the 'White' elite. [3]

Especially in the U.S. Racial inequality can be traced to the very beginning of American history. For example, the struggle of Black people against discrimination and oppression is centuries old. Recognizing the circumstances that led up to contemporar race relations is key to fully comprehending the effects of intergenerational systemic racism.

1 http://www.strategicleadershipinstitute.net/news/your-racist-brain-the-neuroscience-of-conditioned-racism/;
2 http://www.ncbi.nlm.nih.gov/pubmed/16051800; 3 www.unesco.org/webworld/wpfd/presskit_docs/teun_dijk.rtf

My Thoughts

by Andre Cole

photo courtesy of Andre Cole

Whether we are conscious of it or not, racism, prejudiced beliefs, and discrimination surrounds us. However, some individuals, like myself, are more frequently affected by such injustices. Despite being 25% Swedish, 25% Sri Lankan and 50% African American, I am and always will be seen and treated as a Black male before I am viewed as multiethnic.

When I introduce myself, I give a firm handshake, I maintain eye contact and I speak clearly, enunciating every single consonant and vowel. Even though I do my best to display proper etiquette, I know that I am judged differently. My, "Hi, my name is Andre Cole. It's a pleasure to meet you!" is not accepted in the same way as an introduction from an individual who is not a person of color. I believe that when I introduce myself, my appearance speaks much louder than my words. My physical characteristics and my overall appearance are heavily used by many to develop preconceived notions or thoughts about who I actually am, before I have the chance to prove otherwise. I have been labeled as a jock, an athlete-student, when in reality, I only play basketball because it is something I love to do. Indeed, basketball is a part of me, yet, many individuals who are not people of color believe that basketball is the entirety of me. I actively refuse to be classified and defined by what I do for fun rather than by who I actually am.

> Despite being **25% Swedish, 25% Sri Lankan and 50% African American**, I am and always will be seen and treated as a **Black male** before I am viewed as multiethnic."

This discriminatory and prejudiced mindset, whether it be a subconscious or conscious action, is due to a lack of appreciation for diversity. Having gone to an elementary and middle school where there was only a small handful of students who identified themselves as Black, I have always been interested yet mindful of the differences between individuals. In the winter of my junior year, I was fortunate enough to travel to Tampa, Florida to attend the Student Diversity Leadership Conference, a conference designed for students at private high schools, dedicated to raising awareness about diversity in their own respective communities. Everything from the guest speakers to the affinity group workshops was overwhelming because it was amazing to see over 2,000 students, all in one auditorium, devoted to the cause. The lessons and information I learned along with people I met completely transformed my outlook on life.

Brian, a White, homosexual male from rural Minnesota, was one of the very first people I met at SDLC. Even though I am a black, heterosexual male from Princeton, the differences between Brian and me unexpectedly made our friendship much more interesting.

Brian and I shared our experiences in creating favorable environments that foster and demonstrate appreciation for diversity in our communities at home. While my experiences lay more with racial discrimination, Brian enlightened me about the severity and the extent of other forms of diversity in this day and age.

He told me that he attempted to commit suicide two weeks before SDLC because he was physically, emotionally, and mentally drained from being bullied and assaulted by conservative classmates, in his hometown, due to his sexual orientation. Brian even mentioned that his guidance counselor at school would call him "the fag" when talking to others.

Three months after SDLC, I travelled to Cuba for a dance and culture immersion trip, which left me speechless. Having asked if racism and discrimination existed in Cuba, all of the natives gave me the same answer. They said something similar to "we are all happy people, everyone is equal, and everyone loves and treats each other with respect. Discrimination is not present in Cuba." This answer confused me because Cubans are extremely diverse; some natives looked European while others looked Jamaican. Considering the plethora of skin tone variations, I would have expected some form of racism, yet none seemed to exist. I left Cuba with an entirely new mindset and new hopes for what I would want U.S.A. to eventually become, at least on the social level and the interactions between individuals.

Oftentimes, when I am alone, I like let my mind wander. I think about Brian, and how his guidance counselor made Brian's life much more miserable. I think about Cuba and how it is equally as diverse as U.S.A., yet is not riddled with discrimination. Finally, I think about my own struggles as a Black male in the 21st century. In all honesty, because of all of the altercations between people of color and the police, I GREATLY fear for my own life and the lives of my Black brothers and sisters across the nation. As much as I feel that the police and other figures in society fear us Black people, I know that I am not the only one left equally as afraid of those who fear us. The fear is a two-way street. As a result, while our justice and legal system needs drastic change, humanity as a whole needs a novel outlook on life. We must not fear the diversity to the left and right of us. We must openly accept everyone's differences for what they are. We must STOP letting preconceived notions, fears and prior beliefs dictate our actions and control our receptivity toward multiculturalism and diversity. Thank you.

> "... I GREATLY fear for my own life and the lives of my black brothers and sisters across the nation."

Here are a few quotes that resonate with me:

> "Until the killing of black men, black mothers' sons, becomes as important to the rest of the country as the killing of a White mother's son, we who believe in freedom cannot rest."

Ella Baker
1964

> "Our lives begin to end the day we become silent about things that matter."

Martin Luther King Jr.
1965

> "Love, Itself is a Revolutionary Act."

Rodney Glasgow
2014

"I'm from Guatemala. In Guatemala City, they just make fun of the natives because they don't speak Spanish, they just have like 25 dialects—one of them being Quechua—and they tend to have darker skin from working in the sun. There is a lot of racism against natives over there. But [the natives are] very important; they make everything for Guatemala. Most people only come to Guatemala for tourism to see the natives and their culture. They're not teaching that in schools so people don't understand their value, and that's why there's racism. But it's because of them and what they make, their artwork, that helps our country."

There is a lot of racism against natives over there.

Indigenous people, like those in Guatemala, were pushed aside and marginalized by White European colonizers, whose arrival led to drastic results. For example, the pre-Columbus population of indigenous people in North America was around 10 to 12 million. In the 1890s, that number fell to around 300,000 people. Latin American countries experienced similar drops in their indigenous population. Today indigenous people are still disadvantaged and largely unwelcome from their stolen land, because of their race and different cultural traditions.[1]

1 http://www.un.org/WCAR/e-kit/indigenous.htm

It was at a food store and it was in a different state down south, and I felt that this person who happened to be from another country, did not speak English well, was treated differently than I was.

Language-based discrimination against immigrants in the United States exemplifies racial prejudice and underlies many workplace conflicts. In Houston, Texas, a phone-line which took calls from victims of language-based workplace discrimination claimed that in just one month it received 100 phone calls from native speakers of Chinese, Vietnamese, Tagalog, Spanish, and French Creole. In contrast, Swedish, Dutch, or Gaelic speakers did not file complaints; in fact, their accents were often perceived as charming and sophisticated. Thus, language prejudices are often driven not by the lack of English fluency, but by the background or national origin of the accent. This mistrust also sprouts from racism against minorities who, in the eyes of many Whites, historically came to America to steal White jobs.[1]

I think we're having a greater influx of Asians that we haven't had before.

From 2014 to 2015, the immigrant population in the United States grew by approximately one million. Asian Americans accounted for 573,439 of the increase, and India (171,000) and China (136,000) together accounted for over half of those. Although people from Mexico still make up the highest proportion of immigrants in the United States, Middle Easterners are growing at a faster rate.[2,3]

INTER-PERSONAL

1 http://community.miamioh.edu/writingcontest2007/node/58
2 http://www.ijreview.com/2015/09/427749-new-census-shows-new-immigrant-group-fastest-growing-america/; 3 http://www.latimes.com/nation/la-na-immigrants-census-20150923-story.html

“It was at a food store and it was in a different state down south, and I felt that this person who happened to be from another country, [who] did not speak English well, was treated differently than I was. The person was ignored, the person did not get serviced, and I ended up saying something. I think New Jersey, in general, is so diverse. I've grown up here, so for me to experience that was odd, even back then—and this was in the 80s—I thought that was still not acceptable. New Jersey in itself I think is very open. And I think we're a wonderful example of what this country could be. I've grown up in a very diverse population. I think we're having a greater influx of Asians that we haven't had before, but I think we've always had people of color, and definitely different languages. So for somebody to not be treated well because they didn't speak English well—that was kind of very upsetting. And Princeton in general? I think Princeton's always been very open because of the educational component, where it draws students from everywhere. Einstein's a prime example. Coming from Germany, he didn't speak much English when he got here. So if you look at just Einstein, and the brains he could draw from all over the world, I think that's great. ”

"Stop Touching Her Hair, White People!"

"Humans always fear what they don't know, or what is different from them, and a lot of the time, this fear turns into hate."

Humans always fear what they don't know.
Identifying ignorance through exposure and education is the first step to overcoming prejudice.

CHOOS

So for me, it feels really odd because I do enjoy math and science, and I don't know if I'm adhering to these kinds of stereotypes. Self-induced stereotyping can occur when stereotypes become the new norm, or become integrated into the standards of the community. When, throughout their lifetime, minorities suffer from the pressure of racial profiling, the line between what the stereotype influenced them to do and what they chose to do can become blurry. However, as in this case, just because an individual hobby or passion aligns with a societal stereotype does not mean it is not worth pursuing.

❝ The biggest thing [for me] is probably the perception of what fields I'm going to be studying in, what I'm going to do later on in life. When people ask me, 'What do you want to do when you grow up,' they immediately jump to the conclusion that I'm going to be an engineer, or a doctor, or do science, or go into finance and banking. But ultimately, it all revolves around math and science. So for me, it feels really odd because I do enjoy math and science, and I don't know if I'm adhering to these kinds of stereotypes. In reality, it is something that I've chosen independently, and I want to do myself. **❞**

CURRENT EVENT

originally a CHOOSE Facebook post
graphic credit: www.zap2it.com

April 27th, 2016

"Lew [Treasury Secretary] also announced Wednesday that Andrew Jackson will move from the front of the $20 to the back, making way for Tubman. She'll become the first Black woman ever to front a U.S. banknote."

Read more:
http://money.cnn.com/2016/04/20/news/10-bill-hamilton-20-tubman/

 CNN- Tubman on the twenty-dollar bill

"I'm Hispanic. I came here in 1986, and back in those days I felt quite a lot of the racism that was here, especially because the community from [Witherspoon Street] down is almost segregated. You see Hispanics living on one street, African-Americans living on another street. And so in those days, the 80s and the 90s, it was mostly like that. But now, I see a change in the new people that are moving into the city—they're more inclusive. I see the activities done by Princeton University—they give the opportunity for different races to sell their products, offer their services to whatever Princeton University does. So, I think it's changing, it's getting better in terms of giving opportunity for other races to act as communities."

"Do you think that an uneven balance of opportunity between races still exists in Princeton?"

"Well, with illegal immigrants, it's always existed and it will exist. Princeton is more open, but even with illegal immigrants it persists. For business owners and Latino small businesses, that's no longer the case. There's always opportunity for everyone here."

You see Hispanics living on one street, African-Americans living on another street.
Historical economic and social inequalities resulted in segregation of neighborhoods, physically dividing the community into different sections. These disparities are intergenerational and still exist today.
Refer to the first discussion point on page 144.

With illegal immigrants it's always existed and it will exist.
There are approximately 11 million undocumented immigrants in the United States.[1] A 2009 study showed that 26% of undocumented workers were paid below minimum wage, largely because their legal status allows employers to sidestep U.S. labor laws.[2]
Refer to page 54.

1 http://www.pewhispanic.org/2014/12/11/unauthorized-trends/
2 http://www.nelp.org/content/uploads/2015/03/BrokenLawsReport2009.pdf?nocdn=1

"It means understanding that different kinds of oppression are interlinked, and that one can't liberate only one group without the others. It means acknowledging kyriarchy and intersectionality—the fact that along different axes, we're all both oppressed and oppressors, privileged and disprivileged."

—Shiri Eisner

"First they came for the Socialists, and I did not speak out—
Because I was not a Socialist.

Then they came for the Trade Unionists, and I did not speak out—
Because I was not a Trade Unionist.

Then they came for the Jews, and I did not speak out—
Because I was not a Jew.

Then they came for me—and there was no one left to speak for me.
—Martin Niemöller

Written Reflection
Burst Bubble
by Claudia Orostizaga

My family moved to the United States when I was a little more than a year old so that my dad could be the minister of a Hispanic church in Jersey City. Because of the fact that I was in a small bubble surrounded by people that looked like me and spoke the same language, I thought that was the way the entire world was. Consequently, I was never really aware of my race nor the fact that I could be perceived differently because of it for most of my childhood. In my mind, Dora the Explorer was a strange anomaly because everyone was already bilingual, everyone knew fútbol was definitely not synonymous to football, and everyone had family that they missed dearly thousands of miles away.

Fast forward a couple of years into fifth grade: My safe bubble began to burst while I attended a predominantly White private school, revealing the hurtful realities and indubitable differences that had passed me by completely unseen. My most vivid memory was when my history class was debating Arizona SB 1070, which was basically a new legislation being implemented in Arizona that allowed officers to ask to see a person's registration documents when there was reasonable suspicion that the person in question was an illegal immigrant. Of course, these were only just a bunch of fancy technical terms to justify racial profiling.

After explaining the law, my teacher asked the class to stand on the left side of the room if they believed the law was ethically sound or to stand on the right side if they thought it was discriminatory. Without a second thought, I swiftly walked toward the right of the room, confidently crossing my arms and waiting for my classmates to follow suit—except they didn't. I stood there, with my arms still crossed, watching as they marched to their places on the left side of the room. The only two people by my side were another Hispanic classmate and my teacher. Afterwards, I tried debating the topic with one of my peers to which she responded, "You can't really have a position about it because you're illegal, aren't you?" To this day, it doesn't make me angry that her racist assumption was incorrect, but the implication that somehow, if I were undocumented or if my parents were, it meant my opinions and views were not as valid as hers.

As I got older, something that had been invisible to me for so long, was instantly impossible to ignore. When racism was brought up, I thought about the time my parents were followed in a store because the manager thought they would steal something, the time a cop asked to see my dad's driver's license for no apparent reason, the time a little boy on my school bus taunted me for being a darker complexion, the multiple times I've been complimented for being articulate as if it's not to be expected. On a broader scale, Latina women in media that are either oversexualized or exclusively housekeepers, the colorism and idealization of European beauty standards in Latin American countries, the growing xenophobia of immigrants not just from Mexico, but from all over, and the list can go on and on and on.

Despite all these things that have happened to me, my loved ones, or the Hispanic community, I am dumbfounded when asked whether I would change my race if given the chance because in doing so, I would be changing my identity. The bubble that had kept me from seeing racism burst a long time ago, but it left behind a hope for a better world instead of resentment for that which I cannot change. The solution to racism is not changing who we are as races, but it can start by changing the way we view ourselves and the people around us; realizing that although we may be different, we are undeniably equal.

EDUCA-
TIONAL

"When I tell people I hate a certain subject, or that I really am doing poorly in it, they kind of look at me like, 'You should be be better at this,' not just because I'm Asian but [because] when you have parents or siblings that are really smart, they just kind of expect that you are similarly intelligent. And then for people to hear that I'm struggling in subjects that they think I shouldn't be struggling in, it's weird. It's kind of mind-boggling, but there's nothing I can do about it. I've tried my hardest, and unfortunately that doesn't mean I get everything the first time I tried it."

"I go to Lafayette College, and we're very White. We have a lot of international students, but not so many American minority students. People are really aware of that and wonder why that is. Part of it is because we're a small liberal arts college on the East Coast, so if you just think about what kind of demographic that draws, it's a lot of middle class White kids. It's a really accepting community, and a lot of people are curious about other cultures and different races, so when there are students of diversity, race never really comes into the question."

"I definitely noticed that in high school too. But for international students, partially because they're from the same place and speak the same language—a lot of times they [stay in] their own friend group and other students don't reach out to them, or they don't reach out to other students, which is unfortunate. I think the language barrier is a big part of that. So, maybe as we all get older, since I'm a freshman in my first semester, we'll do more together and be able to overcome such barriers."

We have a lot of international students. People are really aware of that and wonder why that is. In the past decade, foreign college and university students on F-1 visas have greatly increased, reaching 524,000 students in 2012.[1] Certain colleges set quotas for international students, and in some cases, like that of MIT, this decreases the acceptance rate for these students.[2] Despite evidence that increased diversity benefits the cognitive performance of all students, some students have resisted measures to increase diversity, citing them as unfair.[3] In the case Fisher v. University of Texas, a White student sued one of the schools UT for rejecting her, citing that her rejection was the result of unfair measures to improve diversity. In June 2016, the Supreme Court ruled 4-3 in favor of UT.[4]

A lot of times they [stay in] their own friend group. Research on the diversity of social groups finds that "in a 100-friend scenario, the average White person has 91 White friends; one each of Black, Latinx, Asian, mixed race, and other races; and three friends of unknown race. The average Black person, on the other hand, has 83 black friends, eight White friends, two Latinx friends, zero Asian friends, three mixed race friends, one other race friend and four friends of unknown race."[5] Long after the Brown vs. Board of Education decision to integrate schools, the segregation of schools and friend groups continues to thrive.[6]

1 http://www.brookings.edu/research/interactives/2014/geography-of-foreign-students#/M10420; 2 http://mitadmissions.org/blogs/entry/international_men_women_of_mys; 3 http://www.nytimes.com/2015/12/09/opinion/diversity-makes-you-brighter.html?_r=0; 4 http://www.supremecourt.gov/opinions/12pdf/11-345_l5gm.pdf; 5 https://www.washingtonpost.com/news/wonk/wp/2014/08/25/three-quarters-of-Whites-dont-have-any-non-White-friends/; 6 http://www.usatoday.com/story/news/nation-now/2014/05/15/school-segregation-civil-rights-project/9115823/

Graphic Credit: Ayesha Qureshi

❝ Tomorrow I'm turning ten, but I feel like I'm way older than that. Maybe because I always have to help out at home, and take care of my siblings.

My mom is from Costa Rica, and she speaks mostly Spanish to me. She always tells me I'm special and brushes my hair, which she says is special too. My dad works really hard at this store near my house, and he speaks Spanish also. I learned English from school, and I think my English is better than my mom's!

But I'm very quiet in school. I don't usually talk about anything that is going on at home. Everyone's just really busy all the time, and me too—I've never been on a playdate after school because I help my dad out in the store then. There's also clubs and tutoring stuff that meet after school which I can't go to. But it's okay, because I'm happy to spend time with my family. **❞**

There are some races [and ethnicities]—people of Muslim descent for example—that people tend to move seats and stay away from.
Refer to the first discussion point on page 42.

Some of my friends have even told me that "You're so lucky— when you go into college they'll probably put you in instead of me because you're Hispanic." It's not like that at all.
Refer to the second discussion point on page 141.

EDUCA-TIONAL

" I don't think I've ever experienced [racism] myself, [though] I've seen it around, especially on the bus. There are so many different races that come onto the bus. [However], there are some races [and ethnicities]—people of Muslim descent for example—that people tend to move seats and stay away from. It's very upsetting that that's still going on, and there's not really much you can do to stop that from happening.

There are also some instances in school where the successes of minorities are undermined. White people say that [minorities] have everything handed to [them], like in competitive club and sport leadership programs. For instance, at our school, leadership positions are available for a peer-to-peer sexual health education program called Teen PEP, the Teen Prevention Education Program. This year, there was a lot of talk about how some people's auditions were probably not good; however, because they were minorities, they got in regardless. It's really annoying that people see us as incapable people who do not have the capacity to do much or amount to anything.

Some of my friends have even told me that 'you're so lucky—when you go into college they'll probably put you in instead of me because you're Hispanic.' It's not like that at all. If you do not have good grades or extracurriculars you are not just going to be admitted because you're Hispanic. Some people don't realize that and they're just thinking, 'Oh well, she's Hispanic, so she's gonna get in.'

I would like to say that I mostly push off any doubt coming from being in this constant atmosphere of people discrediting [minorities'] successes. I'd say it makes me work harder, because that way I can prove to them that just because I'm Hispanic, it doesn't mean I am going to get everything handed to me. I can show you my grades, I can show you I'm smart and I can prove that is why they're putting me in. "

134

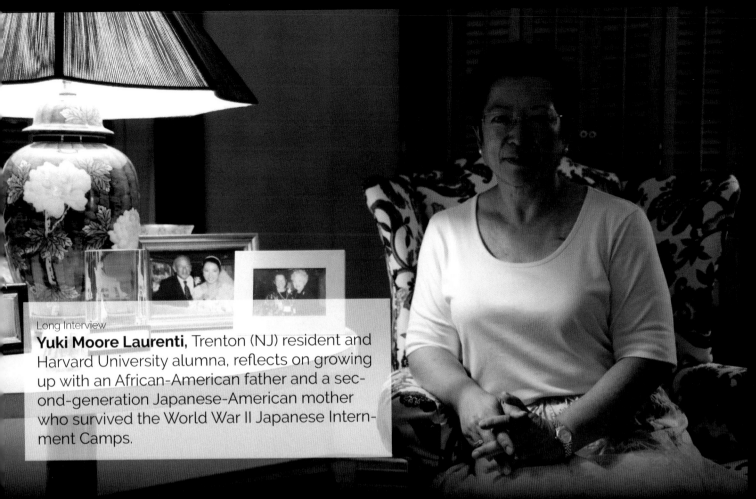

Long Interview

Yuki Moore Laurenti, Trenton (NJ) resident and Harvard University alumna, reflects on growing up with an African-American father and a second-generation Japanese-American mother who survived the World War II Japanese Internment Camps.

" My mother was born in Seattle, Washington. She was one of three children; her parents had come from Japan, and they met in the United States and got married here too. When the war came, when Pearl Harbor was bombed, they had to leave their home.

As she got older she got more nostalgic. Her view was that she actually grew up and become a stronger person because of their internment.

So the night of Pearl Harbor the FBI knocked on the door of every home of somebody who [was] Japanese American. She distinctly remembered having someone knock on the door when her parents were not home. I guess she was 15.

She was able to deter them from coming into the house before her parents came home. When her parents came home and found out that somebody was gonna come, they went up through all the apartments in their building and burned everything they had that was from Japan before the FBI came back. They were then forced to leave their home with only two trunks.

First, they went to the state fair grounds and basically lived within horse stalls. Until they were then shipped by train from Seattle, Washington out to Minidoka, Idaho.

There was a lot of dust in Idaho, and my mother, to the day she died, didn't like to go to the beach because it reminded her of being at the internment camp. There was just grit and dirt everywhere there; she even eventually got hay fever. They also ate in a mess hall, and there are certain foods she told me she refuses to eat. For instance, when she sees cans of Vienna sausage she always said, 'I hated that, that was the worst thing ever in the camps!'

She often did not talk about it. It was not something, in fact, you talk [about] to other Japanese Americans. Most Japanese did not talk about this because [it] was an embarrassment; it was a black mark. A lot

> " ... my mother, to the day she died, didn't like to go to the beach because it reminded her of being at the internment camp."

of kids would one day randomly go to their parents and say, 'were you interned?' The parents would tell them yes and the kids would ask, 'well, why did you never tell me?'

While she was in the internment camp through the Quakers, through the American Friends Service Committee, she was able to actually leave and go east to college.

When she was in Chicago, waiting to catch a train, a woman came and sat by her and started talking to her and said, 'Well, you're Chinese, aren't you?' My mother didn't say anything and the woman chatted on and finally my mother said, 'I'm Japanese–American,' and the woman was horrified and rushed away.

So she came east, and she went to Boston first. When she went to the president of the school once and he asked her why she had come east, she talked about the internment and he knew nothing about it. Therefore, she formed the Friends' service community that she thought this was not the school for her.

My mother then was transferred to Arcadia and that's where she went to school for one-and-a-half to two years. When the internment ended she went back to Seattle with her parents and went to Univer-

> **"**... my mother said, **'I'm Japanese American,'** and the woman was **horrified** and rushed away."

sity of Washington to get a degree in sociology.

Ultimately, [my mother] ran her own business, and so she felt her ability to stand up for herself and negotiate—all of those were characteristics that were developed traits of hers that came out in her during this.

My mother came out to Harlem a number of times and worked at the settlement houses, and through that volunteer work she ultimately met my dad. My mother was a Presbyterian from a Japanese Presbyterian church and my father's Presbyterian and they met during one summer out here.

When she got together with my dad she was disowned. She was one of three children, she's the middle child, she had an older brother and a younger brother. Her older brother disowned her when she married my dad, didn't want to have anything to do with her. She was left to sort of be on her own.

When I was born my grandfather told her, 'well, you're bringing this mixed child, and that's your challenge... you have to bring her up so that she's gonna be able to be successful.' My mother would often say that her father challenged her to raise me to

> **"**In my own personal experience, **the fact that I came from a mixed family meant that there were children who would not play with me...**"

try to be a successful young person and to get beyond the fact of what I look like and the combination of races that I am.

Nonetheless, she really wanted to prove both to her brother, father, and her friends out in Seattle that even though she decided to marry somebody who was not Japanese, and who was Black, she could still do a good job.

Unfortunately, my parents did get divorced. In the end, she earned all the money from her business and was there on her own. But for her there was a sense of being uplifted, the challenge of her life and her ability to have made it.

***

My mother and father both felt that as a mixed child, if I was gonna get ahead in the world, education was one of the most important things. So I was able to go to [a private school] on scholarship. I was one of very few minorities who were at that school, and I was on financial aid there until I went to Harvard.

In my own personal experience, the fact that I came from a mixed family meant that there were children who would not play with me— there were families who did not invite me to play at their house. It's

interesting, because as I progressed in life and became more successful in school and ultimately went on to Harvard, people then thought, "Oh, Yuki's okay." But back then, my father was Black and so it was not acceptable for me to go play. I was a good student, but I was never included.

So my father was a postman, and he delivered to what was called the "number one route," which was [a street with] all of the big houses. My mother stayed home with me at first, when I was young, and then decided to start her own business. She started a catering business—she's very good at cooking. My husband thought I was doing all the cooking while we were dating when really it was my mother; he found that out later. My mother actually became sort of "the caterer" in Princeton. We started catering Japanese [food], so I would dress up in a kimono and I would go out and serve people while my mother would cook all the food. I mention this because that's how my mother and father put me through [private school]... a lot of hard work.

Regardless, my mother often told me that I should not be bitter. She always said, 'If you hold a grudge it's like a cancer that grows inside.' And her mother had told her that even if people look down on you, you're not doing anything wrong. You're

working hard, you're not trying to be their friends, but you are just trying to get a good education to move on, so don't worry about it. Overtime, I just learned that if people didn't like me for who I was, that was fine.

I will say that when I did get into Harvard, it was sort of a validation. When I went in to talk to the guidance officer about where I wanted to apply [for college], I asked about Harvard, Princeton, or Yale. And they said, 'no, we don't think you're going to get in.' But my mother thought otherwise; she believed in me. So she took me to [another school] and had me talk to the [other school's] guidance counselors. If I didn't have a mother who looked beyond what advice I was given from a school that was predominantly White, I might not have applied. I might not have applied to Harvard, and then I wouldn't have gotten in.

There were divisions within Harvard, when I went. I didn't view myself as Black so I viewed myself as a multiracial person. What I had to deal with at Harvard was that I didn't view myself as a member of the Black Student Association, so I sort of started to slice and dice who I was.

But I will say that Harvard sort of became something. I don't like to say it but I do often tell people that I went to Harvard as a way to sort of even out the fact that I can be on their level, despite my race.

***

[My mother] didn't like to talk about her own personal experience, but I would talk about it on her behalf. Even though she was uncomfortable talking about it, I would talk about it. Because back then there was really nothing in any history books, at least the history books they were using in New York State. There should be something written about it.**"**

INTER-PERSONAL

" In recent times sensitivities towards racism have heightened. I'm a color-blind person. But when people start saying 'Whites are this, Whites are that,' without [them] taking responsibility [for their racism], then I am pissed off. **"**

1 http://www.gallup.com/poll/184193/racism-edges-again-important-problem.aspx
2 http://www.cpt.org/files/Undoing%20Racism%20-%20Understanding%20White%20Privilege%20-%20Kendall.pdf

In recent times sensitivities towards racism have heightened.
Recent dialogue about race in America has largely been sparked by controversy and protest over multiple incidents of police brutality towards Black men, such as Eric Garner (July 2014) Michael Brown (August 2014), Ezell Ford (August 2014), and Paul O'Neal (July 2016). In December 2014, 13% of Americans considered race the most important issue facing the United States, compared with 1% in January 2014. 13% has been the highest percentage since May 1992, when 15% named race the biggest national problem after the verdict of Rodney King's case.[1]

I'm a color-blind person.
Color-blind ideology rejects racial and cultural differences, effectively also refusing to acknowledge racism as an issue. By calling himself color-blind, this man believes that he is not racist. Even if it is true that he wholeheartedly attempts to reject racist beliefs or perspectives, this microaggression nevertheless demonstrates an inability to acknowledge others' racial and cultural differences.

'Whites are this, Whites are that,' without [them] taking responsibility.
This man emphasizes the importance to acknowledge and understand the impact of systemic white privilege, which disproportionately favors Whites in America. While white privilege has been constructed by centuries of White power, it still manifests itself in current society; examples include viewing white as "normal," veiling a real, multi-dimensional truth by teaching from a White man's perspective, discounting people of color, choosing whether to listen or to reject, and refusing to recognize privilege.[2]

Police brutality is very common. Refer to page 108-109.

I just did my school project on colorism. Refer to page 60-61.

So, I feel like with the Black movement going on, like Black is Beautiful, there's melanin poppin' and stuff.
"Black is Beautiful" sprouted from the Black Power movement in the 1960s. Quickly, it permeated American cultural mainstream. After years of poor portrayal by White supremacy, "Black is Beautiful" especially embraced Afro hairstyles and Afro-centric fashion. Blackness, or "soul," started becoming more apparent in films, magazines, and advertising.[1] Melanin is a pigment that gives skin, hair, and eyes a darker color. "Melanin poppin'" is a phrase used in the "Black is Beautiful" movement to express an individual's embracement of their darker complexion or Afro-features.

People love Black culture, and that's seen as a positive thing, but that's kind of ignorant when they don't actually care about the people.
Cultural appropriation occurs when members of a dominant group exploit the cultural traditions of a less privileged group, and often with little understanding of the history behind it. "Black music and dance, Native-American fashions, decorations and cultural symbols and Asian martial arts and dress have all fallen prey to cultural appropriation."[2]

1 http://www.pbs.org/wnet/african-americans-many-rivers-to-cross/video/black-is-beautiful/; 2 http://racerelations.about.com/od/diversitymatters/fl/What-Is-Cultural-Appropriation-and-Why-Is-It-Wrong.htm

POLITICAL & LEGAL, AESTHETIC

"Police brutality is very common. Like Trayvon Martin, Sandra Bland—everything you've seen on TV—and how no justice has been served, and it's common for cops to get like off on a lot of things. It's the same current issues, we need to do better and make sure to train police differently before they go out. You know, not everyone has a gun in their back pocket.

I just did my school project on colorism. I feel like in the Black community there is a pressure to have lighter skin. So, I feel like with the Black movement going on, like Black is beautiful, there's melanin poppin' and stuff. It's like #blackpower and #blackwoman. I mean, if we were all the same we could have no creativity. We'd be boring.

I'm a Caribbean female. When I went to Thailand, I felt like people were surprised and asked if they could touch my skin and my hair because I had braids, so they were surprised and shocked of a dark-skinned person. But I know in Thailand the darker you are, you are seen as having less and less wealth.

I feel pressure to perm my hair sometimes. Also, sometimes skin bleaching is prevalent in the Black community. Like I said, being from Caribbean descent I sometimes feel conscious about my hair and skin. Also, body image too. I feel like Black women are known for being curvaceous and having big lips, and people love Black culture, and that's seen as a positive thing, but that's kind of ignorant when they don't actually care about the people. But, like I said, everybody is beautiful."

Graphic Credit:
Keri Zhang

" My teachers were horrible. I feel like it's really hard to be Black and live in Princeton. First off, it's a very diverse town, but I feel like it's almost like we're not supposed to be here. I mean, I know I was from a low-income living, not saying poor, but we didn't have much. So, I feel like we get looked [at] like we're not really supposed to be here because we're Black.

I have friends that are all different [ethnicities], and they're are like, 'Where you from? Where you live?' And I'm like, 'Princeton,' and they're like, 'Princeton? What? You got money?' And I'm like, 'No.'

I know coming up I had to challenge myself more because the teachers didn't give me what I needed. I was in small classes at first. I didn't mainstream until like junior year, and I feel like my teachers wanted me to stay there. 'Cause the majority of the people that do live in Princeton—I know the people I was coming up with—were in small classes, and I feel like Princeton [did not] really gear nothing towards us, for us. Like there's nothing for us. I was in things like GenerationOne. That was like a program for, I'm not going to say minorities... other kids that were White or Asian, whose parents didn't go to college. There's nothing, no programs really for us. We have to kind of make our way. There's is no extra. There's nothing. It's hard to be in Princeton. Don't get me wrong, it's a great area. I have a daughter—it's a great area to raise your child. I know now I probably wouldn't stay because... I feel like [Blacks] down ourselves because we feel as though we don't have the fortune, the options that Whites do. We always say something about having a single mom or something. There's always an excuse, but we could be just like everyone else. I tell people all the time, it shouldn't matter because we're Black, White, Asian. Like whatever, it doesn't matter. But I feel like living in Princeton don't make it any better. It doesn't help... It's hard. It's hard as hell. "

My teachers were horrible. I feel like it's really hard to be Black and live in Princeton. First off, it's a very diverse town, but I feel like it's almost like we're not supposed to be here. Princeton, New Jersey is often considered an elite, privileged town. Its population consists of 67.8% White, 16.1% Asian, 6.3% Black and 6.2% Hispanic people, compared to the nation's 63.7%, 4.7%, 12.2% and 16.3% respectively.[1,2] Despite its high percentages of minorities, Princeton has historically been subject to racism, and it still is. Princeton University, being the heart of the town and the most southern Ivy League, attracted many Southerners and discriminatory policies. A Princeton graduate in 1928 wrote, ''Princeton is popular through the South because it is the one eastern school which does not enroll negroes.''[3]

Princeton Public Schools was not desegregated until 1948, and the University opened up to African Americans only in the 1960s. For example, a local named Paul Robeson was denied an education at Princeton University despite his many academic, athletic, and artistic achievements. However, he was given the first scholarship to Rutgers, graduated as Valedictorian, was elected to Phi Beta Kappa, and received a law degree from Columbia University. Afterwards, he was a pivotal activist in the Civil Rights Movement.[4]

Over a century ago, the African-American population came to Princeton to serve as butlers, maids, cooks, and chauffeurs for a "university and town with a nearly Southern fondness for segregation." Since the 1960s, when schools desegregated, Black and Hispanic students were often subject to low expectations from teachers, thus fueling the achievement gap. As of 2005, 37% of Black students in Princeton High School failed to meet standards in English, and 55% of Blacks and 40% of Hispanics failed in math.[5]

That was like a program for, I'm not going to say minorities... other kids that were White or Asian, whose parents didn't go to college. There's nothing, no programs really for us. President Lyndon B. Johnson said, "You do not take a person who, for years, has been hobbled by chains and liberate him, bring him up to the starting line of a race and then say you are free to compete with all the others, and still just believe that you have been completely fair."[6]

However, in a Washington Post survey, 75% of Americans opposed affirmative action programs for minority youth. For example, in the case of Fisher v. University of Texas, a White high school student applied to the University of Texas for an undergraduate program, expecting admission. When denied entry, she claimed it was because she was White and sued the school. According to her, it "was in violation of the equal protection clause of the Fourteenth Amendment."[7]

The Supreme Court ruled in favor of the University of Texas. However, the case raises the question of what extra help minorities should or should not be given. Are universities right in considering race to protect a level of diversity within their student body? How should we create equity for disadvantaged minorities, but not take away opportunities away from others?

1 http://www.city-data.com/city/Princeton-New-Jersey.html; 2 http://www.infoplease.com/ipa/A0762156.html; 3 http://www.nytimes.com/2001/09/03/nyregion/as-princeton-changes-a-black-community-fears-for-future.html; 4 http://www.encyclopedia.com/topic/Paul_Robeson.aspx; 5 http://www.nytimes.com/2005/09/28/nyregion/the-achievement-gap-in-elite-schools.html; 6 http://www.civilrights.org/resources/civilrights101/affirmaction.html

CURRENT EVENT

originally a CHOOSE Facebook post
graphic credit: www.independent.co.uk

May 29th, 2016

Sponsored by Representative Grace Meng, a Democrat from New York, HR 4238 bans "oriental" and "negro" from being used in federal law.

"Oriental" will now be changed to "Asian American" as "Negro" with "African American."

Read more: http://www.independent.co.uk/news/world/americas/president-obama-removes-oriental-and-negro-from-federal-law-a7041701.html

❝Our school is really diverse and accepting. Racism in society is now more of an undertone, something that you don't usually just outright face, it's something more in the system. Acknowledging it does exist is the first step to actually fighting it, because if you don't think it's there, you're in denial. **❞**

It's something more in the system. Both individuals and institutions (such as the government or national media) can enact racist practices.[1] Just like individuals, institutions can behave both overtly racist (for example, before being struck by the Supreme Court in Brown v. Board of Education in 1954, school districts often maintained separate schools for White and non-White students) and covertly racist (for instance, in a 2013 report found that Black men received prison sentences that were 19.5% longer than White men who committed similar crimes).[2,3]

If you don't think it's there, you're in denial. According to a survey by the Public Religion Research Institute, 56% of White Millennials believe that the government pays excessive attention to issues of race, and 58% consider discrimination against Whites and other minorities to be an equal problem.[4] The widespread but ungrounded concept of a "post-racial America" is popular despite contradictory evidence. The commonly held notion that the solution to racism is to be "colorblind," or to ignore that people of different races are treated differently, only ignores the underlying factors of racism and results in the stagnation of racial progress.

1 https://archive.org/details/healthcarechalle00unse; 2 https://academic.udayton.edu/race/2008ElectionandRacism/RaceandRacism/racism02.htm#_edn1; 3 http://www.huffingtonpost.com/2014/07/02/civil-rights-act-anniversary-racism-charts_n_5521104.html; 4 http://www.huffingtonpost.com/dr-david-j-leonard/White-denial-and-a-cultur_b_1817557.htm

"Let us all hope that the dark clouds of racial prejudice will soon pass away, and that in some not too distant tomorrow the radiant stars of love and brotherhood will shine over our great nation with all their scintillating beauty."
—Martin Luther King, Jr.

Credit: Barry Deutsch, leftycartoons.com

INTER-PERSONAL

"A lot of people like to study. Montgomery is a tough school, you have to study. It's just academically-oriented. It doesn't have to do with race. It's predominantly Asian, but it's not correlated. I think I study more than you, actually!"

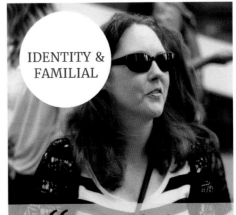

IDENTITY & FAMILIAL

"Maybe I don't notice [racism] as much because I'm Caucasian. If you don't experience racism that often, then you don't really notice it around you."

At the time I was getting Section 8. So I asked if I could have a better apartment and they go, 'Well, you're in Section 8,' like they thought that I was some kind of drug addict or prostitute or something like that.

During the Great Depression, Franklin D. Roosevelt and his administration expanded the use of government programs to aid and assist struggling citizens. One major program was the Federal Housing Act, which worked to build houses for the many people who needed assistance in order to pay rent and reside in a home. The project was amended throughout the years, and in 1974 Congress passed the Housing and Community Development Act, which included Section 8 housing.[1]

The interviewee describes the Voucher Program, which allows tenants of low income to pay for a portion of the property bills from a predetermined location. This expansion was necessary after "White flight" in the 1960s, during which Whites moved away from cities to more suburban locations to avoid the influx of minorities, leading to increased poverty in urban areas. Today, nearly half of all residents in Section 8 housing are African Americans, and in some cities even more. In Detriot 99% of the Section 8 population is Black, and 98% of New Orleans and Washington DC are Black as well.[2]

The houses are typically poor quality with broken utilities (that never get fixed, according to the interviewee).[3] Slowly, the purpose of these programs changed from their origin as "a kind of reward for the working-class family trying hard to make it" into "more of an aid of last resort for the poorest."[4]

As the majority race in Section 8 housing, which is now tagged with extreme poverty, many Blacks living there—like the interviewee—have been tagged with negative stereotypes associated with crime.

" I was first living in an apartment nearby, and it was small enough for a rat. It was dirty and it was shabby and broken. At the time I was getting Section 8. So I asked if I could have a better apartment and they go, "Well, you're in Section 8," like they thought that I was some kind of drug addict or prostitute or something like that. But they wouldn't even get to know me. They didn't really get to know me to find out what I was like. They were automatically [like] 'Boom, she's Black... We are going to put her right there, and that's where she's going to stay. We are not going to give her nothing better.' And that was when I first encountered [racism].

[The places Section 8 found] were like the worst places... They put me in an apartment right across from the Princeton Airport. And I was like the only one there... [It was] bad because I had heart issues, and I had to climb up all these steps, and I had something wrong with my leg. And when something broke hardly anyone would come and fix it. Eventually I had to get out of there. It took me three years to get out of there.

[When I would ask for something better], they [would] go, 'We can have you stay until a place opens up, and it will be within in your price range.' And that's how I ended up near the airport and for three years. I called and they would be like, 'There is nothing open.' They would never [say] a place [was] open even though I knew they were open...

Sometimes you feel like you want to get angry and do something, but then you don't know what to do because you're afraid to do something because you don't want to cause a problem. And sometimes you just have to keep yourself quiet and hope things get better, and they don't.

Sometimes, with housing or going shopping or in restaurants or something like that, you get the weird look like, 'Oh God, she's going to steal something,' but I'm not.

I think the most important thing is that people should learn to talk to each other. And get to know a person and then make the decision whether to be their friend or not... I like to talk to get to know a person. I feel better because now you know me and I know you... We'll go 'Hi, how ya doing?' And that's how things should be. **"**

Sometimes, with housing or going shopping or in restaurants or something like that, you get the weird look like, 'Oh God, she's going to steal something,' but I'm not.

According to research, retailers follow people of color more closely than Whites. In 2015, 24% of African-Americans felt treated unfairly in stores—the highest percentage of all locations, including their place of employment and in law enforcement buildings.[5] According to a University of Florida study, of 1,365 shoppers in a drugstore, Blacks and Hispanics were no more likely to be shoplifters than Whites. This research indicates that many employees are racially profiling customers.[6]

1 https://www.gpo.gov/fdsys/pkg/STATUTE-88/pdf/STATUTE-88-Pg633-2.pdf#page-30
2 http://www.massresources.org/section8-rent.html
3 http://www.abcactionnews.com/marketplace/law-tv/section-8-housing-destroying-home-values-and-driving-up-rental-prices
4 https://www.washingtonpost.com/news/wonk/wp/2015/06/15/how-section-8-became-a-racial-slur/
5 http://www.gallup.com/poll/184439/despite-unrest-blacks-feel-mistreated-police.aspx
6 http://news.ufl.edu/archive/2005/08/study-shows-shoplifters-more-readily-identified-by-behavior-not-race.html

"I was born and raised in Princeton. Back then, there used to be a school that was segregated. Back then it was only Black and White. Now it's a whole mix—there are Whites, Blacks, Asians, and Hispanics. In fact, this whole neighborhood used to be Black. Later on, I don't know if it was because of taxes, or they just couldn't afford to live here, but most of the Blacks moved out.

Now, they're tearing up all these historical houses, houses of historical Black people, and putting these odd-looking modern buildings everywhere. I think the massive plan was to raise taxes, build more houses, so Blacks couldn't afford it and push us out. They're just tearing things down."

I think the massive plan was to raise taxes, build more houses, so Blacks couldn't afford it and push us out.
To read about gentrification in Princeton, refer to page 167.

CHOOS

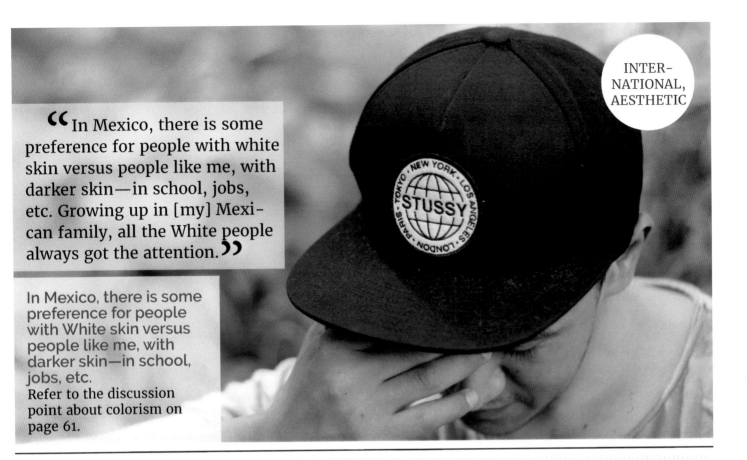

"In Mexico, there is some preference for people with white skin versus people like me, with darker skin—in school, jobs, etc. Growing up in [my] Mexican family, all the White people always got the attention.**"**

In Mexico, there is some preference for people with White skin versus people like me, with darker skin—in school, jobs, etc.
Refer to the discussion point about colorism on page 61.

It is with heavy hearts that we must join together in the mourning of the boxing legend, Muhammad Ali. The world has not only lost a talented and ambitious athlete but also a motivated and outspoken activist. As British Prime Minister David Cameron tweeted, "Muhammad Ali was not just a champion in the ring — he was a champion of civil rights, and a role model for so many people."

"Why should they ask me to put on a uniform and go 10,000 miles from home and drop bombs and bullets on brown people in Vietnam while so-called Negro people in Louisville are treated like dogs and denied simple human rights? No I'm not going 10,000 miles from home to help murder and burn another poor nation simply to continue the domination of White slave masters of the darker people the world over... I have nothing to lose by standing up for my beliefs. So I'll go to jail, so what? We've been in jail for 400 years."

Read more:
http://heavy.com/sports/2016/06/muhammad-ali-dead-vietnam-war-draft/; https://www.washingtonpost.com/sports/boxing-mma-wrestling/people-of-the-world-famous-and-common-pay-tribute-to-muhammad-ali/2016/06/04/3fcfd598-2a66-11e6-a3c4-0724e8e24f3f_story.html; http://www.aljazeera.com/news/2016/06/muhammad-ali-life-quotes-160604094217123.html

CURRENT EVENT

originally a CHOOSE
Facebook post
graphic credit:
Ayesha Qureshi

June 5th, 2016

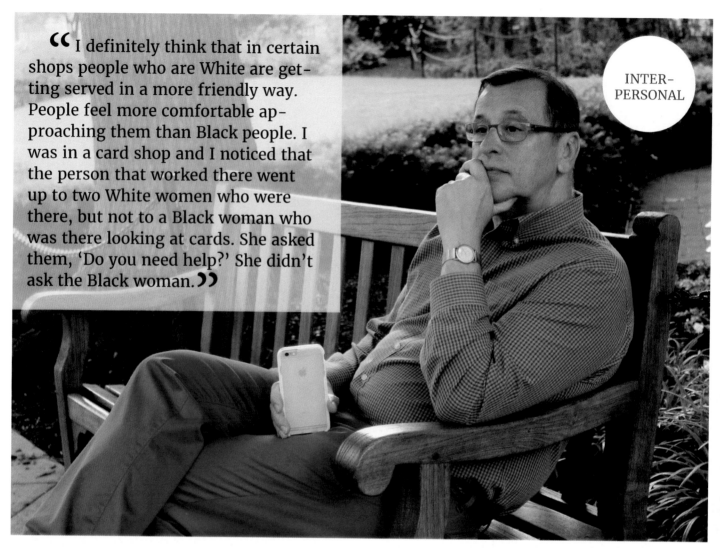

> **"** I definitely think that in certain shops people who are White are getting served in a more friendly way. People feel more comfortable approaching them than Black people. I was in a card shop and I noticed that the person that worked there went up to two White women who were there, but not to a Black woman who was there looking at cards. She asked them, 'Do you need help?' She didn't ask the Black woman. **"**

I noticed that the person that worked there went up to two White women who were there, but not to a Black woman.

Numerous U.S. clothing companies and retailers have been accused of racially-insensitive products or prejudiced treatment of minority employees and customers. For example, a June 2015 study investigated complaints to New York City branches of Zara, the world's largest fashion retailer. According to the report, Black and/or dark-skinned employees who also made up 68% of lower level working roles are "more than twice as dissatisfied with their hours as White employees," "report that they are least likely to be promoted," and "state that they are reviewed with harsher scrutiny from management than White American and European employees."

Surveys also demonstrate that Black Zara customers are 7 times more likely than White customers to be racially profiled and targeted for thievery.[1] Other major retailers—Hollister, Best Buy, Walgreens, and Macy's, to name a few—have faced similar charges.[2] A study by Dr. Shaun L. Gabbidon discusses potential reasons for racial discrimination against customers, such as a "Black thief stereotype" which originates from American slave history, the racialization of crime, and individuals' unconscious biases.[3]

1 http://populardemocracy.org/sites/default/files/Zara-Report_web%20june%200215.pdf
2 http://www.ibtimes.com/shopping-while-black-americas-retailers-know-they-have-racial-profiling-problem-now-2222778; 3 http://www.stopracialprofiling.net/wp-content/uploads/2014/04/Prof.-Gabbidon-UNCALECTURE.pdf

"The path to glory is rough, and many gloomy hours obscure it. May the Great Spirit shed light on your path, so that you may never experience the humility that the power of the American government has reduced me to. This is the wish of a man who, in his native forests, was once as proud and bold as yourself."

—Black Hawk

CHOOS

Society's False Façade

Aadil Rizwan

You'd expect the "average brown boy" when you looked into my glistening eyes. The brown pupils dilated as they carefully observed their surroundings. Those who saw me for the first time automatically classified me as the typical "Asian nerd". My thick black-rimmed glasses sat flat on my nose. The newly born peach fuzz covered my oily skin. There was one distinct factor that set me apart from the hundreds of students in my class. It wasn't the prepubescent look. An engine full of willpower and ambition roared on the inside. But no one could see that because what was on the surface—my skin color— was apparently the only factor that could be used to judge me.

Middle school was one of the most testing times in my life. Every day felt like an everlasting cycle that brought mere torture. Many of my fellow peers disliked my dedication to the classroom environment, constantly mocking me as the "typical brown nerd." My work always demonstrated my true potential, impressing my teachers. And to me, my devo-tion was a symbol of myself, not a symbol of my race.

The United States of America. The words bring forward images of diversity and freedom. My father, a huge fan of American patriotism, ensured that a ten-foot American Flag always hovered in front of our house. To me, the red and White stripes mingled in with the blue represented diversity. Nevertheless, individuals tend to remain in groups throughout high school. As far as my observation went, students formed cliques based on their ethnicity. Up until the end of sophomore year, I had always stuck to my "Brown Clique," as that had been established as my comfort circle.

However, junior year, I was able to step outside that circle. I had taken up the hobby of selling shoes and I found that the shoe culture breeds so many people from all over the world. Individuals come from different states and countries to sneaker expos to portray their love for the hobby. Meeting a variety of individuals may prove daunting at first. Oftentimes people are tempted to judge others because they are different. None of my peers took the time to see beyond the superficial stereotypes I carried. Hence, I always ensured to try to understand others before jumping to conclusions.

The hobby gave me the opportunity to meet people who were outside of the closed interiors of the cliques I'd always been apart of. The customer whose body was covered with tattoos from head to toe had a moving meaning behind each and every one. The fellow African sneaker head who was naturally buff was one of the kindest individuals I had ever met. All the stereotypes that I had grown about hearing in high school were directly proven wrong. I learned: never judge people based off of their appearance, especially the color of their skin, for looks are deceiving.

Branching off and meeting new people is a pivotal social skill that helps one progress forward. I've been blessed with having friends from all different backgrounds and ethnicities. They all contribute to my overall personality and add to its flavor. If I had stuck with the brown clique throughout my entire high-school career, I'd be nowhere near the multifaceted individual I am today. Growing among all sorts of people has given me the opportunity to mature faster and appreciate various minority cultures that are often overlooked. In today's day and age, it is unacceptable to judge someone based off how they look or where they are from. These barriers only divide us as a community and cause disarray.

Just like numbers should never limit a student's potential, ethnicity and appearance should never limit social interaction. Open your eyes and make the effort to really know people outside of your own race. Step out of the comfort circle that has been created for you.

Make your own colorful circle. Stay awake. Think clear cut. Think broad.

Because once you do, you'll realize just how beautiful diversity is.

> " Make your own colorful circle. Stay awake. Think clear cut. Think broad. Because once you do, you'll realize just how beautiful diversity is."

IDENTITY & FAMILIAL

When I was younger, my sister and I would always deny the fact that we were Asian. We would say, 'No, no, no, we're American, we live in America, we speak English, we don't even know Korean, we don't want to be part of that lifestyle.'

Minorities that suffer from internalized racism can loath the physical characteristics that make them stand out from the majority—characteristics such as skin color, hair texture, or eye shape. Victims of internalized racism often refuse to associate with one's own racial group.[1]

Over time, I've slowly embraced my Asian heritage and my culture, and I've actually really grown to like it.

Cultural heritage is the active and cumulative ways of life and patterns of behavior—knowledge, experiences, capabilities, morals, habits, etc.—that encompass a society.[2] Understanding cultural heritage is important in establishing and embracing identity. This story describes the transition from conformity—desire to assimilate into the dominant culture and simultaneously reject individual background—to security in racial identity.[3]

1 http://racerelations.about.com/od/understandingrac1/a/internalizedracism.htm
2 https://www.tamu.edu/faculty/choudhury/culture.html
3 http://www.pierce.ctc.edu/staff/tlink/development/theme_identity_and_cohort/race_stages.html

" When I was younger, my sister and I would always deny the fact that we were Asian. We would say, 'No, no, no, we're American, we live in America, we speak English, we don't even know Korean, we don't want to be part of that lifestyle.' Over time, I've slowly embraced my Asian heritage and my culture, and I've actually really grown to like it. I used to hate going to Korea over the summer. I still don't like Asian stereotypes, and I don't consider myself part of them at all. [Being Korean-American is] not something I consciously think about a lot, it's just part of who I am. **"**

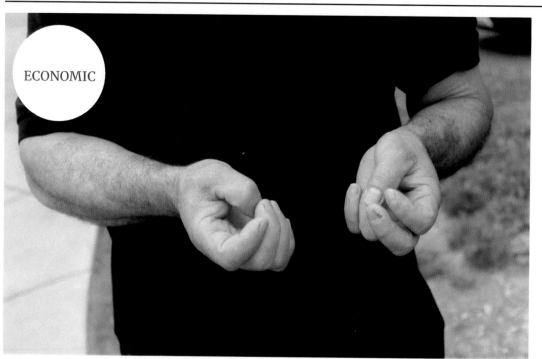

ECONOMIC

... managers make Hispanics work more than others.

As of 2011, Hispanic individuals made up 15% of the American labor force. 58.9 percent of Hispanics aged 16 and over were employed and just under 1 in 5 of those employed was working part-time.[1]

1 https://www.dol.gov/_sec/media/reports/hispaniclaborforce/

" Racism exists at the workplace, where employers and managers make Hispanics work more than others. **"**

CHOOS

"I've definitely been called a White girl. It's used as slang, but it can be derogatory."

"There [are] cases of casual racism, like positive stereotypes, that are harmful as well. People use racial stereotypes to denote and mitigate someone's achievements like, 'Oh you're fast, you ran this really fast, but it's not important because you're Black, so you should be fast.' So that's making their achievement worth less, based on something that shouldn't even matter. Or, for example, getting good grades, and being like 'It's not important because you're Asian.' That happens a lot."

"[Racism is] out of the norm. Well, in a real life example, in [my history teacher's] sociology class, we were talking about whether babies are racist or not. And so far, the general consensus is that they're not racist. So as you grow up anything around you, anything that's not yourself, makes an effect on you."

"I also think that parents have a big influence on you. Especially parents who were raised in the 50s or 60s... I don't have any stereotypes that are preset in my head, whereas somebody who was raised by or someone of an older generation already has a thought."

"There's no point in fighting ignorance with more ignorance. We should be different, but together. We should celebrate our differences and have them bring us closer."

INTER-PERSONAL, IDENTITY & FAMILIAL

There have been cases of casual racism, like positive stereotype, that are harmful as well. Stereotyping, whether "positive" or "negative", is harmful. Statements that portray so-called positive stereotypes, such as "all Black people are good at sports," or "all Asians are good at mathematics," inherently lump individuals into groups, depriving them of their sense of individual identity.[1] This was confirmed by a series of studies in the January 2013 issue of the Journal of Personality and Social Psychology.[2]

Especially parents who were raised in the 50s or 60s.
The Civil Rights Movement during the second half of the 20th century marked a watershed period in the struggle for racial justice. Significant events include the elimination of the "separate but equal" legal doctrine, the Voting Rights Act of 1965, the Civil Rights Act of 1968, and the rise of leaders such as Dr. Martin Luther King Jr. and Malcolm X.

We should be different, but together.
The retention and celebration of cultural differences has long been embodied in the push for multiculturalism. With the rise of cultural assimilation and the "melting pot" metaphor, proponents of maintaining individual and cultural identity to form a harmonious whole have created the "salad bowl" metaphor.[3]

1 https://www.psychologytoday.com/blog/ulterior-motives/201302/the-pain-positive-stereotypes; 2 http://psycnet.apa.org/psycinfo/2012-26176-001/; 3 http://hilo.hawaii.edu/academics/hohonu/documents/vol04x-06fromthemeltingpot.pdf

IDENTITY & FAMILIAL

"I'm from Berkeley, California. On the West Coast, being Black is a different kind of thing than it is here, so that was very shocking to me. I come from a mixed background, but I still identify as Black. Here, everyone is like, 'I'm not Black, I'm Nigerian' or 'I'm not Black, I'm Cameroonian'. Here, it's very nationalistic, whereas the West Coast, either there aren't people with those nationalities tied to them, [or] they don't identify as that. On the West Coast it's very, 'I'm just Black'. Here, people are very attached to their national identities."

"Do you think it shows pride in your nationality and your culture?"

"I definitely think so, but I also think it's a result of how they perceive Black people to be treated in America. Like, there's a way to distance themselves. If you see a minority group that's being subjugated, you don't want to associate with them."

I come from a mixed background.
From 2000–2010, the multiracial population in the United States grew by approximately 32% from 6.8 million to 9.0 million, while the population of a single race grew by 9.2 percent. Many multiracial groups increased by over 50%.[1]

If you see a minority group that's being subjugated, you don't want to associate with them.
Minorities, excluded from the power, prestige, and privileges associated with being White in America, have long been subject to routine subjugation and discrimination. In surveys conducted by the Pew Research Center, 70% of Blacks said they were treated less fairly than Whites in dealing with police, 68% in courts, 54% in the workplace, and 51% in public schools.[2] And in addition to systemic and institutional racism, overt and covert individual racism works together to marginalize minorities. This woman explains how she witnessed attempts to separate from this inequality by clinging to a national identity rather than identifying as the oppressed group.

1 https://www.census.gov/prod/cen2010/briefs/c2010br-13.pdf

2 http://www.pewsocialtrends.org/2013/08/22/chapter-1-i-have-a-dream-50-years-later/#treatment-of-Blacks-by- the-courts-police-seen-as-less-fairthe-courts-police-seen-as-less-fair

INTER-PERSONAL

"Racism is always very subtle, and there isn't usually any large outcry. But even if people aren't part of a stereotype, they have to stand up and just tell [the offender] to stop. People need to stand up for each other."

"When I was in 8th grade, a White classmate called me a spic, and it's this derogatory term, like calling White people crackers or Black people n*****. I literally lost it, and my school wanted to suspend me because I got upset and threatened the kid. But no one ever called me a spic again. I actually ended up becoming the president of my class, even though I felt secluded and didn't have many friends. But people still say I'm loud because I'm Puerto Rican, that I kill people with knives, that my grandmother sleeps with a machete underneath her pillow, that I wouldn't make it to college. But now I'm in NYU, so f*** them. I'm actually the first person in my family to go to college."

A White classmate called me a spic.

The term 'spic' is a derogatory slur towards Hispanics. As far back as the early 1900's, North American laborers labeled Panamanians "spigotty." The headline of the March 14, 1908 issue of *The Saturday Evening Post* (founded by Benjamin Franklin) read "Life in Spigotty Land," and discussed how Panamanians "prefaced their attempts to cheat the Americans out of something—it really made little difference what—with the statement, accompanied by eloquent gestures: 'Spik d' English.' If they couldn't they said: 'No spik d' English.' One or the other was the universal opening of conversation, and those early Americans soon classified the whole race of men who could or could not 'Spik d' Eng.' as 'Spikities,' and from that grew the harmonious and descriptive Spigotty."[1] Use of similar terms still persists today. In January 2015, a White veteran of the Boston Police Department violently attacked an Uber driver after calling him a spic, and later yelled "n*****" at a Black man who assisted the victim.[2]

I'm loud because I'm Puerto Rican.

Hispanics are often stereotyped as lacking in education, wealth, English-speaking ability, and legal residence status in the U.S.. They are also often accused of having a "spicy" personality, being of Mexican origin, and having involvement in drug deals and murder. On the contrary, according to 2010 and 2012 surveys, out of 50.5 million Hispanic people in the U.S., 69% of Hispanic high school graduates enrolled in college, as compared to 67% of White graduates (2012); 63% were born in the U.S., while 37% were foreign-born (2012); approximately two-thirds were of Mexican origin (2010); 65% spoke English solely or very well (2010); and 74% were U.S. citizens (2010). While 16% of the overall U.S. population lacked health insurance and 15% lived in poverty, the respective statistics for Hispanics were 31% and 25%. Median household income was $40,000, $9,800 less than the U.S. median.[3] Hispanics, like Blacks, are twice as likely as Whites to be imprisoned in-state for drug offenses, even with equal rates of drug use proportionate to population.[4]

I'm actually the first person in my family to go to college.

From 2000 to 2012, Hispanic high school graduates enrolling in college increased from 49% to 69%, the highest rate of increase in the nation. Though it has decreased from 28% to 14% from 2000 to 2011, the high school dropout rate for Hispanics is still the greatest in the nation, followed by Blacks, and Whites (7% to 5%), and then Asian-American students.[5]

1 The Saturday Evening Post, Volume 180, Issue 3; 2 https://digboston.com/boston-cop-beats-uber-driver-steals-car/; 3 http://www.pewhispanic.org/files/2012/06/The-10-Largest-Hispanic-Origin-Groups.pdf; 4 Ditton, P.M. & Wilson, D.J. "Truth in Sentencing in State Prisons," January 1999, Washington, DC: Bureau of Justice Statistics.; 5 http://www.pewhispanic.org/files/2013/05/PHC_college_enrollment_2013-05.pdf

"For it isn't enough to talk about peace. One must believe in it. And it isn't enough to believe in it. One must work at it."

—Eleanor Roosevelt

Let's Tune Up

by Darya Tahvilder-Zadeh

Growing up as a child of Iranian immigrants in America has been an illuminating yet confusing experience. There's a certain loneliness to not knowing that many people of your ethnicity. People of Iranian background have a way of "blending" in America; there's not really a distinct group of Iranians that all know each other like there is with other populations. It is quite a distancing experience to grow up seeing the only representation of your culture in popular media involve serious events and discussions about the nuclear deal or the hostage crisis. You look at that and think... that's my country, but that doesn't feel like who I am. My Iranian stepbrother was quite offended after watching *Argo*, a political movie about the Iran hostage crisis in 1979, claiming that "they represented us very badly; that's not what we're really like."

The day before first grade, I remember my dad telling me, "If someone asks about where you're from, remember, just say you're *American*, okay?" I remember being confused and repeatedly asking why I had to say I was American, because at that point my parents spoke exclusively Farsi with me at home and we ate only Persian cuisine.

At the time, I was too young to understand the complicated discourse going on between the two rivaling countries I found myself a part of. It was like having a foot in two worlds that were afraid of each other. My experience felt so different that I wasn't very sure where I fit in when it came to racial groups and discussions involving racism. However, I am so very lucky to have grown up in a diverse population, where the people are so willing to pursue a deeper understanding of racial tensions and issues.

Speaking out about issues involving race is the only way to make progress. The way I see it, the melting pot of America can be compared to an orchestra. Different races, different instruments. Members of an orchestra have to stay aware of their part in the piece. If your part doesn't have the melody at a certain point in the piece, you have to make sure your voice isn't overpowering the people who do have the melody, but supporting them.

This is what we have to do with race relations as well. Especially now, in the midst of tragic, unjustified deaths in the Black community and the rise of the Black Lives Matter movement, we need to listen to African-American voices in the community and work

> **"It was like having a foot in two worlds that were afraid of each other."**

with them instead of speaking over them. Injustice cannot be allowed to continue, and when we ignore it or worse, and begin to see it as normal, it only spreads.

My orchestra director has a phrase she repeats quite often when she's trying to get the different sections of the orchestra to play in tune with each other. "Why doesn't that *bother* you? When a chord isn't in tune, it should bother you. You need to be bothered, it's the only way to get any better." To tune properly, everyone has to listen to each other and adjust their pitch until it sounds correct. But to even get to that point, we have to recognize that something is wrong in the first place.

When we witness unjust events, we need to be bothered, because apathy is a force that only makes racism stronger. We need to stand up and say, "Hey, that's not right, how can we fix it?" With more careful listening, awareness, and understanding of each other, I hope that humanity can one day finally achieve harmony.

"I'm biracial—Roma and Caucasian. I can't go to parts of Europe because that would probably result in me being deported or discriminated against. But here, the Roma are very, very highly romanticized, so there is a lot of appropriation that happens just completely out of ignorance. Like when people wear things like "gypsy skirts" or call their belly dance group something to do with "the gypsy." It's usually fine, but sometimes it can turn into conflict, even in classes when your teachers have no idea how ignorant they are.**"**

Like when people wear things like "gypsy skirts."

This form of cultural appropriation results from ignorance of culture and prejudice stemming from colonial White power. Unlike people of color, White people can choose to engage in these cultural expressions without the associated stigma and discrimination, and often step over the line from appreciation to appropriation.

In addition to donning culturally-specific clothing without understanding their significance, examples of cultural appropriation include donning certain hairstyles (see Amandla Stenberg's "Don't Cash Crop on my Cornrows" video), dressing up as an ethnic stereotype (read about use of Blackface), and substituting sacred artifacts as accessories (see the controversy over Karlie Kloss's "sexy Indian" headdress).

CURRENT EVENT

originally a CHOOSE Facebook post
graphic credit: www.fusion.net

June 12th, 2016

The Orlando Massacre has shaken the nation—it has sent an earthquake trembling through our bodies and minds. It has not only taken human lives and justice from us, but it has also corrupted us.

We have become corrupted because we have labeled the enemy, violence, as "Muslim" and have distracted ourselves from the real issues: homophobia, Islamophobia, and racism just so that we may be more comfortable.

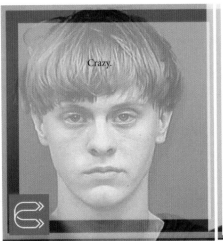

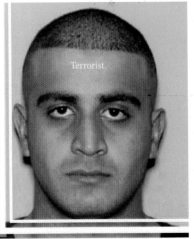

And if you are in denial—in denial of reality, then ask yourself: if we aren't being subjected to lies and propaganda, why has the Afghani Omar Mateen been deemed the terrorist but not the White Dylann Roof, who in June of 2015 was also responsible for taking lives?

Read more: http://fusion.net/story/313760/omar-mateen-orlando-dylann-roof-terror/

Long Interview
Youth Services Librarian
Jocelyn Jimenez talks
about the role of race in
her career and in the publishing industry, as well as
her family background,
culture, colorism, and her
interracial relationship.

❝ As a child, race wasn't a big thing for me. I didn't realize I was different until I was much older. I grew up in a pretty diverse city and neighborhood. There were other Latinos and there were always other races around me, so I never felt different. Then I went to Rutgers, which even President Obama says is one of the most diverse colleges in the country, so again I just felt like I was surrounded by so many different people. But once I went to graduate school and one step further, into the working world, it started to hit me that I was the only person of color in the room a lot of the time and I think it was a big wake up call for me.

Even though I never felt different growing up, when I look back at my childhood as an adult I remember specific events and think about them differently. I remember when I was in Kindergarten, I was placed into an English as a Second Language class. I was a huge reader. I loved to read and I was reading before a lot of other

❝ They literally looked at a sheet, saw my last name, and put me into an ESL class, and it didn't make any sense—to anyone— why I was there."

kids. I spoke English really well because my brother is five years older than me, and while my parents didn't speak English very well, he was ten years old, he was already in school and English was the language he was most comfortable with and so, that's the language he used to communicate with me. My love of reading, my brother's guidance, and, frankly, television, shaped my English skills, but they were strong enough that I didn't need extra help in school. The school hadn't asked my parents, they didn't clear it with anyone—I mean this was the early 90s—so, things were different, but the fact that nobody cleared it with my parents or even bothered to test my literacy skills is extremely disconcerting. They literally looked at a sheet, saw my last name, and put me into an ESL class, and it didn't make any sense—to anyone—why I was there. The only reason I even got out of the class as fast as I did was because my teacher fought for it. She was livid, so she was the one who fought for me.

My parents couldn't fight for me, because they didn't have... they couldn't—they just didn't have the voice to. I mean, I was five, so it didn't occur to me that anything was wrong, and that wasn't something that I learned until much, much later, and it clicked in my brain that, 'Oh wow, that was a really awful thing that happened—that shouldn't have happened, and luckily, someone did something about it.'

As someone who works with books and reading and literature, to think back to that moment and realize that people have made assumptions about my level of literacy based on my race—that kind of cuts me to the core, because that's obviously what I've always loved. I remember when I was applying to college and I had an interview with an admissions officer, and he kept making a big deal about the fact that I was a Latina looking to become an English major. He kept saying, 'Do you know how awesome it is that you want to be an English major? Do you know that there aren't a lot of Hispanic English majors?' I was a teenager so it made me feel very self-conscious and embarrassed at the time because it was one of the first times my differences were

ever acknowledged. I understand where he was coming from and he meant it as a compliment and as encouragement, but I was just a kid and I hadn't learned how to celebrate or embrace my culture, yet.

I mean, even I was uncomfortable talking about race, because for so long people just kind of ignored it. I think it's really easy for the people around me to forget that I'm Hispanic and while that meant that I never felt ostracized by my peers, it also meant that I never really learned how to navigate my cultural identity. I can't tell you how many racist Hispanic jokes have been made in front of me and if I did remind people that I, in fact, am Hispanic, I would usually get a belittling response of, 'Oh, but like, not really.' Or when I tell people that I don't like spicy food or onions and I get the response of, 'Wow, you're the worst Latina ever.' It seems harmless and I'll be honest, I've usually laughed it off, but reactions like that perpetuate stereotypes and they're also ignoring and shrugging off an entire part of my life—as if my entire heritage can be voided because I can't handle jalapeños.

I think it's also dif-

> « ...people have made assumptions about my level of literacy based on my race—that...cuts me to the core..."

> « No soy de aquí ni soy de allá. It's a popular saying that means, I'm not from here..."

ficult because I'm stuck in this awful in between that I think a lot of first generation kids feel: *No soy de aquí ni soy de allá.* It's a popular saying that means, I'm not from here, I'm not from there. I was born here. I grew up here. I know American history, I can recite the Pledge of Allegiance, I celebrate the Fourth of July. I feel very attached to American culture because that is the culture I was immersed in. It's what I learned in school. I'm Honduran, but I don't know anything about Honduras history. I don't even know the independance day off the top of my head—I only remember it when my relatives post something on Facebook. But, at the same time, I still think it's more appropriate for me to say 'I'm Honduran,' rather than 'I'm American,' because it feels like I'm not being authentic if I say I'm American, which I don't think it's fair because I feel like I am. But, as I mentioned before, I also get the other side of it, where I'm not 'Hispanic enough' and so I'm stuck feeling like I don't belong in either.

I can walk into a room and be somewhat racially ambiguous. People can assume that I'm white because I have light skin. I feel like even I have benefited from white privilege growing up, because, again, I feel like I can walk into a room and people can just assume that I'm White. But, at the end of the day, when my name is on an application for a job, or for an apartment, or for anything, my last name 100% stands out.

This past summer, I wanted to rent a beach house for my boyfriend's birthday. We were trying to get it with a group of friends, and I was not getting responses. I kept thinking, 'man, we really booked late in the game.' I had been pretty busy one week so I asked him to take over and send out a few e-mails. He immediately got responses back (my boyfriend's last name is very obviously Irish). And it's those little things. You know, I can't prove it. I can't prove that all those people were being racist, but it's that fact that I spent weeks sending out emails—the most articulate, polite, clear-cut emails. And just nothing. If I did get responses from people, it would be a very definitive no, but everyone that e-mailed him, even if it was a no, it was like people wanted to go further for him, they would say, 'I don't have a house that week, but I have another house here for this many people on a different date.' It's just like, 'Really?'

So, it's those little things that are kind of tough. I really never felt it when I was younger, versus now I feel it all the time.

When I was younger, I thought being Latina was cool. I used to travel to Honduras a lot growing up, to visit my grandparents, so I thought it was cool that I got to have these different experiences. I never felt ashamed of my culture. But, for one of my cousins, it was really difficult for him. He moved when he was in first grade and he was going on his first ever field trip. Back in the day, everyone knew that when you had to bring lunch for a field trip, you had to bring Lunchables—that was just the cool thing to do. Being new, he obviously didn't know that, and his mom packed him this very traditional Honduran meal. It was very simple, just this thicker bread, beans, and mantequilla, which is like cream cheese but butterier. He brought it, having been super excited for it since it's delicious, and one of his classmates was like, 'Ew what is that?'

He told me that that was the first time that he felt ashamed about his culture. So, in retrospect, maybe I was also somewhat ashamed because I loved that same meal, but I never brought that to school. I would eat it at home, but

it wasn't something that I would bring around my friends. So, to some extent, there were certain things that you were just like 'this is not what everyone else does, so I'm just not going to talk about it.'

Now I think about it in terms of—I want to talk to people that have the same cultural backgrounds me, because it's nice to bond about things like pan con frijoles y mantequilla. I want to connect to someone else about it. One of the greatest things about the Internet is that you can connect to people whom you didn't otherwise know. I can't imagine being 26, before the Internet, and trying to figure out my cultural identity and understanding how I feel about it without being able to connect to other people, going through the same experiences, via the Internet.

I think you should acknowledge other people's backgrounds, and, honestly, I love when people ask me questions. I mean, there's a way to phrase them—sometimes questions will seem very rude. For example, I celebrate Christmas on Christmas Eve. For us it's always midnight, and it's almost like a New Year's Eve party, but with Christmas. A lot of Hispanic people celebrate it that way, and I love when people are like, 'Oh that's different that Christmas Eve is your Christmas,

> **"I can't imagine being 26, before the Internet, and trying to figure out my cultural identity..."**

> **"But, at the end of the day, when my name is on an application for a job, or for an apartment, or for anything, my last name 100% stands out."**

tell me more about that.' Because once they ask, then I can go into it.

I think we should openly discuss our differences because ignoring it doesn't change the fact that it exists. I do have a different background than other people. We may have all gone to a school in New Jersey, gone to the same college, and all that, but at the end of the day the way I was raised is different than the way you were raised, and we've had different experiences. I think that people get weird to talk about that, and it's almost taboo to actively talk about someone else's race.

I think what makes a question or discussion or statement offensive has everything to do with inflection. If say, 'Oh that's interesting. Tell me more about that,' versus, 'Oh my god... you do that?'

Or, 'That's so weird that you do something different than I do,' versus, 'That's interesting that you do something different than I do. Tell me more.'

I think it comes down to that. Which, again, I think comes down to the issue at hand nobody teaches you how to talk about race.

***

I watched this short video in The New York Times called 'A Conversation with Latinos on Race,' where this guy, who had light skin and green eyes, said that he 100% bene-fited from white privilege growing up because he was also racially ambiguous, but more importantly, because he had light eyes. Having blue eyes is fetishized in society, and that goes with people loving the white aesthetic. Colorism happens within the Hispanic race for sure. Hispanics and Latinos have a wide range of skin tones, and the lighter your skin, the better off you are. People look at you differently, or they find you more attractive if you have lighter skin. I think a lot of times, in Latin America, lighter skin is associated with Europe and Europe is seen as more prestigious than Central or South America.

In the New York Times piece, there was also this woman, and she talked about having two daughters—one was lighter than the other, and when they were very young the one sister turned to her other and said, 'Well, you're Black!' as an insult.

The mom said she just started crying before she took them aside and explained to them that what society had taught them was wrong and what they may have heard, even from their own family members, was wrong.

***

Both my parents are from Honduras, but different parts. My dad is from the capital, Tegucigalpa, and my mom is from Copán, which is known for its Mayan Ruins. I can count on one hand the people in my family that have married interracially. Actually, almost everyone is married to another Honduran. My one cousin and I are the only ones dating interracially right now but both guys were welcomed with open arms—both are blue eyed, White guys.

They'll make a joke about 'improving the race.' It's an offhand joke that they've made about how you should always date up, date someone that is good looking, ideally with ojos claros (light eyes), because those are the genes that you'll pass down to your kids, and it's one of those things that, again, I didn't notice until I was older—that even within people of color, colorism is a big problem.

If you were to look at statistics of your own personal reading, you're more likely to find that a majority of the authors you read are white. Even the books that have diverse characters are written by White authors. I've struggled a lot with this concept where you wonder if it's okay for a White author to write about the experiences of people of color,

> " If you were to look at sta-tisitcs of your own personal reading, you're more likely to find that a **majority of the authors you read are white. Even the books that have diverse characters are written by white authors."**

because is that saying that a woman writer can't write a male character? No, of course they can and there are plenty of books that have done it well, but it's also disheartening to see so many stories told by white people about people of color. Even *The Help*—A lot of people read it and love it, but I think there are a lot of issues with it, too. The author was a White woman writing the experiences of a black woman. Which, I don't know... it can be done, but I just think, 'Why aren't we turning to the Black women to write about Black women?'

I actively sit down and track the statistics of my reading habits because the first time I ever took the time to see how white my reading was, I was shocked. So, now I try my best to read more diverse books. And it's not as if beforehand I had decided to never read diversely. Nobody goes out and says 'I'm only going to read books written by White guys!' It's just the fact that that's what gets advertised and marketed, and when it's marketed more, more people are reading it, and then more people start talking about it, and then all of a sudden those are the only books that you're hearing about. So, I think as a librarian, as someone that is putting books into people's hands, it's important for me to stop and think about diversity.

I actually just listened to a podcast where they discussed a controversy surrounding Sherman Alexie. He wrote *The Absolutely True Diary of a Part-Time Indian.* He is also a gifted poet and he was put in charge of curating the anthology, 'Best American Poetry 2015.' He received a submission from someone who wrote under a Chinese woman's name, but it was actually a white male, and it was one of the poems he picked. So, when he contacted all the poets telling them they were

selected, the guy revealed his true identity and said that he was doing it because he sent his poem out to 10 different places, but nobody published it with his real name, so he started sending it out as a Chinese woman, and it was finally chosen. The man was trying to make a statement about publishing being too politically correct.

Sherman Alexie had a really great comeback. His reasoning for keeping the poem in the anthology despite the deception is that he was specifically making a point to read diversely and so, when he thought the poem was written by a Chinese woman, he made it a point to give the poem a bit more thought before throwing it into a yes/maybe/no pile. That extra moment is what made it a maybe and then the quality of the poem is what pushed him to publish it.

Although this instance is marked with controversy, I think it is also showing us that there are people out there that are finally taking the time to pause and think about diversity and that pause can do amazing things.

The majority of people getting published are White because the majority of people submitting work are White, which trickles down to the schools. Why aren't we encouraging people of color to express themselves more? Why aren't we encouraging them to write stories and why aren't we telling them that their stories deserve to be told? Because I think that's—that's where the real issue is. We need to make people feel like their stories are worth being told, that people want to hear what they have to say. I think too many people get told that nobody will relate to their story because it's different, but there are so many people who feel different that are waiting to find a story they can relate to. **"**

> **"We need to make people feel like their stories are worth being told, that people want to hear what they want to say. I think too many people get told that nobody will relate to their story because it's different."**

She stated making assumptions about who she is just because she was Hispanic.

Media portrayals of Hispanics can diminish or exacerbate stereotypically negative opinions about them. As a result, non-Hispanics tend to believe that these stereotypes are true. Typically, they are displayed as fitting subordinate roles (gardeners, dropouts, maids, and criminals).[1] Assumptions are often made that they are unskilled, undocumented, and dangerous during the hiring process, leading to employment discrimination.[2]

It was really uncomfortable for me. I guess I don't look very Hispanic.

Colorism occurs when someone is treated differently, even among people of the same race, because of a lighter skin tone. Having light skin or Anglo features leads to the interviewee benefiting from white privilege in a way her darker counterpart would not. Refer to page 61.

1 http://www.latinodecisions.com/blog/2012/09/18/how-media-stereotypes-about-latinos-fuel-negative-attitudes-towards-latinos/; 2 http://sophia.stkate.edu/cgi/viewcontent.cgi?article=1436&context=msw_papers

Graphic Credit:
Ayesha Qureshi

**There was a Hispanic woman at my job who came in and asked for an application at the diner. I was in the kitchen, and one of my coworkers who had handed her the application came in. I overheard her speaking with one of her friends about the way she looked. She stated making assumptions about who she is just because she was Hispanic. She mumbled 'it's a good thing we're racist here, she's not getting the job.'

It was really uncomfortable for me. I guess I don't look very Hispanic. I was just standing there, I didn't even say anything. Looking back I probably would have said 'what is it that I'm here for then? Why am I here?' It just made me feel uncomfortable and not as proud to work there. You should be proud of where you work, regardless if it's part-time. You should look like you want to be there. But, after that I kind of got this shady vibe from everyone around because I was the only Hispanic girl. I also heard the owner has a reputation of hiring attractive girls so then I felt like maybe I fell into that category, which still makes me feel really uncomfortable. She never got the job though. I never knew why. I wasn't even supposed to know she applied because I was just overhearing. They were talking pretty loud though so it didn't seem like they cared. It was awful.**

INTER-
PERSONAL

" I live with Turkish, Egyptian, African-American, and Caucasian people. I am a medical student from India staying under one roof with all of these people harmoniously. Can you believe it? Me, an Indian girl, who always was around Indians, obviously, because I lived in India, living with such a diverse group of people. It makes me feel so enlightened, and it's just incredible. "

It makes me feel so enlightened. Coming from a racially homogenous society, the woman in the above interview finds the "salad bowl" of cultures in the United States to be illuminating. As of 2013, non-Hispanic Whites make up 63 percent of the U.S.; Hispanics, 17 percent; Blacks, 12.3 percent; Asians, 5 percent; and multiracial Americans, 2.4 percent.[1] Researchers Sheen S. Levine and David Stark found that, empirically, "diversity improves the way people think. By disrupting conformity, racial and ethnic diversity [prompt] people to scrutinize facts, think more deeply and develop their own opinions."[2]

1 http://usnews.nbcnews.com/_news/2013/06/13/18934111-census-White-majority-in-us-gone-by-2043 2 http://www.nytimes.com/2015/12/09/opinion/diversity-makes-you-brighter.html?_r=0

"Screwing Native Americans Over the Federal Government Way"

Credit: Barry Deutsch, leftycartoons.com

CHOOS

An Experience in Ballet
by Ashlyn Liverman

"I don't know if you would be able to..."

"Why?"

"Because you're this," as she pointed to the color of my skin.

Around three years ago, I performed in the ballet *Sleeping Beauty*. If you do the math, that would mean I was probably around the age of 12. The day of the show, all of the performers gathered inside of a large ball-room filled with numerous amounts of chairs and were sectioned off by what role they were. Most of my friends and I personally love kids, so the day of the show, we traveled from kid to kid, introducing ourselves, and giving them words of encouragement. One little girl that stood out from the rest was named Nina, as she was full of energy and sass. Her sense of humor and individualism helped calm down our nerves before we stepped onto the stage. That portion of dialogue is actually between her and me. I know, right? You would not think that a six year old would even know about discriminating people based off of the color of their skin.

My immediate response was nothing. I just sat there, staring into her eyes, appalled at what I had just heard. My heart stopped for a second, and all I could think about was running home to my parents who would understand how I felt. Since all of the performers were in the room running around and screaming, nobody could hear what she had said except for my Caucasian friends and me. While my reaction was shock, my friends just sat there continuing on with their conversation. One laughed over the situation, while another supported me and told Nina that it was not polite to say something like that. The shock turned to red hot anger as I spoke up, saying "That's so mean!" However, my friends simply said, "Don't worry about it."

photo credit: American Repertory Ballet

> **❝** A little six-year-old just told me that I wouldn't be able to babysit her **because of the color of my skin."**

How was I not supposed to worry about something like this? A little six-year-old just told me that I wouldn't be able to babysit her because of the color of my skin. My good spirits from earlier all went down and I just wanted my friends to understand how negatively the situation affected me. And that's the problem today. People who haven't dealt with racism, don't know how it affects others and just ignore it. From when people call me ghetto for listening to Drake or Kanye, to store managers following me around at stores because they think I'm going to steal something, to teachers treating me as though I'm less smarter than all of the other kids in my class. Even though we try to think racism doesn't exist, it does, and even when it is addressed, it still continues to happen. When people see me, I want them to see me as a straight-A student who has a mom who attended Princeton University, an aunt who's a neurosurgeon, a dad who is council president of Princeton and has worked so hard to get where he is today, and just a girl trying to make it through life. About a month ago, I saw Nina again three years later. I hoped she'd changed.

Tolerance
by Amy Watsky

Coming from a culturally diverse background, I was introduced to difference from a very young age. I was taught to embrace both my Japanese side as well as my American side, which, in turn, allowed me to embrace other cultures and races as well. This has proved to be a very important life lesson, as I have come to realize that people around the world fear difference and, as a result, cause irresolvable conflicts. Being biracial has allowed me to step in other pairs of shoes, and envision life through other sets of eyes in order to recognize the importance of acceptance and the damage of distrust and hate. It has taught me that fear itself can build up walls that cannot be broken by anything but tolerance.

People that really can't stay here, they're being bought out like crazy.

Refer to the first discussion point on page 167.

It's not slavery like we knew it before, it's called modern slavery now.

Racial inequality in the United States has taken many forms over the past few centuries, and despite the abolition of the formal institution of slavery, systems that suppress Blacks and other minorities still exist. For example, in *The New Jim Crow*, author Michelle Alexander explains modern mass incarceration as a redesigned racial caste system, as "like Jim Crow (and slavery), mass incarceration operates as a tightly networked system of laws, policies, customs, and institutions that operate collectively to ensure the subordinate status of a group defined largely by race."

[It's] not only an issue of race—it's about the economy. The rich get richer, the poor get poorer. There's no such thing as [the] middle class.

In 2015, out of approximately 242.1 million adults in America, 120.8 million are considered middle class while 121.3 million are lower or upper class citizens. While middle-income households have fallen to around 50% from 61% of the population in 1971, the share living in upper-income households have risen from 14% to 21%, and from 25% to 29% in lower-income households.[1] Socioeconomic status closely correlates with race: Pew Research Center found that the current wealth gap between Whites and Blacks is the largest since 1989, with Whites having a net worth 13 times greater than Blacks and 10 times greater than Hispanics. From 2010 to 2013, non-Hispanic White household median wealth increased 2.4% from $138,600 to $141,900, while it fell 33.7% from $16,600 to $11,000 for Black households and fell 14.3% from $16,000 to $13,700 for His-panic households.[2]

Educational disparities also play a factor into the wealth gap. The median weekly earning of a high school dropout is $493, compared to $1,341 for a bachelor degree.[3] In a study of U.S. educational attainment from 2011 to 2013 of 23-24 year-olds, Black, Hispanic, and White students earned Bachelor's or higher degrees at a rate of 14%, 11% and 31%, respectively. In addition, while Blacks constituted 4% of the top decile of U.S. colleges, they were 26% of the bottom decile.[4]

I see a lot of stuff at the high school that you have that six miles away the Trenton kids can't afford to have.

The interviewee notes the differences between resources for Princeton High School and Trenton area high schools, or more generally, the disparity between suburban and urban areas. In a Sustainable Prosperity report, suburban households were able to pay $435 to schools, $87 to busses and $72 to libraries. Urban households could only delegate $232, $13 and $38, respectively, limiting funds and resources for local schools.[5]

Less value and emphasis on schools also contributes to a greater dropout rate. A study from the American Promise Alliance found that, in the top 50 U.S. cities, there was a 53% graduation rate, compared to 71% in suburbs. The biggest gap was in Cleveland, where only 38% graduated from urban high schools while 80% graduated in suburban schools.[6] As one of the most segregated cities in America, Cleveland houses more minorities in urban areas, where there is less access to a better quality education; for example, 9% of Blacks versus 22% of Whites received a Bachelor's degree.[7]

1 http://www.pewsocialtrends.org/2015/12/09/the-american-middle-class-is-losing-ground/; 2 http://www.pewresearch.org/fact-tank/2014/12/12/racial-wealth-gaps-great-recession/; 3 http://www.bls.gov/emp/ep_chart_001.htm; 4 https://www.brookings.edu/blog/brown-center-chalkboard/2016/06/06/7-findings-that-illustrate-racial-disparities-in-education/; 5 http://curbed.com/archives/2015/03/09/suburban-vs-urban-infrastructure-costs.php; 6 http://www.americaspromise.org/APAPage.aspx?id=13074; 7 http://www.communitysolutions.com/race-in-cleveland

" There's a lot of money coming in this area right now, and there's a lot of people [who] grew up here in Princeton, [who] after a while aren't gonna be able to live here because it's gonna be too much for them. A lot of people are sick and dying and are being bought out and can't afford it no more. People that really can't stay here, they're being bought out like crazy. And they don't make that kind of money, so they're not gonna be able to stay. You can look right over there [on Witherspoon Street], those houses are like 2 million dollars.

It's not politics, it's politricks. They just do it in a cunning way. It's not slavery like we knew it before, it's called modern slavery now.

Everyone should be paid on a better scale than they are paid now. Now we gotta make ends meet. People are like 'Have a nice day! Now I gotta go to my second job!' You keep hearing that, second job, second job, I got a part time job, I got a second job .... You got people 80 years old and they're still working. You gotta say, 'I'll eat less this week so I can pay my cable bill. I was gonna take my vacation this summer, but nah.' It's hard.

[It's] not only an issue of race—it's about the economy. The rich get richer, the poor get poorer. There's no such thing as [the] middle class. Reagan made sure of that. Every time Obama does something, what do the Republicans do? They don't even respect him, don't call him Mr. President. 'Obama,' like he's one of the guys on the street. But if it was Mr. Bush or something, 'Hello, Mr. President.' It's like Obama's a homeboy or something. They just don't care—I mean, look around you. Everywhere you go someone will get shot and killed, and any time Obama wants to stop with the gun control ... they say, 'Obama go home, we don't want you, get out of here.'

There is [also] no such thing as a childhood. These young kids, they don't cherish life the way I did when we were growing up. Poor kids that can't get access to things that you students all are fortunate to get. I see a lot of stuff that, six miles away, the Trenton kids can't afford to have. I'm a custodian, and I see crayons and pencils and papers being thrown away when they could be donated where kids don't have the notebooks. You could be doing something to help the kids who are not fortunate enough to be blessed to have parents. There are a lot of kids over there, who maybe have one mom who's trying to work, who can't afford to buy even a backpack. "

*second interviewee declined photo

❝I'm from Thailand originally. I came when I was 15... I've been here for about 10 years. It was really hard at first because I didn't really know how to speak English. I remember the first day of school was really hard; I didn't even understand what was going on. Toward the end, it was [still] really hard, but then it got better. Stereotypes happen, stereotypes haven't gone yet.**❞**

I'm from Thailand originally.
According to the Thai Community Development Center, there have historically been three waves of Thai migration. The first, pioneer migration, occurred in a post-war era with primarily educated, middle-class immigrants; the second, group migration, was controlled by U.S. immigration laws and diversified the composition of the population. Since the 1980s, mass migration has marked the third stage, in which many immigrants are exploited due to a lack of education, documentation, and/or English proficiency. Ineligible to receive public benefits, many Thai people are economically disadvantaged and need access to basic health, education, and employment resources.[1]

1 http://thaicdc.org/ourcommunity/

❝I'm part of PHS Studio Band, and we sometimes see other bands that are primarily one race. Race is a surface quality, but you wouldn't necessarily feel comfortable joining a band or going into something where everyone else is only one race.**❞**

Race is a surface quality, but you wouldn't necessarily feel comfortable joining a band or going into something where everyone else is only one race. Being White, the majority race in America, he acknowledges possible racial alienation as the minority in a non-White majority band. This experience is uncomfortable. Possible outcomes include forced conformity, dressing and acting to fit in with majority. On the other hand, related to the scrutiny from being "different" is the burden of tokenism, which puts an individual minority in the position to represent his or her entire group and forces race to consume an entire identity.[1]

1 http://connection.ebscohost.com/c/articles/4612893/fitting-in-issues-tokenism-conformity-minority-women

Gentrification happens multiple differ-ent ways, when wealthy neighborhoods introduce different minorities and those properties lose value.

American cities are changing rapidly. Since 2000, almost 20% of neighborhoods with lower incomes and home values have gone through gentrification (compared to only 9% during the 1990s).[1] Hispanics have displaced Blacks as the dominant urban minority, and Blacks are moving into the suburbs or other regions of the country.[2] The social, economic, and physical impact that gentrification has often results in political conflicts. When prices go up, resulting in tenants to be kicked out and the resulting demographic is typically majority White. Earlier residents, often low-income minori-ties, feel excluded from their own com-munities and subject to racism when new arrivals come in attempting to improve local conditions.[3]

I definitely see that minorities live in less wealthy areas; it definitely has to do with history and here, the history of Princeton.
Refer to page 138.

1 http://www.governing.com/gov-data/census/gentrification-in-cities-govern-ing-report.html; 2 http://www.nytimes.com/2015/02/25/opinion/the-gentrifica-tion-effect.html; 3 http://www.pbs.org/pov/flagwars/what-is-gentrification/

❝ My mom grew up here in the Princeton area. She actually lived up on John Street. She's noticed a huge change—I've noticed it too—between ritzy Prince-ton and not-so-ritzy Princeton, to put it in simple terms. I don't know if you no-ticed, but everything past John Street is ritzy. Especially in John Street there's a lot of gentrification; I've been there and seen what's going on. Lots that were owned by people who weren't as rich are being taken over and knocked down, and multi million dollar houses are being built over there. Gentrification happens multiple different ways, when wealthy neighborhoods introduce different minorities and those properties lose value. Minorities are kicked out and value is so low that White people can buy it back for a lower price. Families don't have enough money for the taxes that are being placed. My grandmother's house—my mother's in the process of selling it and she knows what's going to happen. Someone's gonna buy it, and knock it down, and build something else on top of it; something much more expen-sive, something much bigger.

I definitely see that minorities live in less wealthy areas; it definitely has to do with history and here, the history of Princeton. But I haven't really learned about the history of Princeton [in schools]. ❞

" I was a student in Central High School, Philadelphia—I was born in 1941. During my senior year I took American History. My teacher, Mr. Soslow, got to the 'War Between the States' (that's what they called it in our textbook)—you know, that war that was fought between 1861 and 1865 'over tariffs,' they said. According to the textbook, there was something called slavery, but that was a really a 'minor detail.' Mr. Soslow said to us, 'Well, gentlemen, that is bull shit.' I don't know if that's exactly what he said, but that's how I remember it. He pointed out how the textbook had to be approved by the Texas textbook review board, so the true history was censored. His discussion of the Civil War and Reconstruction were a challenge to textbooks that told us that Reconstruction was a mistake, that the northerners, 'carpetbaggers,' were there as exploiters, and southern turncoats were 'scalawags.'

My experience with African Americans was limited to my school years at Central. Philadelphia schools were segregated because of restrictions on where African Americans could live. Central was an academic high school with students from all over the city. About 15% of the students were African American. At that time it was all boys. It seemed to me that the Black and White students treated each other as social equals, but I've never asked one of the Black students to confirm this. Here's one memory. Elmer Gibson was sunbathing on the south lawn at Central on one of the last days of the school year. I said, 'Elmer, you're going to get a sunburn.'

He said, 'No, no, no. Negroes don't get sunburned.'

The next day I saw that he was really burned badly. He said, 'Guess what? Negroes get sunburned,' and we both laughed.

> " According to the textbook, there was something called slavery, but that was a really a 'minor detail.'"

That's just a small piece of my story. It framed my attitude—plus the kind of family I grew up in, which was very open to racial equality, at least for that time. This may seem like a very small thing now.

My father was a teacher in the Philadelphia public schools. He had a colleague, Charlie Highsmith, who would come to our house as a social equal. This was in the early 1950s. There are very few White people of my age that can tell you that an African American would come to their house as a social equal.

You have to understand what it was like to be Jewish then. We were 'half castes' meaning that we had almost all the rights of White folks. There were residential and employment restrictions and 'Jewish quotas' in colleges. For example, I was a National Merit nominee. One of my White, non-Jewish friends was accepted at Princeton with similar grades and SATs as me. My college advisor said, 'You must be kidding!' when I asked about applying there myself.

***

I was a physics major at Muhlenberg College. I didn't really know what I wanted to do, so I took a couple of extra courses and in 1962 I was admitted to both Medical school and graduate school. The graduate school came with a fellowship. I took that because I could be independent. I was sure I would like it... until I actually did it. And then it wasn't interesting at all. I dropped out and substitute taught in the Philadelphia public schools to earn my way. I reapplied to medical school and entered in September 1963, one week after the great March on Washington.

Much of the years 1962-63 I spent in civil rights activity with CORE—The Congress of Racial Equality. I don't talk about it a lot because people imme-

Robert Karp shares his stories of growing up Jewish in Philadelphia and how his experience as an activist in the Civil Rights Movement shaped his medical career.

diately assume, 'Oh, it must have been like Selma!' But it wasn't even vaguely like Selma. Nobody treated me badly.

One of the times I was arrested with a group of people, they took us to the police station, opened the door of the van, and said, 'Go home.' I remember one cold winter day at a demonstration. There was a freezing rain. I was so cold that I thought my feet would fall off. That's the closest I came to a Selma experience. I spent the last two weeks of that summer of 1963 ordering busses from the CORE office to take people to the March on Washington.

We'd have meetings at the CORE offices every week, and they could be rather boisterous. One of the important things was that African Americans led the meetings—Lou Smith, his brother Joe, Connie Badger, and Alton Lemon. Later, Al initiated the U.S. Supreme Court's case on the separation of church and state. I remember Lou Smith very well. He worked in a vacuum cleaning store as a repairman/salesman. Lou thought things through so well. Given an opportunity, he wouldn't be selling vacuum cleaners. He'd own the company or be a professor somewhere.

The politics of the Civil Rights Movement began to the left of the Dem-ocratic Party. Lou once said, You know, African Americans really appreciate the White radicals for their energy and enthusiasm, but there are times when they put their ideology ahead of the good of the people,' That has stuck with me. Unfortunately, Lou was killed in a car crash years later.

When I was at the March on Washington, I only remember one speech besides King's 'I have a dream.' Rabbi Joachim Prinz spoke representing the Jewish community. He said (I'm paraphrasing here), 'I was a rabbinical student in Berlin, when the Nazis were rising to power. They aren't the ones I think about now. We knew what they were like. It was the good Germans, the good people, who stood idly by that I remember.' That's actually a Biblical quotation; the comment, 'Do not stand idly by.' appeared many times in Rev. King's speeches from then on.

It was really hot that day, and the crowd was restless when Reverend King came up to speak. During the first part he listed the many dreadful things that have happened to Af-rican American people in the United States. And then he started with, 'I have a dream.' A lot of people had portable radios, and there were loud speakers, all off by about a half second. So Rev. King would say, 'I have a dream,' and then it would repeat in the background from the speakers... I... I... HAVE... HAVE... HAVE. The speech lifted us off our feet. We floated several inches above the ground. Some of us never came down completely. These experiences clearly shaped my attitudes and career.

> " The speech lifted us off our feet. We floated several inches above the ground. Some of us never came down completely."

> " One of the important things was that African Americans led the meetings—Lou Smith, his brother Joe, Connie Badger, and Alton Lemon."

***

The war in Vietnam was expanding. While in medical school, I applied for conscientious objector status, which I received rather easily because of my civil rights activity, which showed my commitment. My work then was in nutrition. I continued this as a pediatrician in the War on Poverty for 14 years, and then for 30 years in central Brooklyn, NY. My work flowed very naturally from my experience in the Civil Rights Movement. So, here I am 54 years later. I think that what I've done is for the good, but there is still so much more to do. **"**

originally a CHOOSE Facebook post
graphic credit: Aileen Wu

*In June 2016, a
Princeton sociol-
ogist conducted
a study, which
showed that race is
one of the factors
that may either
impede or bene-
fit your chances of
accessing mental
health care—de-
pending on whether
you are non-White
or White.*

*This was proven
when "two voice-
mail messages were
left for 320 New
York City therapists,
randomly select-
ed from a major
health insurance
company's listing
of providers. One
call was from a
purportedly Black
therapy seeker and
the other was from
a purportedly White
therapy seeker.
Half were middle
class and half were
working class; they
were also evenly
divided by gender.*

From 80 therapists,

16 responses.   1 response.

*The results were
striking: Thera-
py seekers portrayed as middle-class Whites received appointment offers, for any day or
time, from almost 30 percent of therapists. Working-class therapy seekers — both Black and
White, male and female — received offers from less than 10 percent. The middle-class Black
man received appointment offers from 13 percent, and the middle-class Black woman from
21 percent."*

*Read more:
https://www.princeton.edu/main/news/archive/S46/47/86C24/*

Most people do not assume I am Muslim, because I am African-American.

The American Muslim population is, on average, both younger and more diverse than the U.S. population. 23% of the American-Muslim population is Black, 30% is White, 21% is Asian, 19% is other/mixed, and 6% is Hispanic, according to the Pew Research Center.[1]

I would say that there is a stereotype that the International Baccalaureate education system is hard for kids of color.

A 2015 study shows that in U.S. Title I schools, 85% of Black students and 82% of Hispanic students in the International Baccalaureate Diploma Programme enroll in college immediately following high school graduation. The national average for postsecondary college enrollment is 57% for African Americans, 60% for Hispanics, 80% for Asian Americans, and 69% for Non-Hispanic Whites.[2]

[1] http://www.people-press.org/2011/08/30/section-1-a-demographic-portrait-of-muslim-americans/; [2] http://ibo.org/globalassets/publications/ib-research/title-1-schools-research.pdf

"Certain comments are made in class [about] race or terrorism. Most people do not assume I am Muslim, because I am African-American. So beforehand, there are a bunch of comments regarding how all Muslims are terrorist and radical. Then when I make someone aware of my religion they have a different opinion, and I tell them that just like Christians, there are people that misinterpret the religion and hurt other people.

I have grown numb to it. I wear my hijab to school, and people ask questions about why I am wearing it. I then explain to them why, and they become more open and accepting of it. If many people would take the time to have a conversation and befriend a Muslim American, then they would understand that the media and many radical politcians just generalize Muslims and many other minorities.

I would say that there is a stereotype that the International Baccalaureate education system is hard for kids of color. Many kids in IB do not know about the benefits of IB, because many minority parents are not apart of the Parent-Teacher-Student Association. I kind of feel that, because of the diversity problems in IB, many minorities do feel that IB is hard [and] there is less of a support system than many other students receive."

Interviews by and photo courtesy to CHOOSE Chapter @ Atlanta Founder Jordan Williams

"Most of my experiences have been with microaggressions, which is sometimes worse than direct [racism]. Because they're subtle, it's hard to call people out on them. I have dealt with dress code rules that apply to African-American trends and styles, such as dreads. One in particular involves no crop tops; however, a fellow White classmate was able to enter the establishment with it. You can't wear Jordans shoes also. This is covert racism.

Affirmative action is a necessary process in some colleges. It is needed in jobs more than colleges, however. Diversity brings different talent and different perspectives to either the workplace or college. If minority groups (such as African Americans and Hispanics) are under 10%, then the school is not very diverse. Also, because race applies to economics, it in return can show the relation to the disparities in education.

Fair skin in the Philippines and in most countries gives off the perception of class or wealth.
See the second discussion point on colorism on page 61.

In a short documentary on racism in the Philippines, a Nigerian teenager named Alexander Omiunu says, "People treat you differently, just because you're darker. Knowing you in the Philippines, you know that whole mentality of White is superior..." He adds that, for six years, everyone has told him he looks like Dwyane Wade.[1]

[1] https://www.youtube.com/watch?v=tk4w8g-fzh28

" Have you ever been hurt by racism?"

"Yes, both physically and emotionally. When I was in middle school, people would pull my hair and try to cut it. Everyone would want to touch my hair, because I was the only Asian girl in the class, and they saw me as different."

"What is the standard of beauty in the Philippines?"

"You are either a Morena or Mestiza. A Mestiza is a person who has a pale or fair skin tone. A Morena is a person who has a more tan or olive skin. It is the same standard as it is in the U.S.—lighter is prettier. Women in the Philippines go to an extreme to bleach their skin or make their skin lighter than it truly is. Fair skin in the Philippines and in most countries gives off the perception of class or wealth. Never in my life have I tried to alter the complexion of my skin, because I love my skin and accept that it is beautiful... Every color is beautiful and I believe to not change who you are to fit into society. If you are born from the Philippines and have a darker skin tone, then accept who you are and your heritage no matter what people say, because you are equal.

"How important is race in society?"

"I do not focus on race. I focus on myself and trying to get power, so I can change the importance of race in society. It is sad, but that is how society works. The people with power dictate how society is run. **"**

Disparities in education are just horrible. You can't start by talking about them at a district level—it is at a much larger level... Teachers are so important in the process, and we need to listen to what they say. There is some input-output function with the race of the teacher and the race of the students. So this in many institutions is 'I do not want to work with regular kids,' which, in most cases, are minority students.

Also, reverse racism in an American society cannot exist. African Americans economically do not have the power to influence people's life across the nation. Even if we are prejudiced... which we are. **"**

If minority groups such as African Americans and Hispanics are under 10%, then the school is not very diverse.
As of July 2015, 13.3% of the U.S. population is Black or African-American and 17.6% is Hispanic.[1]

[1] https://www.census.gov/quickfacts/table/PST045215/00

" Education covers a lot of ground. I try to remove myself from situations where I don't want to see it, I don't want to hear about it, but I know it exists. And I raise my kids that way and I like the way they turned out, but unfortunately [racism] happens and I don't know what to do. I don't know how you can change these people's minds. I wish there was a way. Education is [more like] education and humanity because you can have an advanced degree but still be race-entitled. So that doesn't correct anything.

School would probably not be a bad place, but I think kids need to be exposed to it early on so they don't grow to be twenty-five and be like, 'Oh, I didn't know I was racist.' We need to [become] the generation that tries to at least cure some of this... Kids y'know are going to be told weird stuff at home, but at least if they get another view maybe we can lessen that. We basically choose to look at everyone the same. Everyone is equal."

"We choose to basically see everyone's regardless of what is it y'know: race, ethnicity, sexual orientation, it doesn't matter. When I was raised they tried to view everything as almost a colorblind society. In a way that's good, but on the other hand, instead of seeing everyone's differences and appreciating the qualities of those differences, they try to gloss over that and say those differences don't exist. But I think it's important that you need to embrace that people are different and those differences come with some really good qualities. And they need to embrace those qualities if we teach these to our kids. "

Education is [more like] education and humanity because you can have an advanced degree but still be race-entitled.

According to Harvard President Catharine Drew Gilpin Faust and cultural critic Leon Wieseltier, the study of humanities is "rooted in slowness" and a lifetime of learning. While Faust and Wieseltier believe study of the humanities is increasingly needed in a fast-paced, technology-centered, and polarized modern culture, from 2012 to 2014 the number of students receiving Bachelor's degrees in literature, history, linguistics, classical study and philosophy declined by over 8%.[1] Improvements and innovation in technology cannot be equated with improvements in humanity, and according to Wieseltier, "What the humanities teach, what literature and art and music and philosophy and history teach, is that the correct description and analysis of human life is not a scientific affair." In addition, Faust says that the humanities "[teach] empathy for people other than yourself," a skill vital in an increasingly diversified nation.[2]

I try to remove myself from situations where I don't want to see it, I don't want to hear about it, but I know it exists.

According to Kristina Olson, Ph.D., "Decades of research suggests that even if parents are not talking about race, children are noticing it, so avoidance will not make it go away."[3] Discussing race and promoting social justice education is crucial from a young age, when children are particularly sensitive and impressionable. For example, a 2006 report by Yair Bar-Haim found that children of 3 months who do not grow up in a multiracial environment will already develop preferences for people of their own skin color.[4]

When I was raised they tried to view everything as almost a colorblind society. In a way that's good, but on the other hand, instead of seeing everyone's differences and appreciating the qualities of those differences, they try to gloss over that and say those differences don't exist.

After the 2008 election of President Barack Obama, many Americans have claimed to live in a "post-racial" nation where the solution to racial inequality is to ignore it, or be "colorblind." However, this discourse actually perpetuates and reproduces inequality by obscuring the issue and the necessity of reconciliation and active change. In addition, a refusal to acknowledge physical differences creates a culture unappreciative of background and ethnicity.[5]

1 http://humanitiesindicators.org/content/indicatordoc.aspx?i=34 ; 2 http://www.theatlantic.com/entertainment/archive/2016/06/learning-to-be-human/489659/; 3 https://www.psychologytoday.com/blog/developing-minds/201304/are-kids-racist; 4 http://pss.sagepub.com/content/17/2/159.short; 5 https://hbr.org/2013/07/the-costs-of-racial-color-blindness

ECONOMIC, RESIDENTIAL

I do think that there is a lot of subtle racism in Princeton—it's a pretty segregated [and] homogenous town. Refer to page 130.

"I do think that there is a lot of subtle racism in Princeton—it's a pretty segregated [and] homogenous town. In addition to racism, it's more of a socioeconomically segregated town and the town could do more to get people from different backgrounds together. For example, there are more neighborhoods that are Black [and] Latino, and there are other neighborhoods that are White and Asian. A little more mixing would be nice, because people would benefit and learn from that."

Christian Joachim, Wheaton College Class of 2019, shares four personal stories from private school, a trip to the Dollar Tree, and construction jobs.

"In my high school there was this kid named John. John was kind of the same physical build as me, Black, and he was a freshmen while I was a junior. There was this one teacher who would always call me John. It doesn't sound like a big deal, but when it happens to you daily and you go to a boarding school where there's no escaping it, it gets pretty frustrating. It was pretty clear why he kept calling me John—I was also Black.

This one time when I was on campus, I saw the teacher and he was like, 'Hey John, do you want to go play ping pong?'
Was distinguishing Black people so hard for him? He called me this name like a million times, and I've corrected him a million times. After he asked me to play ping pong, I saw him an hour later, and he still called me John. Sometimes, I feel like people group minorities together and make them all look the same.

***

Last semester, it was 7:30 at night, and I went to a Dollar Tree that was close to my school. My sister took me, and they were supposed to close at 9 PM, but when I went in the lady working there suddenly told me they were closing. So, when she told me that, I didn't want any trouble and told her that I would come back tomorrow. But then she said I could take 10 minutes in the store, and I was really confused. I knew what time the store actually closed, and I said, 'What? You guys close at 9:30, I should have an hour and 30 minutes left.'

But the woman kept saying she's only giving me 10 minutes, and I had to get supplies for school so I just kept quiet. I went in and got my stuff, but every aisle I went into she followed me. I didn't know what to think. She just kept following me through every aisle. I'm pretty sure she thought I was going to steal something. Eventually, she ordered me to leave, saying that it was time to go. Like I said, I didn't know what to think. And I didn't even buy anything, I just had to leave.

***

Once we were talking about slavery in class, and this teacher turned to one of my friends who's Black and asked her if she ever experienced any racism in front of the whole class. I know the teacher was well-intentioned, and I think he just wanted a first-hand example, but it was wrong. It's an uncomfortable question that puts her in an awkward place. No student wants to talk about that in front of their peers, because any story that deals with racism is either embarrassing, hurtful, or scary, and you can't ask a student to just become that vulnerable in front of everybody. To me, that was crazy, and I sat in class thinking I never want this to happen to me. But it did.

Last year, my business teacher pulled me aside. He asked me, 'How is your time being at college?' And then he eased his way into asking whether, as an African-American male, I have ever experienced anything outside of my comfort zone. And that was weird because it was out of the blue, and he's my business teacher, and I wondered why he needed to know that. I guess I just don't like how people think if you're Black, then you're open to talking about race at the snap of a finger. Because most of the time, I'm just minding my own business not thinking about my race until someone else brings it up.

Also, since I've been going to private schools, I noticed how most of the pictures are staged on school websites. In order to attract people, they like to show diversity even if it doesn't exist. They have to include pictures of diverse groups, and since they can't take natural photos they have to stage it. So they just put in a brown person, a Black person, an Asian person, and throw in a couple White kids and then that goes onto the home page. I always thought that it was really dishonest.

***

This summer I've been doing a lot of construction jobs. The people I work with say racist stuff all the time, but I kind of just nod and try to stay out of it. For example, there was a black bear spotted somewhere close by, and the authorities were going to tranquilize the bear. And while we were talking about it, this guy goes and says, 'Yeah, they shouldn't shoot the bear because black bears matter right?'

I was shocked. It's not cool to just joke about a serious movement—the Black Lives Matter one—like that. But, as usual, everyone just laughed it off. ❯❯

"I'm Puerto-Rican, Irish, and German... married to an Asian woman. Grew up in Manhattan, had nothing but other races around me. It was a melting pot of many different races caught up in the same struggle, so we were all an even plane, there was no 'oh, that's better,' or 'we're worse,' or 'this is where we want to be.' We had sections, I lived in Washington Heights, so it was predominantly Spanish, Domini-can, Puerto Rican, some Cuban, not much. But if you went three blocks, there were the projects, predominantly Black at the time, now completely integrated. Inwood was primarily White, Jewish—but they were all within eight blocks of one another. You're engulfed in one culture, you cross the street and you're engulfed in another. You're never without, you never came to a point where that's all [you] saw.

But street smarts [is important], you make a left and you know that doesn't feel right. There's situations that you get a gut instinct about, and you know that's not somewhere to be. I don't think that's correlated with race, but with culture.

You can't fight ignorance. Even though I'm the way that I am, my father grew up in Jersey, and his grandparents are racist. I know it. They don't ever say the word, but they don't like Black people. They were a product of their environment, so growing up I know we just had to be a lot more tolerant.

One time, I'm in the Bronx with my wife, and she picks up one of my friend's chil-dren. This woman says, 'how do you get your nanny to work on weekends?' Some ignorant s*** right there.

Ignorance is an ugly, ugly thing. We live in the internet age now, and you can't ig-nore anyone. When I was younger, people could stay by themselves, live alone with their own. They had no reason to integrate... but now you can't avoid people. If I'm so close-minded that I don't want to talk to someone because of the way they look or where they live, I'll be dumb forever, I won't grow, I'll be a small-minded person for the rest of my life. There are so many things that you have to share, if I didn't give you a chance, that would just be really sad."

Grew up in Manhattan, had nothing but other races around me.
While Manhattan used to have a rich ethnic and racial diversity, as of 2010 new census figures show its diversity is decreasing.[1] Gentrification being a factor, the island's Black and Hispanic population has decreased in the last decade and the number of Whites has been increasing.[1]

One time, I'm in the Bronx with my wife, and she picks up one of my friend's children. This woman says, "how do you get your nanny to work on weekends?"
As of 2006, 40% of nannies in New York are minorities—meaning that the majority of those in the work field are not racial or ethnic minorities.[2] Yet, as exemplified by this experience, minorities are often victims of racial profiling. Being mistaken for a service worker by a White person occurs more frequently as minorities climb out of the lower socioeconomic level that years of systemic discrimination has placed them in and rise into higher employment positions. Pathological stereotypes about minorities making less money than Whites fuel racial profiling. For example, while African Americans are in reality 29% poorer than their White counterparts, White Americans believed that Blacks were 50% poorer when surveyed.[3]

1 http://www.nydailynews.com/new-york/manhattan-diversity-ebbing-city-demographics-evolve-new-census-figures-show-article-1.475650
2 http://www.nytimes.com/2006/12/26/us/26nannies.html
3 https://www.psychologytoday.com/blog/culturally-speaking/201112/african-americans-and-pathological-stereotypes

In some ways it's good because it pushes you to try harder, but then it's also horrible because who wants to be profiled in a certain way? "Positive" stereotypes—such as assuming all Asian Americans are good at math, Blacks are good at sports, Hispanics are hard working, and Whites are wealthy—do not necessarily make people feel good. Studies show that positive stereotypes can make individuals feel as though they are being stripped of their individuality. In addition, it can cause an overload of pressure. It can become frustrating for one to know that others see him or her as a generalized member of a group, and not as an individual.[1]

On the opposite side, being a White kid in a school where everyone kind of thinks Asians are the only smart kids, you feel average all the time. Changing the sociological perspective of racism can lead to improved understanding of others' circumstances and the degrading effects stereotypes have on them. Since stereotypes are often targeted at one race, open discussion can lead to a change of perspective and greater empathy.[2]

1 https://www.psychologytoday.com/blog/ulterior-motives/201302/the-pain-positive-stereotypes
2 http://www.soc.ucsb.edu/faculty/winant/Race_and_Race_Theory.html

" Being an Asian American at a school that's as competitive as Princeton, it sometimes feels like there are a lot of stereotypes about being Asian and getting good grades. You know, being that stereotypical kid. In some ways it's good because it pushes you to try harder, but then it's also horrible because who wants to be profiled in a certain way? Especially now with all the protests happening in Missouri and the Eric Garner case in New York—it gives you a very big perspective on even though in America we think things are different, especially in Princeton, we're wrong. There's definitely still racism in Princeton, but like we don't see it as much.

"On the opposite side, being a White kid in a school where everyone kind of thinks Asians are the only smart kids, you feel average all the time."

"I don't think you're average! "

180

INTER-
PERSONAL

There were only about 10 people that were minorities in the entire school. Though the legal ruling in Brown v. Board of Education of Topeka (1954) overturned the segregation of public schools, first established under the doctrine of "separate but equal" by the Supreme Court's decision in Plessy v. Ferguson (1896), the segregation of schools persists today. The de facto racial division of American public schools is largely attributable to the discriminatory practices of the Federal Housing Administration during the 20th century, which led to African Americans residing in poorer neighborhoods and attending poorly resourced schools.[1]

They would compete to have the token Black kid, and it was so degrading... no one stopped it. Tokenism refers to the "practice of making only a perfunctory or symbolic effort to do a particular thing, especially by recruiting a small number of people from underrepresented groups in order to give the appearance of sexual or racial equality."[2] In the situation above, minority students were treated as "novelties" by the fraternities and sororities to which they belonged to. Without upstanders intervening, racial abuse by groups that perpetuate tokenism continues unhindered while a false sense of progress is simultaneously encouraged.[3]

It's judgmental and labeling, and they don't even think about it. Even though microaggressions (see definition on page 203) occur frequently in everyday conversation, many cannot recognize them when they occur. Examples include asking minorities where they are from and assuming they are alien to the country, comparing someone with others of the same race, identifying as color blind, and mistaking a person of color for a service worker.[4]

❝ I went to a very White school, and there were only about 10 people that were minorities in the entire school. In the fraternity and sorority system, they would compete to have the token Black kid, and it was so degrading... no one stopped it. It was like a novelty, and then they would call the kids racist names. There was this one African-American kid who they called 'cotton.' [Here], around the store, usually older people also make comments, but they don't realize they are derogatory. So they say, 'Oh, that oriental lady back there left her receipt.' It's judgmental and labeling, and they don't even think about it. It makes others feel a little wrong inside. **❞**

1 http://www.epi.org/publication/
the-racial-achievement-gap-segregated-schools-and-segregated-neighborhoods-a-constitutional-insult/
2 http://www.oxforddictionaries.com/us/definition/american_english/tokenism
3 http://www.clutchmagonline.com/2013/04/dealing-with-tokenism-in-Black-america/
4 http://www.uwsp.edu/acadaff/NewFacultyResources/NFSRacialMicroaggressions_Table.pdf

"Americans believe in the reality of 'race' as a defined, indubitable feature of the natural world. Racism—the need to ascribe bone-deep features to people and then humiliate, reduce, and destroy them—inevitably follows from this inalterable condition. In this way, racism is rendered as the innocent daughter of Mother Nature, and one is left to deplore the Middle Passage or Trail of Tears the way one deplores an earthquake, a tornado, or any other phenomenon that can be cast as beyond the handiwork of men. But race is the child of racism, not the father."

—Ta-Nehisi Coates

The Identity of a Terrorist
by Jawaher Abuhammoud

My name is Jawaher Abuhammoud. I am a born and raised American, my nationality is Palestinian, and my religion is Islam. When people look at me, they can't really tell because I "look White," but when someone reads my full name, sees me in a hijab, or hears me speaking Arabic, they can probably infer that I'm Muslim—or as some others would like to call "a terrorist."

I'll never forget the day in the sixth grade when a boy came up to me and called me a "terrorist" and asked, "Is your next plan to blow up the school?" Since he was Mexican, I responded, "at least I'm not the one who had to cross the border illegally." Now at the time I was only 11; my first experience of racism fueled my own racist thoughts. Reflecting back on that, I realize racism is embedded in society and kids at a young age (I thought it was normal to retort back like that). In other words, not only was it disturbing that I had been judged based on my ethnicity/religion, but that I had also used derogatory language as a reflex.

I learned there is no point in going back at the person with a negative comment. People have asked me "Do you know where your uncle Osama is?" and as a reaction, I tend to either ignore them or show them directly that I'm offended.

Another time I experienced racism was when I went to go visit my own country. My brother and I, at the ages of 13 and 14, went to visit Palestine alone for the first time. We went on the plane by ourselves, and when we got off with the flight attendant and the many other children our age, we knew we were being treated unequally. We checked in at a booth once we landed in Tel Aviv, all the children went through quickly, but my brother and I were questioned for almost an hour. After that, our luggage was nowhere to be found.

> "No child should have to grow up thinking it is okay to be called a "terrorist" because of his or her religion or race."

I have many family members who go to visit back home and often they are left in rooms for "questioning" for 7 hours about why they are visiting the country. People will yell, shout, and swear up and down that Muslims are terrorists. In reality, the real terrorists are the ones who call names, make assumptions, judge, and invade your privacy because of the way you look or because of how you worship.

A terrorist knows no religion or specific race. Treating a person as a terrorist for those reasons is more than unjustifiable.

No child should have to grow up thinking it is okay to be called a "terrorist" because of his or her religion or race.

ECONOMIC,
RESIDEN-
TIAL

Talk Teacher

"My English as a Second Language students have to pass the same test that all New Jersey students have to pass—the PARCC—in order to graduate. They have to take the English part in English. They can take the math in Spanish, but if Spanish is not your native language, they only have a few substitutes for English. If your native language is Vietnamese, you have to take it in English. It's not necessarily fair. This makes it very difficult when and if they get rid of portfolios; it adds an extra step. Certain students will not be able to pass the test given the fact that they may arrive here at 15, 16, 17 years old, and they're going to be required to learn enough English to pass a test that assumes that you've learned English your whole life."

"How many of your ESL students do pass the test and are able to graduate?"

"Most of the time, kids who pass the test are no longer in ESL. In other words, if they could pass this test, they no longer need the ESL services. I had eight seniors in ESL this year and all eight did not pass the PARCC—but one student got the minimum score for the PSAT for English, so she did not need to do the portfolio in order to graduate. If they switch to not allowing kids to take a portfolio test, none of these kids would have graduated. The portfolio tests are in math and in English, where they take equivalencies. They have to show they have the ability to do work at the test level, but are given more time to complete the task and given more help with the language, so that they have a way to graduate without passing PARCC. All of my students were able to use portfolios this year and pass. However, they spent a lot of extra time during the school day taking the portfolios in order to graduate. So instead of giving them the regular curriculum, we had to stop and give them a portfolio assessment, which took a lot of time because of their abilities... It really hurts those students who do not perform well on these kinds of tests. And in the past, more minorities have struggled with these types of tests, especially ESL students without English as their first language. You can't have one test that is going to represent all students. By all means have a test, but it shouldn't tie into graduation."

—Rob Emison, ESL teacher

"I'm from Charleston, and they still have that slave mentality. Charleston is where they have a history. They have a nice history, but to Blacks it's not so good, because they were brought as slaves over from Africa. They have a place down there called Kunkletown where they sold a lot of them. In the marketplace, they stood them on the tables and bid and sold them. My husband, who works for a moving company, said he would sometimes move families in and out of those big mansions down there. He said when they go to the basement, you can smell it; it smells like must. Like where they piled them up. Where they kept them... They say you can still smell that."

My friends applied... one Asian, one Black, same grade... [the Black student] got accepted.
Refer to the discussion point about affirmative action on page 39.

"My friends applied to Ivy Leagues all over the country: one Asian, one Black, same grade... [the Black student] got accepted. I don't think it's fair. It's not fair for them, the ones who aren't the smartest, at the top of the top. It's crazy. They should really stop asking for your race on college applications."

"The Story of Bob and Race"

Graphic Credit: Barry Deutsch, leftycartoons.com

"Ask yourself seriously—who do you think is attractive? We want to be with people who we feel comfortable with, so [we consider] skin color or the way they look."

Ask yourself seriously—who do you think is attractive?
In 2013, out of 3.6 million adults who got married, Pew Research Center reports that 58% of American Indians, 28% of Asians, 19% of Blacks and 7% of Whites married someone of a race different than their own.[1]

1 http://www.pewresearch.org/fact-tank/2015/06/12/interracial-marriage-who-is-marrying-out/

ECONOMIC

"Racism in Princeton? It's alive! That's all I got for you. Racism in Princeton it is alive. It's alive. When it comes to jobs, opportunities, it's alive."

"Just yesterday I came here from India. India is really, really nice. The Indian culture is great. But this my son's restaurant, I'm so proud of him. He came here 20 years back to start a business. It was scary, but I didn't have any worries."

CURRENT EVENT

originally a CHOOSE Facebook post
graphic credit: Eddie Cai

July 6, 2016

More than 200 lives have been lost within the past few days due to terror attacks on civilians—yet there has been no #standwithBaghdad or #standwithIstanbul or #standwithDhaka or #standwithMedina filters buzzing through the media.

Jerusalem's Old City Wall was not illuminated for flag colors of any of the four countries. News channels such as CNN did not come close to investigating and discussing these unfortunate events as they did with the Paris shooting. These innocent lives have barely been acknowledged outside their home countries because the media chose not to value non-White lives.

So as lights and cameras are flashing towards White countries, constant tears and spilled blood in Baghdad, Istanbul, Dhaka, and Medina are left to be dried by themselves—until another unnoticed attack opens unhealed wounds.

> **"** I feel like I can't really comment [on race relations] because I'm White, my opportunities have not been affected in the same way, and you know, who the hell am I to talk about it? There are problems everywhere... and I think it is a very difficult issue, because obviously there are horrible racist people out there and a lot of the current events that have been happening have been because of that. But it's hard because there is also the backlash against the cops, but the majority of cops are good people. People need to learn that there are some bad cops, but the majority are good. It's a tough time for everybody. **"**

INTER-PERSONAL

But it's hard because there is also the backlash against the cops, but the majority of cops are good people.

When asked whether "police officers tend to unfairly target minorities," 69% of Blacks, 54% of Latinx, and 29% of Whites agreed.[1] While national discourse should reflect the important discriminatory practices and laws that lead to racially-disproportionate mass incarceration (see page 164), labeling all cops as racist is also a stereotype. Victims of racism should not reciprocate with prejudice, even though individual prejudice and structural racism are not on an even playing field.

I feel like I can't really comment [on race relations] because I'm White, my opportunities have not been affected in the same way, and you know, who the hell am I to talk about it.

Whereas minorities tend to be forced into the issues and conversation about race relations without a choice, white privilege shelters Whites from it. America was institutionally built to favor Whites. Whether it be the white color of band-aids or the reality that Blacks are three times more likely to be arrested than Whites, racism often takes no part in the daily concerns of White people, causing many to become oblivious to the reality of minorities.[2]

1 http://blogs.reuters.com/great-debate/2015/01/15/one-third-of-americans-believe-police-lie-routinely/
2 http://www.huffingtonpost.com/good-men-project/why-its-so-hard-to-talk-to-White-people-about-racism_b_7183710.html

Racism does not have to approach you on the street and slap you across the face for you to feel its stinging, ringing effects. It can exist in your peripheral vision and whisper in your ear, so you always know it's there. It can dig into your flesh and hold on, perhaps giving a little shake from time to time. Likewise, our community may be relatively sheltered from the brashest, crudest, most direct forms of discrimination, but subtle and subconscious prejudice continue to thrive—so much that you realize it doesn't matter how racism is delivered—the effects will be the same.

> " Still, subtle racism is similar to **smoke**—it comes in wisps and surrounds you but you don't realize how **potent and dangerous** it is until it accumulates."

I can only tell my own understanding of the degrading nature of knowing that someone, somewhere WILL perceive you differently simply because you come from a different heritage. Most of the time, these experiences can be contributed to a lack of sensitivity and abundant ignorance. The people that I have come across typically do not have bad intentions and probably wouldn't consider themselves hurtful. Still, subtle racism is similar to smoke—it comes in wisps and surrounds you but you don't realize how potent and dangerous it is until it accumulates.

I'm taken back to a middle school sleepover, where the girls somehow reach the conclusion that *"Asian guys [in our school] aren't attractive."* Then, as if compensating for something, they tack on, *"Oh, but Asian girls are SOOOOOO pretty!"*

Or those times my closest friends remarked to me, *"Hey... you know, you don't really look like other Chinese people! When I think of Chinese people they look more like this..."*

Perhaps the moment when someone saw me doing my math homework in school and offhandedly commented (or complimented?), *"All Asians are good at math."*

When I tried to correct her unbelievably generalizing statement, she laughed, *"No—trust me—all Asians are good at math."* Whatever that's supposed to imply.

Subconscious, unintended racism is just as impactful as its more straightforward and obvious counterparts. It shows that racism is so embedded into society that now people don't even have to try to succeed at being stereotypical.

Why is racism so dangerous? Because it impairs one's sense of belonging. It doesn't matter if it's physical or verbal, accidental or intended, or—very ironically—given as a "compliment." If it can estrange a person and make her feel like an outsider then it has accomplished its goal.

"What if All the Defaults Were Reset?"

Graphic Credit: Barry Deutsch, leftycartoons.com

"I know what the world has done to my brother and how narrowly he has survived it. And I know, which is much worse, and this is the crime of which I accuse my country and my countrymen, and for which neither I nor time nor history will ever forgive them, that they have destroyed and are destroying hundreds of thousands of lives and do not know it and do not want to know it. One can be, indeed one must strive to become, tough and philosophical concerning destruction and death, for this is what most of mankind has been best at since we have heard of man. (But remember: most of mankind is not all of mankind.) But it is not permissible that the authors of devastation should also be innocent. It is the innocence which constitutes the crime."
—James Baldwin

❝ If I ever meet someone new here, there's always that question of what school I go to. And sometimes we don't even get to that point, they just immediately say, 'You're Asian, you must go to Princeton.' Good schools like Princeton or NYU or any Ivy League, there's that affirmative action, and there's that stigma that if you're a certain race, you're dealt certain cards. In terms of Princeton, it's the same way any school would affect a community, setting a bar and asking how close can you get to it. There's also always that assumption that I am good at science and math, that I want to be a lawyer. There's a subtle moment from that other party when they hear you're not into that."

"So what are you into?"

"I love music. Independent and acoustic, stuff like that. But mainstream media and famous musicians are usually White, Black, or Hispanic. You don't see an Asian face there a lot, and when people do see me as an Asian, they are like, "hey, you look like a K-pop star." And I just don't want to be associated with that just because I'm Korean. **❞**

There's always that assumption that I am good at science and math, that I want to be a lawyer.
While they are often stereotyped as excelling in scientific or mathematical fields, approximately 41% of Asians Americans with a science or engineering degree are currently employed in a STEM occupation, followed by biracial or multiracial (24%) and non-Hispanic White (23%) individuals. Although it is important to acknowledge that Asians are the leading race in STEM employment, 59% of Asians are not involved in STEM-related fields.[1]

If you're a certain race, you're dealt certain cards.
Race and background impacts every facet of an individual's life. Nevertheless, individuals are often accused of "playing the race card," or exploiting racist or non-racist attitudes by accusing another of racism. Often, minorities are blamed for using their race and the circumstances associated with it as an excuse for any of their actions or words. According to Luke Visconti, founder of DiversityInc, minorities by definition cannot be racist to a White person, and while some may "play the race card," White people inherently do so every day of their lives due to the systemic privilege associated with being White in America.[2]

You don't see an Asian face there a lot.
Breaking into a new industry in which the vast majority is or a different race or background may be daunting or alienating. In the 21st century, 81% of Billboard's top selling albums are by artists who are White, African American, or Hispanic.[3]

1 https://www.census.gov/prod/2013pubs/acs-24.pdf
2 http://www.diversityinc.com/ask-the-White-guy/does-playing-the-race-card-make-you-racist/
3 www.businessinsider.com

It was very, very separate and segregated within my high school. But it was the groups themselves that kinda made it like that.

Racial homogeneity is common in America. While being around the same race might be comfortable because of cultural similarities, a lack of diversity impacts social behavior negatively. Around 40% of White Americans and 25% of non-White Americans surround themselves exclusively by friends of their own race. Furthermore, 30% of Americans are not mixing with others of a different race.[1]

Refer to page 45 to read about another important benefit of racial diversity in schools.

1 http://www.reuters.com/article/us-usa-poll-race-idUSBRE97704320130808

INTER-PERSONAL

Interview by CHOOSE Chapter @ Penn State Founder Papakojo Kuranchie

"Basically it was a race war in my high school every single day. And it was bad. There were always fights breaking out between the different races within the school, and there was this group of White kids who didn't want the Black kids sitting with them, or even near them at lunch, and if they did, it turned into a huge fight. There was a group of Black kids who didn't want the White kids sitting with them, or the Puerto Ricans. It was very, very separate and segregated within my high school. But it was the groups themselves that kinda made it like that. It was odd. I was just chilling, though. I would just chill with everybody."

"Did anyone try to stop the fights?"

"I mean there was, there was me and my group of friends who pretty much had friends of every race and ethnicity. And we never really made any effort to stop it just because we had seen other people try and stop it before. All [they would do] was ... get their teeth knocked in and then wanna start another fight. It was getting to the point where there were fights two or three times a week over race. So, we just kind of were protecting ourselves and each other within our own friend group. And then the administrators never made any effort to stop it either."

"How did the fights usually start? Was it just like name calling, or confrontation?"

"I remember a really big rift was between the Black kids and the Puerto Rican kids. If a Puerto Rican kid would get too close to where they sat, then the Black kids would start hassling them, and, before you knew it, names were getting thrown, racial slurs were getting thrown around, and then it just turned into fist fights. By the end it usually ended up with someone with a broken nose at least."

CHOOS

ECONOMIC

" I'm a Black guy from the Caribbean. I came here in 1972 to go to the first fashion school. But you've got to understand that, in America, sometimes the very best don't get the bread. For example, I'm a talent, but I haven't made it big. That doesn't bother me though. I just believe in one thing—God. Men think they're in control, but they're not. "

Talk Teacher

"I would love to do the play 'Rag Time,' because it has beautiful music and a beautiful story. But there aren't enough African-American students. Right now I have no African-American students—or of any color—in musical theatre, so I can't do that show and it makes me really sad. Even West Side Story would be hard to do."

"Do you notice that not a lot of African Americans are trying out for musical theatre, or is it something else?"

"That's one of the reasons why I started the musical theatre class: I had kids that took class with me, but never got to be on stage because they couldn't rehearse after school with jobs or other stuff. There have been years when I do have African Americans in musical theatre class, but it's only one or two. At some point, when it's almost time for the musical and we need to rehearse everyday after school, some of them have jobs, some of them have sports."

"Would you put in White kids for African-American parts?"

"That's totally inappropriate. That wouldn't be fair; a playwright writes a play and you have to respect the casting that they laid down, because it influences the material."

"What do you think of #oscarssowhite?"

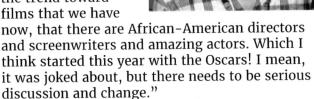

"The Oscars has such a long history, and it just hasn't kept up with the trend toward films that we have now, that there are African-American directors and screenwriters and amazing actors. Which I think started this year with the Oscars! I mean, it was joked about, but there needs to be serious discussion and change."

"Have you ever discussed it with your classes?"

"This year we did, because everybody was talking about Kevin Hart and if he went too far. I don't think he did go too far. There has to be a little wake up call."

—*Patricia Wray, performing arts teacher*

"The single story creates stereotypes, and the problem with stereotypes is not that they are untrue, but that they are incomplete. They make one story become the only story."

—Chimamanda Ngozi Adichie

❝ 40 years back, we came to America from India. We love the culture, we love the food. There's an Indian restaurant [where I live], and a lot of Americans go there. They like Chinese food also. It's good, because there definitely should be an appreciation of different foods and cultures that way. **❞**

There definitely should be an appreciation of different foods and cultures that way.
According to numerous sociologists, food and the context in which it is found, prepared, and consumed do not simply satisfy "physiological and psychological needs," but also reflect social systems and cultural values that often fall along the lines of status, class, and ethnicity. Thus, diverse foods should be viewed—and respected—as a matter of cultural significance.[1]

1 http://journals.cambridge.org/download.php?file=%2FPNS%2FPNS41_02%2FS0029665182000342a.pdf&code=0e33ba9330b813efbe3d4e84592ebdd3

"O ye who believe! stand out firmly for justice, as witnesses to Allah, even as against yourselves, or your parents, or your kin, and whether it be (against) rich or poor: for Allah can best protect both. Follow not the lusts (of your hearts), lest ye swerve, and if ye distort (justice) or decline to do justice, verily Allah is well-acquainted with all that ye do."

—Holy Quran

Talk Teacher

❝ Do you try to get books with a greater diversity of authors into the library?"

"Yeah! That's actually a big push that we've had, the last two years particularly. There's an entire thing that's being run by the American Library Association called We Need Diverse Books—it's a hashtag—and so they've been really good about providing lists. We've tried to do different disabilities, mental illnesses, races, ethnicities, sexual orientations, and gender identities."

"Why do you think that has been such a big push recently?"

"I think it's just discussed a lot more often now. Honestly, various library schools have been doing a lot to recruit various minority candidates and so forth, so that's broadened awareness to librarians who weren't there before. It's something I always felt was personally important, but there is a dearth of people—authors themselves—who are represented over various groups. But some are rising to prominence, so it's starting to pick up. There's a lot more resources now for people to pinpoint how to get those books that weren't there before. **❞**

—*Jennifer Bigioni, media specialist*

194

So if I see someone who is Hispanic or Black, I already have this [assumption] that they come from low-income backgrounds.

While the stereotype that all Hispanics or Blacks are poor is false, there is a significant wealth gap along racial and ethnic lines. Refer to page 164 for statistics.

Her mom is Black, and she doesn't know what [race] her dad is.

Although perhaps not relevant to this individual, the "fatherless" discourse has become more and more prominent as extremely high incarceration rates deprive Black families of fathers. Princeton University professor Imani Perry writes: "The problem with the fatherlessness talk is not that fatherlessness isn't an issue. But it misidentifies the issue and locates the resolution in a traditional patriarchal model of head-of-household status for fathers. The cruelty of this gesture is that men who have been incarcerated, for example, have virtually no opportunities to acquire the head-of-household status without working in the illegal economy (because it is so difficult for ex-offenders to find employment) or by performing patriarchy via physical and social dominance." She offers a solution: "To begin with, talk in communities should not be framed around whether people 'need' fathers while growing up to become good citizens and should instead be framed around how these men can and should fit into families and communities as loved and loving members and how all families, however they are constituted, can work effectively under what are often quite difficult circumstances. In order for this shift to translate to more productive policy initiatives, we must encourage policy research to extend beyond quantitative data, which in their minimalism often fail to provide information about substantive human relations, to qualitative research such as extensive surveys about relationships and values and to ethnographic research that assesses what structures of support provide necessary and sufficient condition for effective individual and co-parenting."[1]

1 Imani Perry, More Beautiful and More Terrible: The Embrace and Transcendence of Racial Inequality in the United States

"I work with people who are disadvantaged and homeless. Many people we see come from racial minority backgrounds. The biggest thing I've had to learn how to do is learn how to fight stereotypes we already have of these young people, and listen to their stories. So if I see someone who is Hispanic or Black, I already have this [assumption] that they come from low-income backgrounds. I ask them a lot of questions about their past. A lot of the time it is really traumatic, and I can't relate to them. Just yesterday, I saw this 20-year-old girl fighting through college. Her parents left her when she was 2 years old, she's been in foster care her whole life. She's homeless, but she's trying to go to school, pay for school. She's studying to be a physician, and taking her MCAT soon. She was a full-time student and full-time employee; she said she never sleeps, not only because she has nowhere to sleep, but because she doesn't have time. Her mom is Black, and she doesn't know what [race] her dad is. It's hard because I have certain expectations of what I want, and they know what they want; for example, they will say they'd rather be on the street than in a shelter. And I think they're crazy, but just being able to listen is important. For a lot of these youth, it's their first time telling their story—they'll start crying in front of you, and you won't know what to do. So listening, but also personal time to reflect—I live in Boston, and it's a pretty fast-paced culture, so everyone's just like 'go, go, go.' We have to be introspective."

Painting by Nora Wildberg

CHOOS

HISTORY

1. Do Not Gloss Over the Country's Racist Past

Use your history textbook as a tool, not a crutch. A lesson can be learned from the mistake of a widely-distributed, mass-produced textbook company, McGraw Hill: "The Atlantic Slave Trade between the 1500s and 1800s brought millions of workers from Africa to the southern United States to work on agricultural plantations."

Africans "brought" to America were not "workers or indentured servants," they were enslaved. Tuning out America's racist history begins by replacing the truth with softer, more vague words like these. Another example: The College Board revised its AP U.S. History standards in 2015, substituting more blurred language after the Republican National Convention complained in 2014 that it was "a radically revisionist view of American history that emphasizes negative aspects of our nation's history while omitting or minimizing positive aspects."

What is there to learn from all of this? Do not be afraid to go off script. Dive into race-related history discussions, and avoid stunting students' growth by offering warped, sugar-coated translations of history.

2. Avoid Whitewashing

Whenever you are teaching a significant historical event, make a point to be inclusive. Instead of only focusing on the role of White men in history, expand your efforts to include what minorities were up to. Talking about the Declaration of Independence? In addition to teaching George Washington's subsequent accomplishments, mention the position his slaves were left in, too. Is there only a paragraph about the Japanese Internment Camps in your textbook? Then spend some extra time teaching it on your own.

Make a point to not leave anyone out of history, no matter how gruesome their experience, and only teach White achievements. If we do not teach history in its entirety, we are in danger of repeating it.

3. Understanding Trumps Memorization

Students will not sincerely grasp race's role in shaping history if you throw numbers at them. Some teachers dust their hands off, thinking they conducted an adequate race-related discussion after spitting out facts with no ensuing discussion. Just mentioning how many enslaved Africans there were, how many natives died, or how many Chinese immigrants were denied citizenship does not characterize an effective lesson on historical racial tensions. To encourage understanding, try conducting in-class discussions that center on these facts but also discuss their repercussions.

Furthermore, to enhance a student's understanding, connect historical racism with contemporary context.

Students can be misled to believe that because it happened so long ago, it does not exist today. However, by encouraging students to connect the dots and investigate the aftermath of the past's racism, they will be able to identify its existence today too.

4. Show Historical Evidence

Students are more likely to take discussion of racism seriously if they see evidence. Yes, they will read it in a textbook and acknowledge racism's existence, but it will truly hit them if they see proof. Print out some primary sources as examples for students: letters, photographs, paintings—anything that represents the state of race-relations in that time period. If an online search does not work, try reaching out to your local historical society or library for some primary sources.

5. Be Careful with Terminology

Choosing the appropriate historical terminology is tricky. As times changed, so did names. Enslaved Africans, during the colonial time period, were not African Americans. Not only was America not created yet, but those enslaved were denied citizenship, so "America" cannot appropriately be used. Furthermore, the use of Native American versus American Indian is highly debated. There are many other terms that you should be careful with, but that comes easily with preparation and consciousness.

Credit: Barry Deutsch, leftycartoons.com

Outline of Core U.S. History Curriculum

Acknowledging key components of U.S. history provides context for addressing contemporary individual and social issues

Created by Roberto Schiraldi as part of the Not in Our Town Princeton curriculum team

A. Genocide of Native Americans

1. Mass killing of Native Americans
2. Manifest Destiny and ties to economic advancement for Europeans
3. Seneca form of tribal government used as model for democracy.
4. Removal Act of 1830
5. Intentional exposure to small pox
6. Slaughter of buffalo, starvation, and social and cultural disintegration of many Plains tribes.
7. Present situation: Still mostly confined to reservations, poverty, poor education, and minimal job opportunities.

8. Contributions by Native Americans to American culture.
9. Understanding and acknowledging resulting intergenerational trauma from the aforementioned is necessary for healing and trust building to begin. (Truth and Reconciliation Commission of Canada, South African Truth and Reconciliation Commission as examples).
10. Many Native Americans in NJ, for example the Nanticoke Lenni-Lenape, many African Americans have Native American ancestry, many multiracial people with Native American ancestry.

Bibliography: 1. NJ Dept. Of Education. Amistad Commission http://njamistadcurriculum.org 2. Zinn Education Project http://zinnedproject.org 3. An Indigenous People's History of the United States (ReVisioning American History) by Roxanne Dunbar Ortiz (2014) 4. Truth and Reconciliation Commission of Canada http://www.trc.ca/websites/trcinstitution/index.php?p=3

CHOOS

B. Slaves Viewed as Property, Not as People and the Legacy of Slavery

1. Africans intentionally chosen to be kidnapped because they were seen as strong, smart, and master farmers.
2. Major difference between Africans, the only group forced to come here, and immigrant groups that came to America by choice.
3. Original U.S. Constitution was written for land-owning, White males
4. Atrocities of slavery: forced labor, torture, murder, rape.
5. Identifying the U.S. Presidents who owned slaves.
6. Civil War/economic reasons for Civil War/freeing the slaves (slave labor undergirded the U.S economy.)
7. Policing system and bounty hunters
8. Post-emancipation and Reconstruction sharecropping virtually re-establishing the plantation system and Jim Crow laws (loitering, etc.) resulting in chain gangs (penal slavery).
9. Voting rights /still an issue
10. Mass incarceration and killing of young Black men.
11. Contributions by African Americans to American culture.
12. Understanding and acknowledging resulting intergenerational trauma is necessary for healing and trust building to begin. (Truth and Reconciliation Commission of Canada, South African Truth and Reconciliation Commission as examples).

Bibliography: 1. NJ Dept. Of Education. Amistad Commission http://njamistadcurriculum.org 2. Zinn Education Project http://zinnedproject.org. 3. Slavery by Another Name: The Re-Enslavement of Black Americans from the Civil War to World War II by Douglas Blackmon. (2009) 4. The New Jim Crow: Mass Incarceration in the Age of Colorblindness by Michelle Alexander (2010)

C. White Privilege

1. Definition of White racial privilege (and how it contributed to above sections A and B).
2. Definition of racism
3. Role of institutional power. (Internment camps for Japanese Americans as example of treatment of other marginalized groups).
4. Effect of "unhealthy" White heteronormative male values (superiority, power, wealth control, elitism, entitlement, success, competition to be number one at all costs, defining beauty by European standards, etc.).
5. Internalized oppression of people of color.
6. Colorblindness
7. What to do?
a. White people need to acknowledge their privilege and take responsibility to speak out, support, and advocate, if there is to be substantial, sustainable change. This is not about guilt or shame; it is about taking action.
b. Teach core value that all life is valuable, worthwhile, important, that all individuals have worth, regardless of grades, money, possessions.
c. Teach importance of Dr. MLK's speech, "I have a dream that my four children will one day live in a nation where they will be judged not by the color of their skin but by the content of their character."

Bibliography: 1. Teaching Tolerance/Teaching the New Jim Crow by the Southern Poverty Law Center. http://www.tolerance.org/publication/teaching-new-jim-crow 2. Teaching for Change http://www.teachingforchange.org 3. White Privilege Conference Course Curricula 4. NJ Dept. Of Education. Amistad Commission http://njamistadcurriculum.org 5. The Great White Elephant; A Workbook on Racial Privilege for White Anti-Racists by Pamela Chambers and Robin Parker. (Beyond Diversity Resource Center, 2007 http://beyonddiversity.org/books. 6. The Complete Guide To Resilience by Glenn R. Schiraldi, http://www.resiliencefirst.com (2011) 7. The Self-Esteem Workbook by Glenn R. Schiraldi, pp. 29-37 (New Harbinger, 2001) 8. I Have a Dream Speech, Dr. Martin Luther King, Jr., August 28, 1963.

D. Racial Microaggressions and Intersectionality Theory

Racial Microaggressions

1. Definition
2. Examples: Myth of meritocracy (statements which assert that race, gender, class, sexual orientation do not play a role in life success); "Color blindness" (Denying a person of color's racial or ethnic experience; the implicit message is "They should just assimilate"); Assumptions (Asian Americans and Latinx are assumed to be "foreigners;" assumptions of intelligence based on race, gender or perceived abilities).

Intersectionality Theory

1. Examination of factors (gender, race, class, economic status, ability, sexual orientation, etc.) of identity which intersect on multiple and often simultaneous levels
2. Recognition that people can be privileged in some ways and definitely not privileged in others and aware of one identity and not others
3. Multiple identities and systems of oppression at work
4. Importance of increasing awareness and not reinforcing deficit models of cultural groups.
5. Lack of experience in interacting with individuals from different groups can lead to over- or under-emphasis on cultural factors, ("Broaching").
6. Important never to assume, but to ask, if appropriate, about individual identities ("Broaching").

Bibliography: 1. Race, Class, Gender: An Anthology by Margaret L. Andersen and Patricia Hill Collins (8th ed. 2012) 2. "Demarginalizing the Intersection of Race and Sex," The University of Chicago Legal Forum 140:139-167 (1989), by Kimberle Crenshaw 3. Black Feminist Thought: Knowledge, Consciousness, and the Politics of Empowerment, by Patricia Hill Collins. (2008) 4. "Racial Microaggressions In Everyday Life: Implications for Clinical Practice," by Derald Wing Sue, American Psychologist, pp. 271-286 (2007) 5. Diversity and Oppression, Graduate MSW Course taught by DuWayne Battle, PhD, Rutgers University/MSW Culture Competence Certification Program. 6. "A Journey through Alienation and Privilege to Healing," by Roberto Schiraldi, White Privilege Journal (2013) http://www.wpcjournal.com/article/view/6457.

ENGLISH & LITERARY STUDIES

Decolonize the Book Selection

The global spread of the English language is connected to the power of White people, making English and Whiteness thornily intertwined—and students are noticing. For example, Yale University students wrote a petition in 2016 saying that predominantly reading novels by Shakespeare, Milton, and T.S. Eliot, among others, "creates a culture that is especially hostile to students of color."

Chances are, your English class also consists of novels primarily by White, male, and European authors. If you have a required curriculum like this, do not let it hold you back. Today's world includes a diverse group of people, so choose novels that reflect this diversity. Even if you can not fit in entire books, at least include excerpts by minority authors to supplement what you are required to teach.

Why? Many minority students miss the chance to connect with literature as intensely as their White classmates. Furthermore, students of all identities suffer from receiving no exposure to other traditions, cultures, and races because of their current selection of literature. Bias has created an English course content across generations that's discriminatory, and it is time to mix it up.

Utilize the Story

English teachers are lucky. Normally, when conducting a discussion on race, teachers risk singling out a student by putting them in a position to speak on behalf of their entire race. However, with a novel in hand, you can shift the focus onto the character's racial struggles.

Successful racial dialogues depend heavily on sharing personal experiences. Utilizing the character's story, instead of being dependent on a student's, allows for more freedom to pick the story apart, analyze it, and discuss its implications without hurting anyone.

Recommended Teacher Reading

1. Racial Domination, Racial Progress: The Sociology of Race in America **by Matthew Desmond and Mustafa Emirbayer**

2. Teaching for Diversity and Social Justice (2nd ed) **by Maurianne Adams, Lee Anne Bell, and Pat Griffin**

3. Whistling Vivaldi: How Stereotypes Affect Us and What We Can Do **by Claude M. Steele**

4. Refer to the recommended reading for high school on page 202

color brave: to acknowledge the color of one's skin and see it as a positively defining factor.

communication: a message that is given to someone.

community: a unified body of people.

cultural appropriation: the adoption of elements from another culture without permission.

cultural pluralism: when the minorities of a society integrate themselves with the majority all while maintaining their cultural differences.

derogatory: attempting to lessen the reputation or merit of someone by showing a lack of respect.

dialogue: a conversation started by two or more people.

diaspora: people who live outside an area where their ancestors lived.

discrimination: the practice of unfairly treating another person or group of people.

disenfranchisement: the act of depriving someone of a privilege.

diversity: the state of having a range of races and cultures in a group.

divisions: separation among groups.

empowerment: to receive power over one's self or others.

equality: the state of being treated fairly.

exploitation: to selfishly utilize someone or something for profit.

freedom: the state of having liberty.

Graphic Credit: Tina Kugler, foreveryoungadult.com

Recommended Reading
Multicultural literature listed as top choices by Scholastic, Teaching Tolerance, etc.

Elementary & Middle School

All for the Better: The Story of El Barrio **by Nicholasa Mohr**

Hairs/Pelitos **by Sandra Cisñeros**

Rabbit Wishes **by Linda Shute**

¡Viva México!: The Story of Benito Juárez and Cinco de Mayo **by Argentina Palacios**

From Miss Ida's Porch **by Sandra Belton, illustrated by Floyd Cooper**

Meet Danitra Brown **by Nikki Grimes, illustrated by Floyd Cooper**

Alvin Ailey **by Andrea Davis Pinkney, illustrated by Brian Pinkney**

Lift Ev'ry Voice and Sing **by James Weldon Johnson, illustrated by Jan Spivey Gilchrist**

Trombone Shorty **by Troy Andrews**

Seed of Freedom: The Peaceful Integration of Huntsville, Alabama **by Hester Bass**

The Glory Field **by Walter Dean Myers**

When Shlemiel Went to Warsaw & Other Stories **by Isaac Bashevis Singer**

Sheltering Rebecca **by Mary Baylis-White**

One Afternoon **by Yumi Heo**

Molly's Pilgrim **by Barbara Cohen, illustrated by Michael Deran**

grassroots: originating from the common people.

harmony: a peaceful and pleasing integration of people.

healing: to make whole and sound.

heritage: The traditions that make up part of the history of a group.

homogenous: made up of a similar kind or nature.

identity: the qualities or beliefs that make up an individual or group.

ideological racism: racism based off commonly heard or seen stereotypes.

ignorance: the state of being unaware due to the lack of knowledge.

individuality: having distinctive characteristics.

institutional: racism that occurs from the way institutional policies and practices create different outcomes for different racial groups; see systemic racism.

interdependence: to be mutually reliant on others.

intergenerational: of or between different generations.

internalized: racism that occurs when an oppressed group adopts the racist mindset of the dominating group.

Intersectionality: the intersections between different social identities and systems of oppression; examples include race, gender, ability, religion, sexuality, class, etc.

justice: systemic fair and equitable treatment for all races.

melting pot: metaphor for the assimilation and blending of different races, cultures, ethnicities, etc.; often contrasted with the salad bowl metaphor.

Elementary & Middle School
cont.

The Journey: Japanese Americans, Racism, and Renewal **by Sheila Hamanaka**

Hiroshima **by Laurence Yep**

Grandfather's Journey **by Allen Say**

Freedom's School **by Lesa Cline-Ransome**

High School

Black Boy **by Richard Wright**

"Master Harold"... and the Boys **by Athol Fugard**

The Absolutely True Diary of a Part-Time Indian **by Sherman Alexie**

The Other Wes Moore: One Name, Two Fates **by Wes Moore**

I Am Malala **by Malala Yousafzai**

Yaqui Delgado Wants to Kick Your Ass **by Meg Medina**

Under a Painted Sky **by Stacey Lee**

Copper Sun **by Sharon M. Draper**

Under the Blood-Red Sun **by Graham Salisbury**

The Color Purple **by Alice Walker**

The Fire Next Time **by James Baldwin**

Song of Solomon **by Toni Morrison**

Out of Darkness **by Ashley Hope Pérez**

Taking Flight **by Michaela DePrince**

America Is the Heart **by Carlos Bulosan**

Democracy in Black: How Race Still Enslaves the American Soul **by Eddie S. Glaude Jr.**

The Latte Rebellion **by Sarah Jamila Stevenson**

Lies My Teacher Told Me: Everything Your American History Textbook Got Wrong **by James W. Loewen**

Cuba 15 **by Nancy Osa**

Why Are All the Black Kids Sitting Together in the Cafeteria: And Other Conversations About Race **by Beverly Daniel Tatum**

American Born Chinese **by Gene Luen Yang**

Three of our all-time favorites:

The New Jim Crow: Mass Incarceration in the Age of Colorblindness **by Michelle Alexander**

Between the World and Me **by Ta-Nehisi Coates**

"What to the Slave is the Fourth of July?" **by Frederick Douglass**

microaggression: common and usually subtle racial slights or insults toward people of color (unintentional or intentional, verbal or non-verbal).

minority (racial): Asian American, Black or African American, Hispanic or Latinx, Native Hawaiian and Other Pacific Islander, and American Indian and Alaska Native.

multiculturalism: a philosophy that encourages ethnic diversity and pays equal attention to all cultures.

multiracial: having a mixed ancestry of multiple races.

opportunity: favorable chance or occasion that could allow something to occur.

oppression: the act or state of being subject to unjust treatment or authority.

outcry: a strong, public expression of protest.

passivity: inaction in stopping others from doing something.

perspective: a particular attitude or viewpoint.

postracial: describing a theoretical era of no racial prejudice or discrimination.

power: ability to directly influence others through control and/or authority.

prejudice: negative preconceived feelings toward a particular group.

privilege: advantages granted to a limited group of people

profiling: the use of race in targeting a suspect of a crime.

racism: the attitudes, actions, or institutional structures that subordinate a person or group because of their color or assigned race

reconciliation: a social, political, and spiritual process of solidarity and positive movement towards equality.

respect: deep and genuine admiration.

salad bowl: metaphor for the coexistence and harmony of diverse groups that retain unique characteristics and individuality; often contrasted with the melting pot metaphor.

scapegoat: an individual or group unwarrantedly singled out, blamed, or negatively treated.

self-determination: right of a person to control his/her own life, without outside influence.

slur: an insulting remark or characterization based on race.

socioeconomic: involving social and economic factors.

standard: a quality or level that is the established norm.

stereotype: a common, oversimplified image of a certain type of person or thing.

stigma: disgrace because of certain characteristics; disapproval of someone or something different.

subjugation: the act of dominating, controlling, and/or enslaving another group.

supremacy: a position of ultimate authority.

systemic: racism and inequity enshrined in society's policies, ideas, behaviors, and practices; see institutional racism.

tolerance: fair and objective acceptance of differing views, beliefs, and racial or ethnic origins.

tradition: an established custom, belief, or practice.

underrepresentation: represented disproportionately and/or inadequately.

unity: the state of being together, joined as a whole.

upstander: a person who stands up in defense of certain beliefs or other people.

victim: a person negatively subjected to others' actions.

white privilege: the unearned societal advantage given to White people.

xenophobia: unreasonable hatred of other countries and cultures.

"Once social change begins, it cannot be reversed. You cannot un-educate the person who has learned to read. You cannot humiliate the person who feels pride. You cannot oppress the people who are not afraid anymore."
—César Chávez

PERFORMING & VISUAL ARTS

Art is Not White Property

Racism is not entertainment. To this day, songs in choir are typically sung in European languages, and the casts of plays typically consist of White leading characters. Unable to connect to the material, minorities feel left out. To create a more accepting performing arts environment, introduce more minority figures into the limelight and be conscious of maintaining diverse content.

For visual arts, initiate racial dialogues by utilizing art history. For example, you could mention Islamic geographical patterns or the style of Chinese landscape paintings and how they influenced current aesthetic trends. Otherwise, as minorities typically appear as slaves or exotic novelties, spark a racial dialogue by challenging the racism in art history .

Act it Out

The arts provides the opportunity to transport students to an emotional state, geographical location, or time period. Acting out tricky racial scenarios and how to handle them can prepare students to combat real racism. After all, practice makes perfect. For example, you could educate students on intent vs. impact, and how to properly speak about racial issues without offending someone, by play-

ing out this scenario from Teaching Tolerance (applicable to younger students):

Apple: *Wow, Basil! I'm so impressed with your presentation. You're so smart! Every time you present, I can't believe you're a product of public schools.*
Pause (ask students): *What is Apple's intent? What does she want to convey to Basil?*
Basil: *[to his peer, Luisa] I can't believe Apple would say that. I love my school! I love this city. She is so insensitive and judgmental. She should know better. I can't stand to be around her anymore.*
Pause (ask students): *What is the impact of Apple's comment on Basil?*
Luisa: *[to another peer, Jett] Did you hear what Apple said to Basil? He is so offended. Which is too bad—they were good friends. I don't think Apple meant to be insensitive.*
Jett: *[to a new student, Leila] Everyone here is pretty cool, except for Apple. Avoid her at all costs!*
Pause (ask students): *What are the ramifications of Apple's initial comment? What is the relationship between intent and impact?*

Furthermore, if you are teaching theater, you could have your students perform a race-related play (with a moral) to help increase the racial literacy of your audience and students. An example that is commonly used in high school classrooms is "Master Harold"... and the Boys by Athol Fugard. Also, check out Hamilton!

Use the cartoons by Barry Deutsch in this book for role play exercises or visual art inspiration.

WORLD LANGUAGE

Travel with Your Language

Studying a second language for at least one year is compulsory in more than 20 European countries, but not in the United States. However, learning world languages increases cultural appreciation. Furthermore, it fosters the development of global citizens.

As a world language teacher, you have the unique ability to travel with your language—whether you are teaching Spanish, Mandarin, Italian, Zulu, French, Swahili Japanese, Hindi, or even Latin. You have the ability to travel in time or through geographical locations to start a racial dialogue. For example, by locating the country that speaks your language, and researching the human rights issues

of that region, chances are that at least one racial group (typically the indigenous people) is facing discrimination. Go a step further by comparing and contrasting race and ethnicity in other countries with the United States.

Even if you are teaching a language that is not commonly used today, such as Latin, try investigating historical racism and the lingering effects it has in contemporary society. Either way, you have the unique opportunity to delve into global racial conflicts. This will not only increase awareness and a deep understanding of the language's accompanying culture, identity, and history, but it will also simultaneously develop the student's language skills.

MATHEMATICS

Extra effort

STEM fields, including math, need more minority participation. According to a 2011 National Science Foundation report, STEM fields in the United States consist of 55% White men and just 1% Hispanic women. In schools, a similar trend is illustrated as few Black and Hispanic students are in advanced math courses.

Too often, to increase minority participation in math classes, the pace is slowed down. However, assuming minorities cannot handle high-level content only makes it worse. Instead, try expanding enrichment opportunities such as peer-tutoring and after-school help.

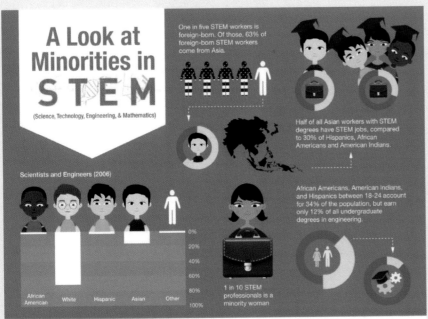

Credit: onlineuniversities.com

Increase involvement

The lack of minorities in professional science fields can be traced back to the classroom. Increasing feelings of inclusion, and therefore minority involvement, can be achieved by simply referring to a diverse group of minority historical figures. For example, there was Charles Drew, who invented the blood bank, or the man who invented the microphone, James West. By including minority historical figures in your classroom discussions, students can better identify to the subject.

Make it relate

If you want to discuss a current event, but are wondering

Know your history

If you are going to credit mathematical inventions to Pythagoras, Newton, and Einstein, then it is only fair to shine some light on minority mathematicians, too. It is not that they do not exist, or what they accomplished is not significant enough, it is just that they are overlooked. To name just two examples, you could talk about Muhammad ibn Musa Al-Khwarizmi, one of the creators of the Hindu-Arabic numerals, or Katherine G. Johnson, a NASA mathematician who won the Presidential Medal of Freedom.

Careful with word problems

"Leroy has 2 ounces of cocaine. If he sells an 8 ball to Antonio for $320 and 2 grams to Juan for $85 per gram, what is the street value of the rest of his hold?"

This was a real math problem given to Alabama middle school students. In this problem, "Black and Latino-sounding names" are assigned to characters dealing drugs. While you might not do something this extreme, do not give students word problems with racial stereotypes. Furthermore, try to make your word problems more inclusive by using names from different cultures.

SCIENCE

how it will relate to science, find a correlation. For example, if a recent racial conflict involving gun violence was on your mind, then you could "have students look at the [graphical] relationship between gun shop access and crime." For more examples of making race relate to your subject, visit NPR's article entitled "Uncomfortable Conversations: Talking About Race In The Classroom."

Race is a myth

Teach students that race is not a biological reality; rather, it is a concept constructed by humans. In 1950, the United Nations Educational, Scientific and Cultural Organization (UNESCO) issued a statement asserting that all humans belong to the same species and that "race" is not a biological reality but a myth.

BUSINESS & ECONOMICS

Understand the significance

Economic disparities based on or because of race relations have been illustrated in healthcare, housing, job opportunities, and education for centuries. The root of this condition—relocating Native Indians for land and enslaving African Americans for labor—was the first American business designed to build wealth. The tradition of minority disenfranchisement continues; for example, research shows that minorities seeking small business loans are treated differently from their White counterparts, despite having similar qualifications on paper. Exploring how socioeconomic status and race are intertwined, and mostly how minorities are disadvantaged, is the best way to leverage a racial dialogue in your classroom. Not only will students be prepared to face inequalities when starting their own business, making an investment, or opening up a bank account, but it will inspire them to expel the systemic racism that keeps most minorities underprivileged. See the personal stories with an "Economic" tag in this book.

Graphic Credit: Barry Deutsch,
leftycartoons.com

Talk about current events

Business and economic events related to race occur everyday. For example, the issue of gentrification in urban areas has impacted minority life since the 1950s. Researching such events and talking about them in class can help teachers stay "on topic" while increasing racial literacy.

TECHNOLOGY & COMPUTER

Reach Out & Research

Aim to have a diverse classroom. According to The Atlantic, out of all the 2014 Advanced Placement Computer Science test-takers, 8% were Hispanic and only 4% were African-American. In contrast, Latinx students make up 22 % of the school-age population in the U.S.; African-Americans make up 14%. Something is discouraging minority students from taking technology and computer-related classes.

Minority students need to know that they can succeed in STEM fields. To demonstrate this, try incorporating some history of the field into your lesson plans. Mention Gerald A. Lawson, who created the first home video game system with interchangeable game cartridges; Marc Hannah, who developed 3D graphics; Floyd Norman, who was Dis-

ney's first Black animator and who still works for Disney; or Patricia Bath, the programmer of a medical probe for ophthalmologists—all of whom are Black. The truth is, many minority accomplishments are overlooked, so you do not hear about them. But, if you look, you will be surprised by the number of accomplished tech and computer game changers there are—people students need to hear about.

Analyze the Impact of Social Media

In the past decade, numerous campaigns for social justice have been spread through digital platforms. Talk about how #BlackLivesMatter, #ITooAmHarvard, #ITooAmPrinceton, #SayHerName, #SayHisName, etc. went viral online, and how technology fueled and continues to fuel social movements.

SCHOOLS AND DISTRICTS:
A PLAN FOR RACIAL RECONCILIATION

1. **All-school announcements** via loudspeaker during major cultural holidays (Dr. Martin Luther King Jr. Day, Chinese New Year, Cinco de Mayo, etc.).

2. A stakeholder committee of students, teachers, administrators, and community members—a **"Diversity Council"**—to promote racial reconciliation, diversity, inclusion, and equity (board members elected and rotated yearly).

3. **Required use of CHOOSE's Engage program** or similar teacher supplement in curriculum of target grade or course (ex. 5th grade, U.S. History, etc.).

4. **All-school annual assembly** with varied formats—for example, a culture fair, student performance, panel discussion, small group conversations, role play, guest speaker, or workshop—in addition to periodic **optional events**; organized by administration, Parent-Teacher Organization, and/or cultural groups on campus.

5. Required yearly **cultural competency training** for ALL faculty and staff (recommended before using this book too).

6. Creation of **Race & Ethnicity in America (or similar) course** in high school for optional enrollment as an elective.

7. Implementing the **Core Curriculum**, or sections, (refer to page 198-199) in all U.S. History classes.

8. **Cross-curricular writing or service** on relevant topic throughout entire school.

9. Assign social justice-related **summer reading** to all teachers (see page 200 for recommendations).

10. Create and hire staff specifically for a **multicultural and diversity office**.

All schools and districts should look into their existing programs and systems to determine what the most effective and efficient path toward racial reconciliation would be.

Sample Truth & Reconcilation Vision Statement for Strategic Planning Committee

Created by Roberto Schiraldi for recommendation to Princeton Public Schools, based on the goals of the Truth and Reconciliation Commission of Canada regarding the Indian Residential Schools

The goals of the Committee shall be to:

(a) Acknowledge social and school experiences, impacts and consequences for students of color living in Princeton and attending Princeton schools.

(b) Provide a holistic, culturally appropriate and safe setting for former and current students, their families and communities to relate their experiences.

(c) Witness, support, promote and facilitate truth and reconciliation events at both the national and community levels;

(d) Promote awareness and public education of all citizens about the white privilege value system and its impacts;

(e) Identify sources and create as complete an historical record as possible of the Black history and legacy of Princeton. The record shall be preserved and made accessible to the public for future study and use;

(f) Produce a report including recommendations to the Princeton Board of Education, concerning the the history and experience of living and going to school in Princeton, experiencing structural racism and white privilege, (including systemic harms, intergenerational consequences and the impact on human dignity) and the ongoing legacy of the Black experience in Princeton.

(g) Support commemoration of former students and their families.

Opinion Pieces

written by CHOOSE team members

CHOOS

Are Racist Jokes or Slurs Okay?

by Simran Kaur
(10th grade)

Everyone loves the classic joke. With the right ambience, timing, and cleverness of thought, a simple joke can lighten the mood and make things more jovial. But, are all jokes completely harmless? Let's consider the following:

Failed my biology test today:
They asked, 'What is commonly found in cells?'
Apparently, "Black people" wasn't the correct answer.[1]

What could possibly be more hilarious than a play on words regarding jail cells and the perpetualization of a stereotype? Let's look at more supposedly 'harmless' jokes.

Q: You know what that little red dot means in the middle of an Indian woman's forehead?
A: Coffee's ready.[2]

Complete ignorance regarding the cultural significance behind a bindi, this "red dot"—and going to the extent of mocking its existence—is clearly comedic, right?

A joke is defined as a thing that someone says to cause amusement or laughter.[3] However, the straight up promotion of ignorance, racism, and offensiveness is definitely not an action that should cause 'amusement and laughter.' Individuals who crack such 'jokes' and individuals that laugh at these jokes are both equally responsible for the furtherance of stereotypes, ignorance, racism, and more. Such distasteful phenomenons are not only heavily present in the racist jokes mentioned above, but also in all other racial jokes and slurs that exist today. And the thought and spread of such phenomenons are what make these 'jokes' harmful.

These types of 'jokes' are not okay, and they can truly hurt numerous individuals. So please, beware of racial jokes and slurs, and take extra precaution to not propagate them. This world needs love, not hate.

1 http://kickasshumor.com/funny-joke/1715/failed-my-biology-test-todaythey-asked-what ; 2 http://www.commonsenseevaluation.com/2011/10/10/joke-of-the-day-309/#st-hash.3Nu1rXFH.dpbs; 3 http://www.dictionary.com/browse/joke?s-t

Should We Be Colorblind?

by Alex Bell
(11th grade)

My friend is colorblind. Most vibrant colors look exactly the same to him. He loses some of the beauty of the world—roses lose their unique hue, and the sky just isn't as blue. How very tragic, right? Being colorblind about race is just as tragic. It lumps everyone together; it says that differences are insignificant. But they aren't. They make up our identity. And while ignoring race also merely veils racial problems and systems in our world, at the individual level it is impossible to truly remain colorblind. People notice things. It's natural. I'm not saying that the problem is impossible to solve. "Should we be colorblind?" and "should we stereotype?" are two completely different questions, but colorblindness was a failed attempt at stopping stereotypes. Humans can't truly stop stereotyping until we celebrate race and ethnicity as an important piece of our identity—not a flaw. We will always see all races. The next step is for us to *love* all races.

by Fedlyne Cleo
(10th grade)

Graphic Credit:
Valeria Torres-Olivares

Does Diversity Harm or Help?

Learning about other cultures—and I mean all (not just Black and White)—will help us truly see the world. Without diversity, our world becomes nothing but monotonous, and life becomes hard when you're closed off from the rest of the world. With diversity, we are no longer ignorant, and we open our eyes to a whole new meaning of being human. It helps us recognize and utilize positive differences, leading to learning and innovation. Diversity should be used to help, not harm, and nurture harmony, not conflict. But while diversity can educate, we must also put our knowledge to good use—to action.

All of it—the bombings, police brutality, hate crimes, stereotypes—ties in with the fact that our society loves labels. Diversity has certainly harmed our world: it can bring out the worst in people, especially in those who don't like change, on both an individual and national level. History shows that one racial group will almost certainly expel, discriminate, and harm another. Take what you learn to promote equity, love, and justice around you by fighting inequity.

"It is time for parents to teach young people early on that in diversity there is beauty and there is strength."

—Maya Angelou

by Abby Emison
(11th grade)

#1: Without broaching, we would never learn. We would take what we believe for granted and never think about others' opinions or beliefs. You will never be challenged. You will only believe what you believe. What if you believe something incredibly wrong? Something that leads you to make the wrong decisions over and over again? Something that makes you miss out on many opportunities? I like to think that if I keep an open mind I can never cut myself out of anything. I can continue to live in harmony with all sorts of other people.

#2: Essentially, broaching is raising a difficult topic for discussion. In it's purest form, broaching should feel uncomfortable, no matter how much you know or think you know on the subject. Feeling uncomfortable is not a bad thing—rather, something people need to experience to be open to new ideas. But if the kid started crying and screaming, you would want to buy them a new one. Same thing with broaching—the level of discomfort helps you to be more empathetic, and that's the goal.

#3: Broaching is especially necessary in the classroom. Classrooms teach students knowledge, and there will never be a more valuable piece of knowledge than acceptance. Broaching in a classroom helps student raise taboo subjects confidently and calmly without being criticized (note that criticized is not the same as challenged). Educators and students alike should be brave, compassionate, and willing to make mistakes, in order to be allies and role models. If you've ever had a teacher that has brought broaching to the classroom in any topic or in any form, thank them—you're a better person for it.

Are You Racist?

by Anonymous

According to the National Education System, "In the United States at present, only Whites can be racists, since Whites dominate and control the institutions that create and enforce American cultural norms and values . . . Blacks and other Third World peoples do not have access to the power to enforce any prejudices they may have, so they cannot, by definition, be racists."

For the White and/or light-skinned, it is crucial to recognize the undeniably benefits from numerous systems put into place in America which unfairly advantage and subordinate by race and color.

However, racism does not just include institutional structures, but also beliefs and actions. It is important to accept that people are not born racist, but everyone becomes racist, even if only through implicit biases. It's inherent in our culture, traditions, and society as a whole. The way our country is set up—whether it be the glorification of lighter skin, the criminalization of Blacks and Hispanics on TV, or the image of terrorists having brown skin—has conditioned us to be racist. So when you're asked that question, don't spit back "NO!" as if someone has accused you of a terrible crime.

Instead, wake up every morning ready to work. Trudge against the systemic racism everyone else considers the norm; take an extra effort to check your thought processes and decisions. Seek community resources to educate yourself; engage. It takes practice and a critical consciousness, but you can do it.

Why "Black Lives Matter" over "All Lives Matter?"

Graphic Credit: Ayesha Qureshi

Graphic Credit: Kris Straub, chainsawsuit.com

What is White Privilege?

by Elaine Ma[1] (11th grade)
and Simona Brickers[2]

If you're born White, you basically won the lottery... A lot of things are easier, and you can get away with more.

White privilege is not a new concept. Many people are hostile to the idea of white privilege because it is a commonly misunderstood phrase; it does not mean that White skin automatically prevents poverty, but that it grants certain privileges that minorities are not welcome to and therefore maintains an elevated societal status that masks racial inequality. This privilege can seem unnoticeable unless, of course, it doesn't apply to you.

It is important to emphasize that white privilege does not prevent hardships. But it does award anyone with White skin the benefit of the doubt, which is something that minorities lack. Black defendants are at least 20% more likely to be imprisoned and sentenced to a much longer jail time than White defendants for the same crime. For example, this happened with Cory Batey and Brock Turner. Not only did they commit the same crime of raping an unconscious woman, but eyewitnesses actually caught Turner in the act. So why did Cory Batey get a minimum sentence of 15 to 25 years in prison while Brock Turner got a six-month jail sentence that could be pushed down to three months for good behavior? How

were these two cases different? Race. One man was White while the other was Black. The difference of race led to a 3000% longer prison sentence for Batey. There are rules, there are laws, but if you are White and privileged, sometimes the rules just don't apply to you. The best thing that White people can do to help change this blatant racial inequality is to accept that white privilege is real. Only with the admittance of white privilege can real change happen.[1]

***

At the cornerstone of the social culture within the United States is a dominant ideology disguised and sustained by White hegemony. White dominance is the cultural social hierarchy identity. The American social structure is depicted in visual metaphors, markers, and social fragments upheld by White identity. The evidence of social inequity is mirrored in the fabric of perpetuated American standards: are the majority of your teachers White? Is the principal White and male? Is the maintenance staff Black or Latino? White privilege becomes obvious when you examine the social hierarchy of what group of people hold leadership positions.[2]

by Anonymous[1] and
Andrew Wong[2]
(11th grade)

What Are Some Common Racial Myths?

The concept of race is a highly emotionally and intellectually charged subject, and it always has been. Ironically, people have been fighting over nothing. Research shows that biological races do not exist. In fact, race is a socially con-structed concept that, for centuries, has pointlessly strained the lives of countless people. According to The Myth of Race by Robert Wald Sussman, the creation of "race" can be traced back to the Spanish Inquisition as a justification for Western imperialism and slavery. Today, many people still mistake bigotry for science. But, the truth is, race is a myth.[1]

***

By definition, a myth is a widely-held but false idea or belief. There are numerous examples of racial myths—one, for exam-ple, is that certain diseases only occur in certain races. When race is being affiliated with medical conditions, it is really just a substitute for other factors like ancestral backgrounds and environmental factors. Despite certain diseases being more com-mon in particular groups, no disease is actually exclusive to one particular race. Another misconception is that a person can be assigned to a racial group on sight. Ever since the year 2000, the government "decided" that people could be more than one race and added multiracial catego-ries to legal forms. It became clear that the multiracial and biracial populations are quickly growing In fact, we can't even agree on the racial label that's assigned to the President of the United States. Race is very complicated, and by delving deeper, I feel that we can look past the myths that have often been attributed to it.[2]

White Privilege by the Numbers:

White Euro-American males are only 33% of the population:

They occupy **80%** of tenured positions in higher education,

80% of the House of Representatives,

80%-90% of the U.S. Senate over few years,

92% of Forbes 400 Executive CEO level positions,

90% of public school superintendents,

99.9% of athletic team owners,

and **97.73%** of U.S. Presidents.[1]

1 Derald Wing Sue. "Micro-aggressions in Everyday Life... and on Our Campus." Powerpoint Presentation.

Racial Literacy **Tests**
for pre- and/or ***post-assessment***

For Elementary School

1. What is an example of anti-Semitism (hatred against Jewish people)?
a) The Holocaust
b) Reconstruction period
c) Civil Rights Movement
d) Ghandi's peaceful protests

2. Of the following, people of which race are put into jail most often because of unfair bias among police officers?
a) Blacks
b) Whites
c) Hispanics
d) Asians

3. Which of the following is a false stereotype?
a) All Muslims are terrorists
b) All Asians are smart
c) All Black people are good at sports
d) All of the above

For Middle School

1. Due to racial profiling, for which physical markers are people stopped most frequently at airport security?
a) Turbans and beards
b) Tattoos
c) Shawls and earrings
d) Religious necklaces

2. If two African-American females, one darker than the other, are treated differently (the lighter-skinned one receives more privileges), what form of racial discrimination is it?
a) Slavery
b) Colorism
c) Supremacy
d) Sexism

3. Discrimination against Muslims in present-day America was most influenced by
a) the 9/11 terrorist attack
b) The Afghanistan War
c) Syrian Refugee Crisis
d) President Barack Obama's election

4. Refugees are _____ to leave their home country while an immigrant _____ to leave.
a) Forced; chooses
b) Happy; rarely wants
c) Welcome; is forced
d) Scared; wants

5. Out of the following options, racial harassment occurs most frequently where?
a) In America, compared to other countries
b) In southern states
c) On the Internet
d) In magazines

6. Most Asian Americans work in STEM-related fields.
a) True
b) False

7. You are thirteen years old, White, and have light skin. If someone asks you whether you are racist, which of the following is the best response?
a) "No! My parents taught me to be colorblind. I appreciate people for people, not color."
b) "No, ever since a Black man was elected to arguably the most powerful position in the world, we are living in a post-racial society."
c) "Of course, everyone is racist. There's nothing we can do about it."
d) "Yes—systemic racism makes my privilege unavoidable and everyone has their implicit biases—but I am actively trying to learn more about race, address my biases, and engage in the movement for justice."

1. Gentrification is most commonly experienced by_____ in _____ areas.
a) Children; poor
b) Whites; suburban
c) Minorities; urban
d) Native Americans; reserves

2. Frequently, members of the following religious groups are wrongly stopped by the Transportation Administration Security for "looking Muslim" (i.e. wearing a turban).
a) Hindus and Arab Christians
b) Jainists and Hindus
c) Sikhs and Arab Christians
d) Arab Christians & Jainists

3. 93% of murders of Blacks are by _____ and 84% of murders of whites are by_____.
a) Hispanics; Blacks
b) Whites; Hispanics
c) Asians; Blacks
d) Blacks; Whites

4. Current-day politics regarding Hispanics primarily involve what topic?
a) Maintaining a primarily Catholic religion
b) Controlling borders
c) Improving trade with Mexico
d) Persecuting Spanish-speaking people

5. Anti-Semitism is defined as which?
a) The Holocaust
b) Lynching during the Jim Crow South
c) Hatred against Jews
d) Restrictions on Catholic immigrants

6. In the 1960s, Black is Beautiful sprouted from what?
a) The Black Power Movement
b) March of Washington
c) 1915 skin-bleaching incident
d) Songs from artists like Nina Simone

7. Which of the following is accurate and best exemplifies the effects of colorism?
"India's population has an extremely high consumption of_____."

a) Hollywood movies
b) American clothing and hairstyles
c) Skin-bleaching products
d) Plane tickets to European countries

8. Racial homogeneity, staying in groups exclusively of one race, is seen most frequently with 40% of
a) Whites
b) Blacks
c) Hispanics
d) Asians

9. One reason that Black families are thought of as "fatherless" is what?
a) Black men leave their wives more often
b) High incarceration rates of Black males
c) The group with the lowest education rate is Blacks
d) 68% of Black couples divorce

10. Because of colorism, members of the same race can still experience different levels of privilege.
a) True
b) False
C) Only true for White people

11. In New York City, the percentage of Blacks and Latinx stopped by police was_____, while the percentage of Whites stopped by the police was_____.
a) 80%; 8%
b) 7%; 90%
c) 50%; 50%
d) 45%; 35%

12. Why are Asian Americans often left out of race-related discussions?
a) All have a high socioeconomic status
b) They are considered to be the "model minority"
c) Out of all minorities, they occupy the most government offices
d) Asian immigration only began in 1987

13. #BlackLivesMatter or #AllLivesMatter?
a) #BlackLivesMatter
b) #AllLivesMatter
c) We should always say both

Notes

About CHOOSE

Our Mission: To overcome racism and inspire harmony through exposure, education, and empowerment.

Our Vision: Racial harmony through a sustainable community partnership.

A note from the co-founders:

During our sophomore year of high school, we were stunned when an in-class discussion about Eric Garner dexterously avoided the topic of race. While we were eager to talk about racism, some felt uncomfortable, and others denied its existence.

Yet, we knew our friends, family, teachers, and peers had stories to tell. We wanted everyone to have the opportunity to share, to listen, and to learn, but at the time, there was no platform to do so.

So we created one.

By early 2015, we had collected over 200 stories internationally, given over a dozen presentations, recruited a dedicated team of student activists, and posted on social media so often that a few friends told us their Facebook feeds were "nothing but CHOOSE—a good thing, of course!"

Back in our high school, we spoke with multiple teachers and conducted district-wide surveys. We learned that over 80% of teachers were willing to talk about race in the classroom, but felt that they couldn't because they did not know how. Simply, they needed the tools to engage.

Around the same time, we received an email from **Not in Our Town Princeton—an incredible racial justice advocacy group we have been privileged to work with and learn from**—applauding the recent tweets of Princeton University professor Dr. Ruha Benjamin. "Most educational institutions are not equipping students to understand, much less intervene in, a world structured by racial vision and division," she wrote. "Racial literacy is not about acquiring the words to have a 'conversation on race'—which too often stay at the level of anecdote and sentiment. Racial literacy is developing a historical & sociological toolkit to understand how we got here and how it could've been/CAN BE otherwise." **We are so grateful to Dr. Benjamin for writing a truly inspiring foreword for this book on page 7.**

We realized that too much of our past work had centered around the "conversation on race." We wanted to do more, to address the initial issues and challenges we had identified in our school and district.

We shifted our primary focus to our Engage initiative, aiming to equip administrators, educators, and students with the "historical & sociological toolkit" for racial literacy. Leveraging all the personal stories we had collected to spark conversations about race and ethnicity would be the first stepping stone to acquiring a larger understanding about the past, present, and future of race relations in the United States.

So here it is: the Classroom Index. **Thank you to Princeton Public Schools, and Mr. Charleston and Dr. Lehet especially, for piloting the first edition; to Superintendent Cochrane for writing an incredible introduction on page 9; to Princeton University's Department of African American Studies and the Princeton Education Foundation for partially funding this book.**

On a final note, our journey of taking risks, making mistakes, learning, and growing to get CHOOSE to where it is today would have been impossible without the tireless support of so many amazing individuals and organizations. Thank you **SO** much. And don't worry, we haven't settled (hint: third edition!). We're still taking risks, still making mistakes, still learning, still growing, still excited to be part of this crucial movement for racial justice for the rest of our lives—**nothing** is more important.

Priya Vulchi
Co-Founder and Co-President

Winona Guo
Co-Founder and Co-President

Ayesha Qureshi

Communications Manager

Visuals Manager

Personal Reflections

Current Events

Papakojo Kuranchie
Penn State
Interviews Team

Abby Emison
Teacher Talks
Essential Questions

Hamza Nishtar
Interviews Team
Writer

Other members of our incredible student team:
Alex Bell
Eddie Cai
Anna Cincotta
Elaine Ma Katie
McCarthy Eli
Meisel Zakaria
Nishtar Mel
Smith Annie
Sullivan-
Crowley Valeria
Torres-Olivares
Izzy Trenholm
Denzel
Washington
Jordan Williams
Aileen Wu
Andrew Wong
Nayha Zahid Keri
Zhang

Yoselin Hernandez
Interviews Team

Fedlyne Cleo
Interviews Team

Simran Kaur
Interviews Team

Charmaine Sello
South Africa

220

Special thanks to our Adult Advisory Board for their tremendous support, guidance, and contribution:

Protim Adhikari
John Anagbo
Ruha Benjamin, Ph.D.
Simona Brickers
Timothy Campbell
Eduardo Cadava, Ph.D.
Stephen Cochrane
Jennifer Cohan
John Cutsinger
Kristina Donovan

Ethan Frisch
Joshua Guild, Ph.D.
Jocelyn Jimenez
Linda Oppenheim
Julie Davidson Meyers
Kareen Coyoca Ross
Shirley Satterfield
Roberto Schiraldi
Nipurna Shah
Saraswathi Shukla
Harini Subrahmanyam Fredrickson
Nina Trivedi

CHOOSE